Leading *and* Managing
Archives *and* Manuscripts Programs

ARCHIVAL FUNDAMENTALS SERIES III

Peter J. Wosh, Editor

Leading *and* Managing
Archives *and* Manuscripts Programs

**Peter Gottlieb &
David W. Carmicheal**

Editors

ALA Editions
CHICAGO 2019

Society of American Archivists
www.archivists.org

© 2019 by the Society of American Archivists
All rights reserved.

This edition published by ALA Editions, an imprint of the American Library Association, 2019.

Printed in the USA by Lightning Source.
POD-1

ISBN: 978-0-8389-4647-3

Graphic design by Sweeney Design, kasween@sbcglobal.net.

Table of Contents

PART II

The Evolution of a Book Series

The Society of American Archivists (SAA) first conceived the notion of developing and publishing "manuals relating to major and basic archival functions" in the early 1970s. Charles Frederick Williams (popularly known as C. F. W.) Coker (1932–1983), a former US Marine Corps captain and North Carolina state archivist who recently had been appointed to head the Printed Documents Division of the National Archives and Records Services, edited the initial Basic Manual Series. The first five basic manuals, which appeared in 1977, illustrated the ways in which archivists defined and classified their core concepts at that historical moment:

- *Archives & Manuscripts: Appraisal & Accessioning* by Maynard J. Brichford
- *Archives & Manuscripts: Arrangement & Description* by David B. Gracy II
- *Archives & Manuscripts: Reference & Access* by Sue E. Holbert
- *Archives & Manuscripts: Security* by Timothy Walch
- *Archives & Manuscripts: Surveys* by John Fleckner

The entire series accounted for only 163 pages of text, which included numerous illustrations, graphics, sample forms, charts, and bibliographic insertions. Each 8.5" by 11" softbound pamphlet contained three holes, punched down the left side, for easy insertion into a loose-leaf binder that might be handily referenced at an archivist's desk. Individual volumes sold for $4, though SAA members received a $1 discount.

Archivists operated within a far different cultural, legal, and professional framework during the early and middle years of the 1970s. In 1973, the same year that SAA began work on the Basic Manual Series, IBM introduced the Correcting Selectric II typewriter as its major technological breakthrough, thereby eliminating the need for such popular tools as rubber erasers, correction fluid, and cover-up tape. This revolutionary product seemed destined to alter the nature of document creation forever. During this period, a few archivists had begun grappling with the challenges of something known as "machine-readable records," but a bibliographer who surveyed this puzzling development could still confidently conclude in a 1975 *American Archivist* article that "only a few archival establishments" appeared to be "developing programs for accessioning" such materials. Other momentous—and occasionally unsettling—changes appeared on the horizon. A new copyright law, which was enacted by Congress in 1976 and became effective on New Year's Day 1978, contained significant implications for how archivists would manage collections and serve researchers. Richard Nixon's resignation in 1974 prompted the promulgation of new legislation in 1978 that declared for the first time that presidential and vice presidential records are public documents. Professionally, the archival landscape seemed to be shifting as well. The Association of Canadian Archivists launched an exciting new journal, *Archivaria*, in winter 1975/1976, a development destined to deepen the discipline's intellectual discourse. Regional archival associations formed, became fruitful, and multiplied in the United States. In addition, a new era in archival education began as library schools and history departments inaugurated archives-based graduate programs in the late 1970s, ultimately resulting in a highly credentialed and formally trained corps of professional practitioners.

Such transformations, and many others too numerous to mention here, convinced the Society of American Archivists that only an active publications program that regularly refreshed the existing literature could provide its membership with easy access to rapidly changing trends and best practices. SAA accordingly published the Basic Manual Series II—a second set of five volumes—in the early 1980s:

- *Archives & Manuscripts: Exhibits* by Gail Farr Casterline
- *Archives & Manuscripts: Automated Access* by H. Thomas Hickerson
- *Archives & Manuscripts: Maps and Architectural Drawings* by Ralph E. Ehrenberg
- *Archives & Manuscripts: Public Programs* by Ann E. Pederson and Gail Farr Casterline
- *Archives & Manuscripts: Reprography* by Carolyn Hoover Sung

Over the years, SAA published scores of other titles, each illustrating the rich diversity of archival work: administration of photo collections, conservation, machine-readable records, law, management, a basic glossary, collections of readings on archival theory and practice, and books specific to archives in a variety of institutional settings (i.e., colleges and universities, businesses and corporations, religious and scientific institutions, museums, government agencies, historical societies, etc.). Even with the proliferation of publications, the bedrock of archival practice rested on the core knowledge represented in the basic manuals, which were reconceptualized and rechristened between 1990 and 1993 as the Archival Fundamentals Series:

- *Understanding Archives and Manuscripts* by James O'Toole
- *Arranging and Describing Archives and Manuscripts* by Fredric M. Miller
- *Managing Archival and Manuscript Repositories* by Thomas Wilsted and William Nolte
- *Selecting and Appraising Archives and Manuscripts* by F. Gerald Ham
- *Preserving Archives and Manuscripts* by Mary Lynn Ritzenthaler
- *Providing Reference Services for Archives and Manuscripts* by Mary Jo Pugh
- *The Glossary of Archivists, Manuscript Curators, and Records Managers*
  by Lynn Lady Bellardo and Lewis Bellardo

A second iteration of the seven books in this revamped series appeared roughly fifteen years later as the Archival Fundamentals Series II:

- *Understanding Archives and Manuscripts* by James O'Toole and Richard J. Cox
- *Arranging and Describing Archives and Manuscripts* by Kathleen D. Roe
- *Managing Archival and Manuscript Repositories* by Michael Kurtz
- *Selecting and Appraising Archives and Manuscripts* by Frank Boles
- *Preserving Archives and Manuscripts* by Mary Lynn Ritzenthaler
- *Providing Reference Services for Archives and Manuscripts* by Mary Jo Pugh
- *A Glossary of Archival and Records Terminology* by Richard Pearce-Moses

Mary Jo Pugh and Richard J. Cox edited these multivolume compilations, which almost instantaneously became required texts in archival education courses and necessary additions to archivists' bookshelves. The Archival Fundamentals Series I and II differed in scope and scale from the initial Basic Manual Series. For example, John Fleckner's comprehensive treatment of surveys did not appear in need of revision and dropped out of the series. Security became incorporated into a broader manual on preservation. SAA commissioned an introductory overview of the field, added a new book that focused on managerial issues, and developed a glossary with the goal of defining and historicizing key archival concepts. Beginning in the 1970s, both Archival Fundamentals Series I and II incorporated and delineated the evolving descriptive standards that defined professional practice, dissected the contentious debates surrounding appraisal and deaccessioning that enlivened archival discourse in the 1980s, and reflected the growing emphases on an expanding user base and more complex reference services that revolutionized reading rooms and repositories in the late twentieth century.

This third edition—Archival Fundamentals Series III—contains important continuities and significant departures from its predecessors:

- A new book, *Advocacy and Awareness for Archivists* by Kathleen D. Roe, reflects an increased understanding that these functions undergird all aspects of archival work.
- The management volume, *Leading and Managing Archives and Manuscripts Programs* edited by Peter Gottlieb and David W. Carmicheal, has been reconfigured to focus especially on leadership and to provide readers with opportunities to explore their individual managerial styles.
- *Advancing Preservation for Archives and Manuscripts* by Elizabeth Joffrion and Michèle V. Cloonan addresses digital challenges and focuses on such current issues as risk management, ethical considerations, and sustainability.
- *Arranging and Describing Archives and Manuscripts* by Dennis Meissner, *Reference and Access for Archives and Manuscripts* by Cheryl Oestreicher, and *Selecting and Appraising Archives and Manuscripts* by Michelle Light and Margery Sly may appear familiar topics to readers of the previous two series, but each book illustrates the innovations in thought and practice that have transformed these archival functions over the past fifteen years.
- A general overview volume which I am preparing, *Introducing Archives and Manuscripts*, provides a broad introduction to the historical, philosophical, and theoretical foundations of the profession.

One contribution that constituted a cornerstone of the previous series has been reformatted to maximize its currency and usability. Although not part of the Archival Fundamentals Series III, the *Dictionary of Archives Terminology* (dictionary.archivists.org) will replace *A Glossary of Archival and Records Terminology* and will be maintained and updated as a digital resource by SAA's Dictionary Working Group.

We hope that undergraduate and graduate students, new professionals, seasoned archival veterans, and others in the information science and public history fields will find the seven volumes in the Archival Fundamentals Series III helpful, provocative, and essential to both their intellectual life and their daily work. As Richard J. Cox observed in his preface to an earlier edition of the series, the time has long passed "when individuals entering the archival profession could read a few texts, peruse some journals, attend a workshop and institute or two, and walk away with a sense that they grasped the field's knowledge and discipline." This series provides an entry point and a synthetic distillation of a much broader literature that spans an impressive array of academic disciplines. We encourage you, of course, to do a deeper dive into each of the individual topics covered here. But we also remain confident that this series, like its predecessors, provides an honest and accurate snapshot of archival best practices at the end of the second decade of the twenty-first century.

The authors, of course, deserve full credit for their individual contributions. The Archival Fundamentals Series III itself, though, constitutes a collaborative enterprise that benefited from the work of SAA Publications Board members, editors, and interns throughout the past decade. These individuals helped to define the series parameters, reviewed proposals and manuscripts, and shepherded various projects to conclusion. Special shout-outs (in alphabetical order) are owed to: Bethany Anderson, Jessica Ballard, Roland Baumann, Cara Bertram, Mary Caldera, Amy Cooper Cary, Jessica Chapel, Paul Conway, J. Gordon Daines, Todd Daniels-Howell, Sarah Demb, Jody DeRidder, Keara Duggan, Margaret Fraser, Thomas J. Frusciano, Krista Gray, Gregory Hunter, Geoffrey Huth, Petrina Jackson, Joan Krizack, Christopher Lee, Donna McCrea, Jennifer Davis McDaid, Kathryn Michaelis, Nicole Milano, Lisa Mix, Tawny Nelb, Kevin Proffitt, Christopher Prom, Mary Jo Pugh, Aaron Purcell, Colleen Rademaker, Caryn Radick, Dennis Riley, Michael Shallcross, Mark Shelstad, Jennifer Thomas, Ciaran Trace, Anna Trammell, Joseph Turrini, Tywanna Whorley, and Deborah Wythe. Nancy Beaumont has been an inspirational executive director for SAA, as well as a brilliant editor in her own right. Abigail Christian, SAA's editorial and production coordinator, has skillfully shepherded design and layout. Teresa Brinati, keenly insightful and good-humored as always, remains the epitome of competent leadership and has transformed the SAA publications program into a model for professional associations. It has been a privilege and great fun to work with everyone on this project.

PETER J. WOSH
Editor, Archival Fundamentals Series III
Society of American Archivists

Introduction

Books about leadership are more likely to start conversations than to provide answers. Obviously, there is no step-by-step formula of leadership that can be learned from a manual and then applied repeatedly thereafter. Yet leadership is an appropriate topic for a series addressing fundamental archival skills. We believe leadership can be taught, though not as a process. Leadership skills are best learned by observing and following the example of leaders; they're best taught through mentoring. For that reason, this is a book about personal experiences.

The leadership of archival programs has much in common with leadership of most other kinds of programs. As in other settings, archival leadership includes the roles of both managers and leaders. Like most program managers anywhere, those in archives must plan, budget, supervise, collect and analyze data, and communicate well. Archival leaders perform the same roles that their counterparts in many other organizations do: projecting vision, inspiring change, forging strategy, building relationships, and communicating. These common aspects of leadership mean that archivists can learn much from the enormous body of literature on leadership, whether it pertains to the for-profit, nonprofit, or public sectors of American life.[1]

This book puts leadership into the framework of archival programs, specifically. We do this by exploring the experience of leading and managing archival repositories. Drawing on our combined fifty years' work in manuscript, government, and state historical society repositories, we discuss in the first section of the book what we found most effective in carrying out significant areas of archival leadership responsibility. In the second section, five authors from a variety of repositories deepen our own perspectives on archival leadership by offering their accounts of the challenges of directing programs in these various settings and of what has proven successful. An additional chapter in the second section discusses the most significant development for archival leadership in the last ten years: the advent of a leadership institute for archivists.

Our book builds on previous publications about archival leadership, particularly Bruce Dearstyne's *Leading and Managing Archives and Records Programs* (2008) and Michael J. Kurtz's *Managing Archival and Manuscript Repositories* (2004). Beyond the prescriptions for program leadership that these books offer, we provide the experiential element to give readers a clear idea of how leadership looks and feels in practice. Throughout the book, readers will learn about actual problems we encountered and solutions we devised for them. In some places, we use scenarios in order to highlight issues, but these also broadly derive from our real experiences in tackling leadership problems. Both in our own chapters about key aspects of program leadership and in the chapters describing leadership in different archival settings, this book focuses on what leaders and managers should anticipate as they direct archival programs and on how they can successfully handle challenges in a variety of situations.

The Contours of Archival Leadership

Leadership encompasses the work of executive leaders and also of program managers and all other influencers, wherever they work in an organization. Leadership is not a role limited to those who are in charge. In fact, heads of organizations who think that they alone provide leadership rarely play transformative roles. Transformative leaders care more about the ideas or people they serve than about being in the spotlight or commanding instant obedience. That's good news for people who don't see themselves as leaders in the traditional understanding of that word. Even followers (a word that slowly may be losing its negative connotations) can express passion and excellence in their work.[2] Such people often "lead from the middle" without even seeing themselves as leaders.

In the archival world in particular, where repositories are often small and the management structure relatively flat, the boundary between leaders and managers is sometimes blurred, but we believe the distinction is no less real and important, and that understanding has informed part I of this book in particular. Following the concepts of John P. Kotter, we view managers' roles as coping with complexity and leaders' roles as coping with change.[3] Managers most often focus on budgets, staffing, planning, providing control, and solving problems. Leaders, on the other hand, concentrate on creating vision, setting direction, and aligning and motivating people. The emphasis in managers' work falls on stability and continuity; the heart of leaders' work lies in new departures, transformations, and inspiration. While the book relies on this conceptual distinction between leaders and managers, it treats both roles as essential and complementary. Further, it recognizes that for many archival program directors, leadership often means combining the roles of leader and manager.

A sizable proportion of archivists direct the repositories and programs where they work. According to the 2004 census of US archivists, 32 percent hold positions with managerial responsibilities.[4] This significant representation of managers among all archivists reflects the modest size of most archival institutions. While several notable archives in the United States are large, complex organizations, the vast majority are relatively small programs. A common personnel configuration includes one to three full-time employees assisted by a few more full- or part-time paraprofessionals, clerical employees, interns, student hourly workers, and volunteers. While the actual scope of authority they exercise in these characteristically small programs undoubtedly varies a good deal, the archivists who lead many repositories frequently must wear both the manager's and the leader's hat.

Though we recognize this reality of program leadership in archives, our chapters in part I often describe the roles of manager and leader separately. We believe there is value in considering how each role plays out in different situations. By distinguishing between their respective functions, we suggest not that the lead archivist can just switch from one to the other but that it is important to understand both roles and, in particular, not to sacrifice the leader's role to the often more pressing demands of the manager's part.

In fact, the exercise of archival leadership is anything but linear. In larger archives, where more bureaucratic organizations include distinct manager and leader positions, managers can gradually grow into leader roles as they assert their desire not just to implement improvement or change but also to influence the direction of the program. Leadership emerges from all parts of the archival staff as well. Perhaps especially true in the overwhelming majority of small repositories, where staff work daily in close association with program heads, it also frequently happens in larger archives, especially when strategies and organizational change invite staff to contribute ideas and carry out projects.

Themes in This Book

As we developed our own chapters and edited those of our contributors, certain fundamental aspects of leadership emerged as recurring themes. Whether we were addressing communication or strategy or budgeting, these traits surfaced repeatedly as characteristics of archival leaders. And in our contributors' chapters, where a diverse group of archivists discuss their journeys to and along the path of leadership, these themes emerged again with enough consistency to be notable. Many of these themes are applicable to all leadership (whether corporate or archival, executive leader or manager):

Leaders are intentional. In effect, leaders are always preparing for the role, often starting to "study" well before they have any formal leadership responsibilities and continuing throughout a lifetime of shifting responsibilities, opportunities, technologies, and cultural norms. Leadership can be learned, but it requires thoughtful intentionality and, like any skill, constant practice. Even as a leader grows, some aspects of leadership remain aspirational, and true leadership comes from behavior and not from a title or a position.

Leaders are self-managing and self-aware. The best leaders and managers are unflinching in their assessment of their own strengths and weaknesses. They conduct regular personal assessment and solicit honest feedback from colleagues, mentors, and even subordinates. They strive to recognize how their own emotions and behavior affect those around them. Having uncovered weaknesses, they do not shy away from self-improvement.

Leadership is fundamentally about relationships rather than ideas. Great ideas are just that: ideas. Leaders manage to transform ideas into results, and that requires the ability to inspire people and focus their efforts on a shared goal. For that reason, all leadership stands on a foundation of relationships. The archival world, in particular, is inherently about people—we collect and preserve the record of human activity, after all—making relationships particularly important to archival leaders.

The engine of leadership is communication. All good leaders and managers communicate effectively to a variety of audiences, and this is also true in the archives profession. In hierarchical terms, leadership is about communicating up, to those who support the organization and provide funding; around, to peers and colleagues whose cooperation is essential for success; and down, to those who must work effectively if goals are to be achieved.

Leaders are agents of change. As noted earlier, management is about stability, leadership is about change. Leaders think often about potential changes that they do not initiate—new technologies, political winds, economic trends—and how to prepare their organization for those changes. But they also think about how to instigate positive change within their organization, never resting on yesterday's success and always anxious to keep the organization nimble and alert.

If archival leaders share certain characteristics with leaders everywhere, they are distinguishable from other leaders in certain ways. Archival leaders face challenges and opportunities not typical in the corporate, for-profit setting that most leadership books address, though many are more typical of nonprofit organizations.[5] These can make archival leadership more challenging and more rewarding than leadership in a corporate setting. At the risk of overgeneralizing, some of the challenges faced by archival leaders and managers include the following:

Archival leadership and programs pursue broad missions. Leaders in corporate settings often lead organizations that have a relatively narrow, well-defined focus and employ staff (or management staff, at least) that have had consistent and comparable training. Ultimately, companies like Apple exist to make money, a focused goal to which everything else is subsumed and from which their understanding of customer service and product quality derive. In addition, the majority of their corporate managers share a common understanding of business skills, such as accounting and strategic planning, because these are mature skills taught with a high degree of consistency from one business school to another. Archival leaders, on the other hand, may find it difficult to define their mission in any focused way, given the scope of their collections and the varied interests or needs of their customers and supporters. It is likely, too, that they employ staff who have an incredible diversity of employment backgrounds and education and who may take a variety of approaches to even basic archival tasks such as arrangement and description.[6]

Archival leadership has limited opportunities to provide staff with financial incentives. One of us worked for several years in a corporate setting, where he earned annual performance bonuses and where he was able to reward his staff with bonuses of 6 to 8 percent of their annual salaries. Such incentives can be very effective but are rarely available to the archival leader. Instead, most archival leaders face the challenge of motivating staff with little or no control over their wages. Fortunately, archivists are often passionate about their work, and leaders can motivate by creating a vision and reinforcing the role each employee or volunteer plays in achieving it.

Archival leadership must make many noneconomic decisions. In businesses where the bottom line is the bottom line, most decisions are predicated on one underlying question: will it increase our profits? Archival leaders, on the other hand, often face decisions that have no economic basis at all. As one of us has said many times (in his government archives): "If we could make money at this, the government wouldn't be doing it." If, as many suspect, 20 percent of the typical archives' collection receives 80 percent of the use, then the cost of maintaining 80 percent of our collections makes no economic sense. Our programs also perform tasks to benefit future users—including ones who have not yet been born. Consequently, archival leaders must muster noneconomic arguments to justify much of what they do. This lack of clear economic benefit means that archival leaders may be subject to more pressure from political interests and competing constituencies than is common in corporations, where the ultimate question about any action is whether it will increase profits and where the success of the leadership is evident in quarterly balance sheets.

One blogger has suggested that the challenges faced by nonprofit (and we would add *archival*) leaders mirror those faced by leaders of startups, where success depends to a great extent on passion sustained by a vision of what the future can hold.[7] Although the word *passion* crops up frequently these days in connection with the conduct of businesses, professions, and occupations, we think it applies particularly to archival leadership.

Overview of Contents

The six chapters in part I of this book cover key archival leadership functions. We do not claim that they include every phase of leadership, but we believe that they are all critical to the success of leaders and managers. While we have each separately written three of these chapters, we have collaborated on all of them by critically reading and commenting on each other's work. More importantly, we began with a strongly shared understanding of the concept for the book and of our goals for it.

Part I of the book begins with a chapter on communication, undoubtedly the key to effective leadership that all the other chapters in the book also discuss in connection with their own topics. The first chapter examines leaders' communications with five different audiences of archival programs and stresses the importance of advocacy. The second chapter discusses leading through strategy. It investigates elements of a strategic approach to growth and improvement of archives while describing the roles of both leaders and managers. Chapters 3 and 4 deal with existential challenges for archival leadership. While chapter 3 looks at how leaders maximize resources and budgets, chapter 4 explores how leaders meet the demands of transformative change and crises. Chapter 5 describes leadership roles in forging productive relationships among staff, between the archives and its parent organization, and among an archives program and other organizations. Chapter 6 concludes the first part of the book by discussing leadership development in archives and ways that all archivists can foster leadership, particularly how they—having assumed leadership roles—mentor others toward becoming leaders.

Our chapters in part I provide many specific examples of leadership tasks and challenges, but they do not address the nuances that arise from different institutional settings for archives. This is what readers will find in part II, where five authors examine their leadership experiences, each one in a different kind of repository. Each of them specifically reflects on her growth as a leader and a manager and on the requirements for effective leadership in their own institution. Part II of the book complements the first part by providing cases through which to examine the leadership functions we examine in part I.

Sarah Koonts discusses her formative experiences at the North Carolina State Archives, which have shaped her view of a leader's ambassador role. Jennifer Johnson, senior archivist at Cargill, Incorporated, examines the most important functions of corporate archives and how her leadership efforts seek to strengthen them. Lynette Stoudt provides a detailed account of how she handled her multiple managerial responsibilities as director of the Georgia Historical Society's Research Center. Samantha Norling explains how her work to expand a relatively new archives program at the Indianapolis Museum of Art has given her valuable leadership experience. Megan Sniffin-Marinoff, university archivist at Harvard University, analyzes leadership in critical areas through the lens of her experience in higher education archives. Finally, Rachel Vagts discusses how archival leaders develop from her perspective as director of the Archives Leadership Institute.

Whom Is This Book For?

We envision this book as being especially appropriate for five related audiences: graduate students in archival and library education programs who desire some introduction to basic theory and practice in the field; younger archivists entering their first managerial positions who have not been exposed to these concepts but now have the responsibility for leading archival programs; mid-career archivists who are transitioning from skills-based jobs (e.g., processing archivists or reference archivists) into middle-management positions where they need to be conversant with best practices in leadership; archives project managers who are leading key initiatives within a broader repository; and even well-established archival leaders who would like to examine their own approach to leadership and who may find here some insight into why they lead as they do or how they might encourage leadership development in others. We also hope that the resulting book will be useful for the Society of American Archivists Education Department, as it builds on workshops from the Archives Leadership Institute.

Leadership is not a process or a formula. While all archival leaders need to strategize and build relationships, be comfortable managing change, and communicate effectively, each faces distinctive challenges. The situations in which you, as a leader or potential leader, find yourself will be unique to your repository, institutional setting, and constituencies. Your responses to those situations likewise will reflect your unique combination of temperament, experience, and skills. This book should be viewed, then, as a tool to help you explore and develop individual approaches to leadership. We hope that the experiences and insights of the eight archivists whose leadership this book recounts will prompt you, leaders and managers in the profession, as well as students and current archivists who aspire to these roles, to explore your own approaches to leadership, to examine your own capacity for leadership, and to discover ways to expand and develop personally as an archival leader.

NOTES

[1] For a good overview of the literature on leadership, see Denise Kwan and Libi Shen, "Senior Librarians' Perceptions of Successful Leadership Skills," in *Advances in Library Administration and Organization*, Vol. 33, ed. Delmus E. Williams, Janine Golden, and Jennifer K. Sweeney (Bingley, UK: Emerald Publishing, 2017), 89–134. Our annotated bibliography includes all the works in a variety of disciplines that we consulted while writing the first six chapters of this book.

[2] See Susan Cain, "Not Leadership Material? Good. The World Needs Followers," *New York Times*, March 24, 2017, captured at https://perma.cc/LW5Y-EU77.

[3] John P. Kotter, "What Leaders Really Do," in Harvard Business Review's *10 Must Reads: On Leadership* (Boston: Harvard Business Review Press, 2011), 37–56. Two authorities on archival leadership echo Kotter's model. See Michael J. Kurtz, *Managing Archival and Manuscript Repositories* (Chicago: Society of American Archivists, 2004), 26–27; Bruce W. Dearstyne, *Leading the Historical Enterprise: Strategic Creativity, Planning and Advocacy for the Digital Age* (Lanham, MD: Rowman and Littlefield, 2015), 26.

[4] Victoria Irons Walch, "A*Census: A Closer Look," *American Archivist* 69, no. 2 (2006): 344.

[5] For a study of the challenges of nonprofit leadership (from which these thoughts are largely derived), see Eric Johnson, "Striving for No Difference: Examining Effective Leadership between Nonprofit and For-Profit Contexts," Northwestern School of Education and Social Policy, December 2012, http://www.sesp.northwestern.edu/masters-learning-and-organizational-change/knowledge-lens/stories/2013/striving-for-no-difference-examining-effective-leadership-between-nonprofit-and-for-profit-contexts-.html, captured at https://perma.cc/T5LQ-VTDR.

[6] The staff and volunteers one of us led over three decades have included a retired soap opera director, a jewelry designer, and a composer who had a published/performed symphony to her credit, as well as archivists whose education ranged from internships to archival certificates to full master's degrees. Such diversity has been both challenging and exhilarating.

[7] Joan Garry, "The Difference between Corporate and Nonprofit Management," http://www.joangarry.com/corporate-nonprofit-management/, captured at https://perma.cc/3YV9-D8G9.

Part I

1

Communication

David W. Carmicheal

Effective leadership requires effective communication. Brilliant ideas alone cannot carry the enterprise forward, nor are well-crafted management tools sufficient. Great ideas can inspire exceptional work, but first those ideas must be communicated to others who embrace them. Good management tools can help ensure fairness and consistency, but the ideas of fairness and consistency must be communicated through words and deeds. The archival administrator may communicate to many different audiences. This chapter will explore five potential audiences and suggest messages and methods for each.

Communicating with Employees and Other Workers

Managers and leaders communicate most often with the people who must get the work done; the staff, volunteers, interns, and others who make up the archives' workforce. Because the success of the program depends so heavily on these people, the leader's own success depends very heavily on this avenue of communication.

Communicating vision and values

All communications in the archives, all of its priorities and programs, begin with the vision and values of its leadership. The repository's mission (discussed below) is critical to communication, but the mission rarely changes with new leadership. Each new leader, though, brings to the repository a new set of values and a unique vision of how the mission will be accomplished. It can be argued, then, that the primary responsibility of archival leaders is to create and intentionally communicate a comprehensive vision and a foundation of shared values. At least one study has suggested that the trait all employees value most highly in their colleagues is honesty but that from their leaders, people expect a second quality, that they be forward-looking.[1] This suggests that an archives' leadership must project both strong values and clear vision.

The repository's values generally spring from the leader's own personal values, so archival leaders, and those who want to become leaders, should spend time considering their personal values and how these might be projected (consciously or unconsciously) through the archives. Leaders might even want to conduct a personal values inventory (an online search will yield many lists for you to consider) to determine their own tendencies. Do you value risk over safety? Independence over collaboration? Are you motivated most strongly by ambition? Home/work balance? Job security? If you are an entrepreneurial risk-taker, you are likely to cast a vision for your repository that values experimentation and accepts a certain level of uncertainty and periodic failure as the price of innovation. On the other hand, if you place a high value on stability and accountability, your repository is likely to reflect that fact. Neither approach is superior to the other, but knowing yourself and your own values will result in a vision for your archives that is clear to your staff, supporters, and administration. Over time, a leader who is passionate about certain values will communicate that to staff members, and they will begin to reflect those values as well.

Early in my career, I worked for an elected official who loved innovation and was willing to take calculated risks to achieve it. He communicated that to me in our conversations, through his own actions, and by bailing me out of a few of my own failures. Over time, I grew more comfortable taking risks and trying new ideas. Gradually, my own staff adopted that same posture and, like a good virus, innovation spread through the archives. After several years, my boss relinquished his post and was replaced by someone who was nearly a polar opposite, an official who valued consistency, traditional methods, and very little risk. Almost immediately the archives began to reflect those new values. Interestingly, both approaches worked. Under the new leader, our achievements no longer scaled the heights of earlier efforts, but our failures were less consequential as well. Regardless of whether one approach was preferable to the other, though, the point is the same: both approaches reflected the values of the organization's leadership. In fact, one official made a point of consciously articulating his values while the other did not, but in both cases the values were communicated plainly and, eventually, the repository reflected them. Over time, an archival repository will reflect the values and vision of its leadership.

To say that the repository will reflect the leader's vision is not to suggest that the vision springs from the leader's mind alone. Those who will help implement the vision—the staff, donors, and others—must share the vision, and for that the leader must solicit their input. As Peter discusses in chapter 2, there are many practical ways leaders can engage staff and stakeholders in developing the archives' mission and vision. Leaders who begin with a strong, personal vision for the future of their repository may balk at involving others for fear that they may cloud the leader's own well-formulated vision, but such leaders can often engage others in their personal vision by helping them understand how their vision was arrived at. Such a discussion can allow the leader to solicit feedback and new ideas and then reshape or restate the vision in a way that strengthens it while giving others greater ownership of the vision.

One such discussion at an archives began with staff envisioning what the archives' services might look like in five years: what patron expectations about online access might be by then, and how archival processing might have changed to address the growing prevalence of digital records. Staff were then asked to think about how resources were currently distributed in the archives: what percentage of time and money was devoted to reference services, what percentage to online access projects, and so on. Finally, staff were challenged to think about how resource distribution might have to change, given the future just envisioned: if a much larger percentage of users would expect to access records online in five years, how much increase in resources devoted to online access projects might be necessary? What services might decrease over the next five years as a result of these changes, and how might resources from those services be redeployed to other activities? And how could resources be redeployed, through transfers of positions from one unit to another, for example, or a shift of responsibilities from one unit to another (with appropriate training)? The discussion extended over several meetings and resulted in greater understanding of what the archives might become and how (absent any growth in resources) some units might need to sacrifice resources in the short term, or take on new responsibilities in the long term, in order to achieve the vision of the future. Through the discussion, the leadership's vision was expanded, refined, and distributed to become a more widely shared vision.

A repository's vision serves as a touchstone for employees, the thing they are all working toward, and it is often expressed in a brief, memorable "vision statement," which expresses what the archives will be or achieve at some point in the future, often five or ten years from now. A vision statement is less static than a mission statement (which may be developed at the founding of the organization and remain constant ever after) and can change as circumstances dictate (though if it changes too radically and too often, it will cease to be a unifying vision and become a source of confusion instead). A vision can be expressed in very concrete terms ("the archives will occupy a new facility that provides adequate space for collections . . . ") or in more aspirational terms ("the archives will be seen as a vital asset by the organization's executive officers . . . "). Vision statements are desires about the future and, as such, progress toward the vision cannot always be measured in concrete terms. But vision statements always reflect the leadership's values and aspirations for the repository. Two excerpts from the vision statement of the National Archives and Records Administration illustrate the aspirational nature of vision statements: "We will be known for cutting-edge access to extraordinary volumes of government information and unprecedented engagement to bring greater meaning to the American experience" and "We will lead the archival and information professions to ensure archives thrive in a digital world."[2]

Notice, too, that vision statements imply the repository's values. The National Archives' vision implies that engagement with government information brings meaning to the American experience and that this is something to be valued. Whether the vision grows out of a clear understanding of what the repository values, or the values become evident while crafting the vision, the two go hand in hand.

The leader's vision for the archives—whether embodied in a vision statement or expressed through less tangible means—is an all-important contribution that only leaders can make. After surveying tens of thousands of workers around the world, researchers James Kouzes and Barry Posner concluded that "being forward-looking—envisioning exciting possibilities and enlisting others in a shared view of the future—is the attribute that most distinguishes leaders from non-leaders."[3] The leadership's first duty is to establish and constantly reinforce the archives' vision and values.

Communicating mission

If vision is about the future, *mission* is about the here and now. Mission statements explain why the repository exists: what it does, who it serves, and how it does its work. Notice how New York University's mission statement succinctly includes all three: "The New York University Archives serves as the final repository for the historical records of NYU *[what it does]*. Its primary purpose is to document the history of the University and to provide source material *[how it does its work]* for administrators, faculty, students, alumni, and other members of the University community, as well as scholars, authors, and other interested persons who seek to evaluate the impact of the University's activities on the history of American social, cultural, and intellectual development *[who it serves]*."[4] Similarly, Eastern Kentucky University Special Collections and Archives provides a succinct example: "Special Collections & Archives supports the research needs and enhanced knowledge *[what it does]* of our community *[who it serves]* through the preservation and accessibility of selected historical resources *[how it does its work]*."[5]

A repository's mission may be predetermined (by enabling legislation or some other governance document, for instance) or by the mission of a parent organization. If a mission statement does not exist, it may be crafted by a leader or through broader participation of staff and other stakeholders. Every repository, though, needs to understand its mission: what it does, who it serves, and how it does its work.

Good leaders make certain that everyone has a shared understanding of the repository's mission and vision. Employees who understand and embrace their repository's mission and vision will share a sense of purpose and are more likely to be empowered to make decisions because they will have a clear method of evaluating the consequences of their decisions. ("How will any given decision support or detract from the archives' mission and the leadership's vision of how we achieve it?")

Archival leaders who communicate a clear vision and mission to their employees are well on their way to crafting appropriate communications to external audiences as well. Higher administrators, donors, and other supporters will be attracted to a clear, meaningful vision and mission. These communications form the foundation of all others.

Communicating work expectations and assignments

Beyond mission and vision, much of what is communicated to employees and other workers is general information about policies, procedures, projects, work assignments, and all the daily information that keeps the archives operating smoothly. In such cases, emphasis will be on delivering clear instructions with measurable outcomes. While a leader's primary motive for communicating may be to inspire and set the archival work within a larger context, the manager's motive is to encourage a stable, consistent, and fair work environment and, to that end, all who contribute to the work must have a clear understanding of how their work fits into the larger picture, what specific work is expected of them, what quality standards are expected, and what the consequences of exceptional or poor performance will be.

Management communication is often directed, or accompanied, by standard forms, such as performance plans, that contribute to consistency and objectivity. No form, though, can substitute for direct, honest communication from manager to staff. If you shy away from confrontation, you may avoid telling the truth about unacceptable performance and behavior; instead, you may be tempted to focus communications on what is succeeding and resist talking about things that are not working. The best way to address this problem is to communicate very clear expectations and performance consequences, even for your best workers. Don't wait until performance slips and then scramble to set expectations. A good practice is to meet with each employee at the beginning of each calendar or fiscal year and lay out, in writing, your expectations for the coming year, then hold checkup meetings periodically (quarterly, or even monthly) throughout the year. At checkup meetings, you can reinforce good behaviors and thank employees for exceptional effort, and you can identify unacceptable behaviors or performance, and communicate plans to correct them, before they become major problems. Wherever possible, information about policies, procedures, work assignments, and expectations should be communicated in writing even if it is communicated verbally as well. Disciplinary communication must always be put in writing.

The purpose of business communication is to impart information in simple, direct language that is easily understood and implemented. The federal government has formalized this principle in its guidelines for plain language, defined as "communication your audience can understand the first time they read or hear it,"[6] and archival leaders, managers, and supervisors should embrace the same principle. When communicating with staff, it is easy to place the emphasis on the writer—to write in a way that impresses the reader with the writer's intelligence or importance—rather than on the reader. Instead, written communications should use everyday language, should not shy away from addressing the reader as *you*, and should try to understand the communication from the reader's point of view. Plain language principles, for example, suggest that if you say something that might raise a question in your reader's mind, answer that question immediately in the next sentence or paragraph. If you don't, your reader may begin skimming the document searching for an answer and miss the point of your communication.

Communications about work expectations and assignments may seem mundane, but even these can reinforce (or undermine) the vision and values of the repository. Work assignments reflect the repository's priorities and will signal whether the archives is focused on, or frequently distracted from, its stated mission. Performance standards and reviews reflect the archives' true vision and mission, so these should be explicitly linked to the repository's formal mission and vision statements to ensure that they align and to reinforce their importance in the minds of employees. Policies indicate the values of the repository: how much it values fairness and staff contributions, for example, or how much it values public access to records or conservation of historical documents. Managers and leaders can use even everyday communications to reinforce the vision and mission of the repository.

Communicating with Administrators and Resource Providers

Administrators and resource providers (as we use them here) are the people to whom the archives' leaders are accountable. Depending on your situation, this could be the head of the agency of which the archives is a component part, a board of directors, a university president, a legislature, or any other officer who has authority over the archives leadership. These are often the people who decide the archives' annual budget or have final approval over policy or direction. Every communication to administrators and resource providers is an opportunity to garner their support.

Communicating vision

Though it may seem counterintuitive that a repository's vision needs to be communicated to higher administrators, these people must share the vision of the archives if they are to support the repository adequately. In fact, the strength of their support is likely to depend on the extent to which they see their own needs and desires reflected in the archives leadership's vision. For that reason, the best question to ask before communicating with people in such roles might be, "What's in it for them?" Archival leaders who can answer that question are likely to communicate effectively.

Aligning the archives' vision to those of a parent organization or other funding resource (such as a legislature or governor's office) normally means restating the archives' vision in a way that makes clear its support for the goals of the target audience. A review of the university's strategic plan or the governor's budget message or the institution's annual report will usually reveal the organization's highest priorities. It is rarely difficult to discover ways in which the archives supports such priorities in ways that further the archives' own vision. For example, a recent list of strategic goals issued by the governor of Georgia included these items to which many archives could link some part of their vision and mission:

Educated: Developing life-, college-, and work-ready students
- Increase percentage of students reading at or above grade level by the completion of 3rd Grade—a strategic benchmark for lifelong learning
- Increase teacher and school leader effectiveness
- Increase the percentage of high school graduates who are college and career ready

Responsible and Efficient Government: Fiscally sound, principled, conservative
- Increase availability of state services through innovative technology solutions
- Enlist community support and public-private partnerships to leverage available resources[7]

Similarly, a major university listed the following among its "Priorities for Excellence" in a recent strategic plan, any of which the university archives might support:

- Enhance student success (with emphasis on interdisciplinary learning)
- Advance academic and research excellence
- Serve the people of the state and beyond
- Use technology to expand access and opportunities[8]

The UCLA Library Special Collections "directions" document makes clear the effort to align its vision with that of its parent agency, the UCLA Library itself: "Our directions align explicitly with the UCLA Library Strategic Plan . . . and underscore Library Special Collections' contributions to advancing the work of the library as a whole."[9] Such an explicit statement sends a clear message to administrators: the special collections unit is part of the larger team and is aware of—and actively supportive of—the parent institution's direction.

After establishing a clear vision for their archives, the leadership must constantly restate that vision in ways that appeal to the self-interest of administrators and resources providers. This should never be a cynical attempt to manipulate administrators into believing that the archives supports their goals; if the archives is part of a larger organization, it was established to support the larger institutional goals, and it should be doing so in tangible ways. The task of archival leaders is to identify how the archives supports the larger mission and then document its contributions in a way that is compelling to administrators.

Advocacy

Communicating vision and values upward to higher administrators generally takes the form of advocacy for the archives and its programs. An advocate is one who defends or promotes a cause or person, and advocacy communication generally assumes limited knowledge on the part of the audience. In your role as archival advocate, you must reduce the message to its simplest form, emphasize the benefits of action, and ask for a specific response on the part of your audience.

Advocacy can take many forms, but it is a mistake to see it as a task you do. Instead, it is a mind-set that you internalize and maintain at all times. You should be so familiar with how your archives contributes to the larger institutional mission—and totally convinced that its contributions are important—that this message becomes part of your everyday communication, whether you are having casual conversations during chance encounters or making formal presentations verbally or in writing.

In my first professional job, I met often with my department's budget analyst and frequently waited outside her office for our meetings to begin. I became acquainted with other budget employees who passed by as I waited, and in short order, every one of them knew that the archives was doing exciting things and, more importantly to them, was engaged in projects that were meaningful to the organization's bottom line. The archives, for example, had scanned and indexed thousands of heavily used historic photographs for the Planning Department, thereby reducing that department's search time from several days to just a few minutes. I talked about the cost savings realized by the Planning Department, citing dollar figures as specifically as possible (these were budget people, after all), and since much of the work had been done by volunteers, I quantified that cost savings as well. Several years later, one of the people I met during that period became the budget director, and by then she was an enthusiastic supporter of the archives because she knew that our vision and mission firmly supported the goals of the larger organization and of her office specifically. Not surprisingly, the archives' budget benefited significantly during her tenure.

As this example shows, advocacy communication can be as subtle as a casual conversation if the archivist has the proper mind-set. But advocacy need not be this subtle. The university archives could easily hold a public talk about how the archives is supporting the university's current strategic plan, or it could write an article for the campus magazine around the same topic (or it could do both). In fact, most advocacy communications should be this direct. Don't assume that if you tell a good story, your audience will draw the obvious conclusion ("Ah . . . that must mean the archives saves us money"). Instead, draw the conclusion yourself, and state it clearly whenever possible.

Archival leaders must be advocates for their repositories, subtly and directly. They should not hesitate to reach out to influential people and request a brief meeting to explain the archives and its value. Such approaches sometimes require formal procedures—legislators, for example, often must be approached through the parent agency's legislative affairs officer—but in other cases, the approach can take the form of a cold call or email to the person of interest. I have rarely had anyone refuse my request for a thirty-minute meeting to discuss the archives. Still, what is to be done if the archivists have no access to the administrators or resource providers? Larry Hackman has pointed out that "[a]n excellent way to initially establish interest [in the archives] is to have information about the archives conveyed by peers, or near peers, of the senior parties rather than from the [archives] program itself."[10] For example, a state archivist may have difficulty getting the ear of the governor, but a cabinet-level agency head who is impressed with the archives and its services—and who believes those services can support the agency head's *own* goals—is sometimes willing to advocate a specific archival program to the governor. Peer groups can be effective as well. In this regard, the national professional associations representing state chief information officers and secretaries of state have been particularly strong advocates for archives in cooperation with the Council of State Archivists.

Communicating return on investment

In their communications to administrators and resource providers, successful archives move beyond reporting activities to demonstrating a clear return on investment. Tracking the number of visitors in the research room or the number of reference requests answered can be important tools to measure workload, and these are appropriate activities for managers, but good managers understand that measuring past activity rarely suffices to increase future support for the archives.

Phil Mooney, the longtime archivist of Coca-Cola, created a tool for measuring return on investment that he called a "Destination Document." Such a document "should project both short- and long-term objectives for the department, showing clear links between resources and results. It should also include a projection of quantifiable results that allows the project to be properly evaluated."[11] Archivists often dismiss any talk of return on investment as irrelevant to archives because the results of archival work cannot be monetized, but this view is simplistic at best. In the first place, much of the work of an archives *can* be measured in monetary terms:

- time saved (increased efficiency in retrieval or access, for example)
- savings generated (through volunteer work or interns or public/private partnerships, through reduction in paper stored, through increased access efficiency, etc.)
- income generated (through out-of-state visitors or other tourism, for example)

Several years later, in another essay, Mooney added a further suggestion for demonstrating return on investment: "Public relations work has industry measurement standards that can be applied to archival work. When a story appears in a newspaper or on. . . television, the costs of advertising in those media will be the standard against which value is determined."[12] Is your archives featured in a local paper or radio program? What would it have cost your organization to buy equivalent advertising coverage in that newspaper or radio program? Such costs are relatively easy to determine and may be used as hard data to sell the value of the archival program.

In the second place, archives can make an effort to express return on investment in social, nonmonetary terms. As Samantha Norling points out in chapter 10, the value of the archives to the Indianapolis Museum of Art became apparent only as the newly organized records began to be used to preserve, interpret, and market the museum building itself. While expressing return on investment in social terms is admittedly more difficult, archivists should be proud of these immeasurable benefits and communicate them whenever possible, often through stories. Records in one state archives, for example, were used to determine where the American chestnut had thrived in the eighteenth and nineteenth centuries so that biologists could attempt to reintroduce the tree at some of these same locations. The benefits of returning these historic trees to the American landscape might not be quantifiable (though their commercial potential might be expressed in terms of dollars), but it would be a significant ecological achievement, and the role of archives in that return should be celebrated.

Archival leaders spend time thinking about, measuring, and communicating how their work returns tangible or intangible benefits to their parent organization and resource providers, as well as to society in general.

Communicating to Customers and Potential Customers

In many archives, it is still considered bad taste to refer to patrons as "customers" of the archives, but there are advantages to thinking of archival users as customers who are "buying"—with their time and their patronage—the services of the archives. It is a cliché to say that the customer is always right, but the cliché carries with it the idea that the customers' needs are foremost in the minds of the service provider, and that is a concept that archival leaders should embrace emphatically.

Reciprocal communication

In the consumer world, placing the customer's needs first means (in simple terms) that the business must discover what the customer wants and then determine how to provide that desire. In itself, this is a worthy goal for archives: find out what our users really want—more comprehensive finding aids, simpler ways of finding records, better lighting, more comfortable chairs?—and try to provide it. But communication and interaction with archival customers is far more nuanced than this simple goal because there is at least one significant way in which archival customers differ from those at the local grocery store: our customers often have exceptional insight into our "products," the records we provide. In many cases, their knowledge and understanding exceed our own, so in a unique way, archival customers are partners with archivists and should be treated as such. Here, more than in many contexts, communication is a two-way street.

Training programs in archival reference place great emphasis on the art and science of locating and providing information to archival customers, but much less time is spent on gathering information from the customers,[15] except during the reference interview, which often takes place before the patron has conducted research. Treating customers as partners means making some attempt to capture their insights *after* they have used your collection:

- ***What did they learn about a specific collection that might be of use to the next patron who looks at that collection?*** This is especially important now, in the age of "more product, less process" (MPLP), where the archivists' own knowledge of their collections may be less comprehensive than it once was, and our patrons may be the only ones who have spent significant time mining their contents.
- ***How did their research help them? What will its consequences be?*** Here is your chance to collect hard data or another story for your advocacy efforts. Did someone just save her agency a great deal of money by conducting research in your archives? Did they discover information that will lead to a great business opportunity? Or did they finally locate a long-lost ancestor?

- *How can the archives do a better job serving them next time?* Face-to-face conversations often result in better or different information than formal surveys, and if we see our customers as partners, we will give them opportunity to communicate their needs to us.
- *Will they allow the archives to follow up with them later (by phone or email) to get additional information?* This is especially helpful if you sense that the patron's research resulted in, or may result in, a significant story. Respect your customer's privacy by asking permission to follow up.

These questions might be answered in formal exit interviews or through surveys and online tools, but if the reference staff members have a mind-set that embraces both customer service and advocacy—a mind-set they've learned from the archives leadership—this information is most likely to be collected in casual conversations before the patrons leave the archives. Communication is always a two-way street, but this is never more true than when talking about the archives' customers.

Archival customers extend beyond the patrons who visit our research rooms. Anyone who depends on the archives for information support—or who *should* depend on us for such support—is a customer as well. In an institutional archives, this might include the employees of various departments and the institution's administrators; for most archives, it would include online users who will never visit our facilities. Archival customers even include those who produce the records we collect, whether institutional agencies or private donors.

As with any successful business, archives should not assume that they understand their customers or potential customers without making some deliberate attempt to engage them. Sarah Koonts describes (in chapter 7) her realization that her archives had not adequately explained to the general public the complexity of its work. Even though the staff believed that they had communicated appropriately and effectively, their intended audience had misperceptions and unrealistic expectations about the archives and its policies. Archivists should never assume that their customers—even those with whom they engage regularly—share the same understanding of their work and its importance. Constant communication about our work in simple terms, using a variety of formats, is essential.

Engaging with customers also assumes that archivists collect data about them.[14] Archives should have a firm grasp of many things, including the following:

- *Who uses the archives?* Where do they live?
- *How did they learn about the archives?*
- *Why do people use the archives?* What benefit do they perceive from using archival collections?
- *Who uses the archives' online resources?* Are they the same people who visit in person? What prompts them to use virtual resources instead of physical resources?
- *Who is not using the archives but could benefit from doing so?* Why don't they use the archives? Are they aware of its resources? Are they aware of how they might benefit from such use?

From such data, the archives can determine better ways to serve its customers. The data may reveal that customers prefer to access specific types of records online and other types in person. Determining how your users learned about the archives may reveal ways to reach new audiences. Surveying nonusers, particularly from audiences that you believe would benefit from the archives' services, may uncover better ways to advertise your services. The archives' data collection should be driven by the desire to provide better customer service, and that will require consistent reciprocal communication.

Communicating vision and values

Finally, no matter how you define *customers* in your archives, every customer interaction is a chance to shine, a chance to share your vision of what the archives means to your users, to your institution, to society at large. Not every encounter will result in a meaningful conversation about the significance of archives, but each interaction is an opportunity to demonstrate your enthusiasm and the importance of your mission, and archival leaders instill that belief in their employees through word and example.

Communicating with Supporters and Potential Supporters

Supporters, defined in this context as those who donate time, money, or documents to the archives, are a significant audience for archival leaders, as are potential supporters, who could donate resources to the archives but do not yet do so.

Communicating vision

Supporters of the archives want to feel that they are part of something bigger than themselves. Like most people who support charities or community organizations, they want to know that their contribution will make a significant difference to others, preferably both now and far into the future. Here the archives has a natural advantage over other types of organizations because our mission is always to extend the life of historical records far into the future. It is left to the leadership, then, to explain how the work of the archives is significant. In short, supporters and potential supporters need to come to share the leader's vision for the archives.

Potential supporters are likely to share the leader's vision only if they see something in it that speaks to their own goals and desires. Here again, research is required to discover what motivates your supporters (so that you can keep them motivated) or potential supporters (so that you can engage them). Professional fund-raisers often create profiles on potential donors that include information such as the prospect's hometown, marital status, education, business and professional interests, hobbies, and even religious and political preferences. While it may not always be possible for archivists to conduct research to this extent, the Internet has made it relatively simple to learn key things about potential supporters and customize a tour or letter that ties the prospect's interests to the archives' vision and mission. Is a legislator or commissioner visiting the archives? A quick search will probably uncover their key legislative interests, their hometown, and their educational attainments. The archives is almost certain to have documents that relate to one or more of these. Similar research can identify ways to connect the archives to a new president, CEO, board member, or someone who might be induced to donate money or collections to the archives. Remember that, while it is interesting for a potential supporter to see, for example, a hometown document, they will be more interested still to learn that their passion for education is incorporated in the archives' own vision or mission statement and to learn what the archives did in the past few months to further that goal.

Communicating repository needs

Once the groundwork is laid by demonstrating that the archives supports some goal of a potential supporter, experience shows that, in a surprising number of instances, the archivist can secure a donation of time, money, or documents simply by asking. Many archivists can attest to being told by donors that "I had no idea anyone would want these records," or "No one ever asked me for [time, money, or documents] before." Archivists often shy away from the specific ask; instead, they should believe in the value of what they offer in return—perpetual preservation, public access to information, exciting educational opportunities—and ask boldly.

Supporters' alignment with the archives' vision can be short-term ("I want to see this particular collection digitized, so I will support the archives financially just to the extent needed to make that happen") or long-term ("I believe in the archives' mission to educate senior adults, so I will contribute my time and money until a formal program is firmly established and stable" or "I believe in the work of the archives to make records accessible, so I will donate some time each week to indexing projects"). In every case, though, the archives gains yet another opportunity to invite people to share its vision and catch its enthusiasm. Supporters may be drawn to the archives for many reasons, but the archives should make every effort to build each one into an advocate for the archives, its vision, and its mission.

Communicating with the Public

The public is a term broad enough to be meaningless, but in this context, it means (in general) a group of people who may not have a direct relationship with the archives but whose tacit support is desirable, or (more specifically) a group of people who are unaware that the archives' resources could benefit them. The former group might include the faculty at a university, while the latter might include undergraduate students majoring in history.

Communicating to the general public

Archivists are unlikely to spend significant time communicating to the general public (those who have no direct contact with the archives), though it is always advantageous if people who hear the word *archives* have an accurate understanding of what an archives does and have a positive image of the work. In one instance, an archives installed a temporary exhibit in the lobby of a nearby concert hall. Large numbers of concertgoers were observed viewing and discussing the exhibit during intermissions, and the hope was that this general public, whose experience of archives was probably very limited, might come away with a better appreciation and positive view of archives in general. Because of the general nature of the goal and the audience, no attempt was made to document the results in any measurable way.

Communicating to a specific public

The archives may spend more significant time communicating with specific publics—those who could benefit from the repository's resources. Since such groups are often clearly defined, communications to them can be very targeted. History students can be shown the benefits of using primary sources in their research and can be informed about the archives' hours of service, website, and other very specific information of interest. Genealogists can be informed about specific resources at the archives, while agencies within the larger parent organization might be informed about how the archives' resources have helped other agencies save time and money.

Communicating with specific, targeted publics requires research, but delivering the message is often easy; the archives may reach history students through a history club newsletter or genealogists through a specific journal or conference, and institutional agencies normally have established communication methods, such as newsletters or regular staff meetings, that the archives can tap into. And, unlike the scattershot approach of reaching the general public, the results of communicating to a specific public are likely to be more measurable.

Conclusion

Communication is the engine of leadership, as witnessed by the frequency with which the contributors to this book return to its importance, whether they are discussing strategy, resources, relationships, or any other aspect of leadership. Communication is the archival leader's most potent resource and a potential stumbling block. The work of the archives—the support it receives from administrators, its users, and the public, and the culture of the repository—flow outward from the leader's own vision and values, carried on a river of communication.

The most critical communication vehicle for any leader is attitude, the unspoken message that serves as the backdrop to all other communications. It has been said that Ron Johnson, onetime CEO of JCPenney, "gave the impression that he wouldn't shop in one of his own stores and didn't particularly understand the people who did."[15] Archivists, unfortunately, are not immune to this pitfall. The leader's enthusiasm—or lack of enthusiasm—for the vision of the archives, its mission, and its work will be telegraphed to staff, administrators, supporters, and the public at every encounter. Communication is the river that nurtures all aspects of the archives, and the leader's vision and values are its source.

Because communication is so important to leadership, we discuss it as an aspect of other major topics in the next five chapters. Peter Gottlieb emphasizes in chapter 2, "Strategic Leadership," that a leader's success in developing strategic approaches to archival work depends to a great extent on constant and targeted communication. He also focuses on leaders' status as agents of change, shaping the direction of the archives and guiding—sometimes pushing—staff and stakeholders to grapple continuously with programmatic change.

NOTES

[1] James M. Kouzes and Barry Posner, "To Lead, Create a Shared Vision," *Harvard Business Review* (from January 2009 issue), https://hbr.org/2009/01/to-lead-create-a-shared-vision/ar/1, captured at https://perma.cc/WEA4-N5LT.

[2] "Vision and Mission," National Archives and Records Administration, https://www.archives.gov/about/info/mission.html, captured at https://perma.cc/Q4NX-RPEY.

[3] Kouzes and Posner, "To Lead, Create a Shared Vision."

[4] New York University Archives, http://www.nyu.edu/library/bobst/research/arch/mission.htm, captured at https://perma.cc/2ZYB-566C.

[5] "Mission and Vision Statements," Special Collections & Archives, Eastern Kentucky University, http://archives.eku.edu/mission, captured at https://perma.cc/M78W-VAXE.

[6] "What Is Plain Language?," http://www.plainlanguage.gov/whatisPL/, captured at https://perma.cc/E6X2-GUKP.

[7] "Governor's Strategic Goals for Georgia," http://opb.georgia.gov/sites/opb.georgia.gov/files/related_files/site_page/State%20Goals%20April%202013%20FINAL.pdf, captured at https://perma.cc/2ERZ-DNG3.

[8] "Priorities for Excellence," Pennsylvania State University, http://strategicplan.psu.edu/priorities_for_excellence/enhancesuccess.html. Since this strategic plan was last accessed, the plan (or the way it is expressed) has changed significantly, demonstrating the need for archivists to remain alert to shifting institutional priorities. The newer priorities continue to reflect goals that archives could easily support, such as digital innovation and increased emphasis on arts and humanities. For the newer version, see "Thematic Priorities," captured at https://perma.cc/GX7F-ET6Y.

[9] "[UCLA] Library Special Collections Mission, Principles, and Direction," http://www.library.ucla.edu/sites/default/files/LSC%20Mission-Principles-Directions.pdf, captured at https://perma.cc/8ZXT-7ZLJ.

[10] Larry J. Hackman, "Ways and Means: Thinking and Acting to Strengthen the Infrastructure of Archival Programs," in *Leadership and Administration of Successful Archival Programs*, ed. Bruce W. Dearstyne (Westport, CT: Greenwood Press, 2001), 45.

[11] Philip F. Mooney, "Corporate Culture and the Archives," in *Leadership and Administration of Successful Archival Programs*, ed. Bruce W. Dearstyne (Westport, CT: Greenwood Press, 2001), 88.

[12] Philip F. Mooney, "Stranger in a Strange Land: The Archivist and the Corporation," in *Leading and Managing Archives and Records Programs: Strategies for Success,* ed. Bruce W. Dearstyne (New York: Neal-Schuman, 2008), 201.

[13] Some archival scholars—Elizabeth Yakel, Wendy Duff, and Helen Tibbo, among others—have created tools to gather information about users and how they use archival collections, but the emphasis here is on gathering much more specific information: how researchers have used *specific* collections in *your* archives and how you can make use of that information.

[14] Collecting even simple data about customers can help the archives make better decisions and advocate more effectively for the program. In one instance, simple data collection demonstrated that Monday was not the archives' busiest research day (contrary to adamant staff opinion) and was, in fact, so poorly attended that closing the archives to the public on that day caused no resistance from the public. In another instance, a simple survey of out-of-state visitors uncovered surprising information (such visitors stayed longer and spent more money than estimated) that was of great interest to local tourism officials, who then became vocal supporters of the archival program.

[15] Lee G. Bolman and Terrence E. Deal, *How Great Leaders Think: The Art of Reframing* (San Francisco: Jossey-Bass, 2014), 4.

2

Strategic Leadership

Peter Gottlieb

In this chapter, I discuss how leaders and managers develop strategies for improving archival programs. By *strategy* I mean a purposeful and disciplined approach to strengthening an archives. A strategy underlies and informs specific plans, programs, or initiatives. In a later chapter, I explore archival leadership for transformational change, so here my focus is almost entirely on strategy that builds on the archives' existing programmatic foundations.

Strategy makes it possible to define and achieve positive change: win an objective, strengthen a position, improve a program. If, in some imaginary world, no such change could happen, there would be no need for strategy. Of course, today's archival world brims with opportunities for progressive change. Even the most effective and reputable repository seeks to improve its work to maintain its position or to stay current with emerging trends. Most archives wish to exceed their own definitions of merely adequate performance.

Especially for the leader's role, I think there are advantages to focusing on strategies instead of on strategic planning. First, it is debatable whether we need more strategic planning blueprints. Archivists today can consult a vast literature on that topic, including excellent works specifically about archives.[1] Second, while many guides to strategic planning for good reason provide extensive directions for implementing goals, action steps, project schedules, staff assignments, and other more detailed tactics, they less often dwell on the strategy framework underlying these specifics. Third, in most designs, plans necessarily come and go according to circumstance and need, while strategy remains the constant requirement for archival improvement.[2] Certain schemes recommend that new plans with revised goals and objectives succeed almost seamlessly the conclusion of an earlier phase of planning, thus implying the need for a continuing foundation of strategy.

Leaders play the pivotal role in developing strategies for their archives. The expansive thinking and long-term perspective required for strategic work directly relate to core leader functions. More importantly, strategy calls for leaders because they are the ones who consistently attune their programs to continual change and improvement.[3] Sometimes through inspiration, often by encouragement, and even with discipline, leaders wed their programs to strategic work and make it the default mode in which the archives operates. For the many moving parts in an archives' strategy, managers provide the coordination and logical sequencing of work as well as the performance analysis that are necessary to sustain progress.

Elements of Strategy

Strategy consists of several key elements:

- setting direction
- choosing priorities
- adapting
- measuring and evaluating

Setting direction

A strategy begins with a certain orientation for change and improvement. Before an archives can decide what it needs to do, it must determine as clearly as possible two fundamentals: what it is now, and what it wants to become in the future. The line that connects these two key points provides the archives' bearing—the direction in which it seeks to grow. A useful way to express these basics is by preparing statements on mission and vision. An archives' mission expresses its essential purpose and values. Its vision succinctly describes what the archives ultimately wants to accomplish through the pursuit of its mission.

Archival leaders and managers are lucky to have any number of good sources on preparing mission and vision statements, both from the archives profession and from related fields, and David Carmicheal provides his own suggestions in chapter 1.[4] These sources emphasize the things that characterize effective statements:

- Mission statements reflect the values and philosophy of an archives.
- Vision statements inspire and motivate archives' staff and stakeholders.
- Brevity is better for both statements, though not at the cost of ambiguity.

Writing mission and vision statements confronts leaders with real challenges. While they need to infuse their own ideas, they must always draw on the thinking of the archives staff and often of its parent organization as well (the director, governing board, financial donors, etc.). They must try to make the statements represent broadly shared concepts without allowing it to become overly general or formulaic. Leaders strive to come out with statements that unite and focus the individual efforts of everyone who can contribute to the archives' success. In trying to fulfill these needs, leaders can also face skeptical staff and supporters.

It is perhaps not surprising that members of an organization are dubious about the effort of writing mission and vision statements. Isn't the archives' fundamental purpose obvious to everyone? Why does the old statement need overhauling? It's really a waste of limited time to compose a blue-sky statement about an ideal future! Leaders should not succumb to these natural reactions or shortchange the effort devoted to mission and vision statements. Instead, they need to find ways to draw the people of their organizations into a creative conversation. For example, to engage colleagues in developing a vision statement, leaders can remind staff that many of them approached their archives career with some idea of what their ideal job could be. They can talk about vision by sharing that mental picture and by generalizing from it to what an archives offering ideal jobs would look like. From there, the thought exercise could project how such a successful program would contribute to its community. Leaders might also encourage staff to list all the things the archives has long wanted to accomplish and then imagine what the archives would be like if it did so. Good vision statements are built from such existing hopes and ambitions as well as from bold new thinking.

In a similar fashion, leaders can stimulate the preparation of a mission statement by asking staff and stakeholders to contribute background information on the archives program. They can dig into the sources on their own and their parent institutions' missions, mandates, enabling legislation, official policies, and administrative guidelines. Sometimes this information contains original versions of values and philosophies that still animate the programs or offers clear formulations that have gone unused for years. Even when outdated or irrelevant, information from these foundational documents might provide a historical perspective helpful to discussing current values and writing or revising a mission statement.

Additional helpful information about core values and mission can come from talking with current senior and former staff and administrators, both in the archives itself, the parent institution, and important partner organizations. Long-term donors might also provide a good perspective on the archives' fundamental purpose and on how it has evolved. As with the brainstorming exercises about the vision, these investigations bring leaders, staff, and stakeholders out of the realm of abstract thought and give them specific ideas and perspectives from the archives' own past and current work to use in writing a mission statement.

Leaders also encourage constructive participation in writing the mission and vision by constantly reminding everyone about the practical benefits of having well-considered and clearly expressed statements. A concise and well-composed mission (firmly based on the archives' values) distills the archives' identity, just as the vision announces its aspiration. These basic markers enable staff, managers, and leaders to steer their program and to make good decisions when options arise. Clarity and confidence in the statements helps to decide questions like the following: Is this alternative in keeping with our mission? What best embodies our values? Will this project bring us closer to our vision?

One payoff for deliberating carefully on these direction-setting questions comes from updating traditional but outdated versions of what the archives is. Imagine an archives that decades ago won renown for its services to scholars but that later intentionally broadened its audience and now welcomes many types of users. Leaders as well as staff might still think of their work in terms of the archives' reputation as a scholarly resource—after all, the archives continues to do excellent work with academic researchers and authors. Nonetheless, what the archives does and what it values overall have changed. To be useful in strategic terms, its definition of itself must change too.

Mission, values, and vision provide the bearings for the archives' future course. Without them, no amount of good and important work could move a program confidently ahead, since "ahead" would remain unknown.[5] Just as surely, even the clearest bearings do not suffice for a successful strategy. If they were all that were required for a strategic approach, the situation would end up looking like signposts in a roadless landscape. The direction to follow would be abundantly clear, but heading that way would be very difficult.

Choosing priorities

Beyond setting a direction for change and improvement, a strategy focuses the resources of an archives on work that must be done in order to move ahead. While the direction itself takes precedence over everything else, it needs selected projects whose accomplishment actually propels the archives in accordance with the mission and toward the vision. Whether these interrelated efforts are termed goals, objectives, tactics, or some other name, they become the first claim on the program's resources and the engine for the strategy.

Choosing priorities can be straightforward and easy, but an archives more often must carefully analyze the values of multiple possibilities and then move ahead only with those relative few that best align with its mission and vision, that seem most feasible, and that promise to yield greatest progress. Committing an archives to a long menu of projects is a common misstep. The essence of strategy lies in making choices that focus an archives' work,[6] and leadership has the responsibility for ensuring that the choice-making process is a rigorous one.

The time and careful deliberation leaders devote to crafting mission and vision statements greatly help when it comes time to choose priorities. Let's picture the leadership, staff, and stakeholders of a university archives compiling and sorting a list of possible priorities for its strategy. The archives already has an enviable reputation as a research resource for students and now declares its mission to serve the entire campus community and its vision to achieve the capability to do so. After listing and debating many appealing priorities, the archives comes up with a set of ten that have wide support. Since launching work on ten priorities would clearly be daunting, leadership examines each one according to the direction defined for the strategy. How well does each priority on the list help the archives expand the number of campus groups and offices it serves? Which priorities can best leverage more operating funds, staff, and space for the archives?

The purpose of the exercise is to maximize alignment between the overall strategic direction and the work that the archives focuses on. In rating each priority on the draft list according to mission and vision, some proposals that originally looked quite commendable (e.g., starting an online campus newsletter) will end up proving less valuable. Some changes that had appealed to many in the university archives before work on the strategy began (refurbishing the archives reading room) in retrospect look like they do not sync at all well with the trajectory for the archives. Grounding the priorities firmly in the mission and vision avoids dressing a strategy in the clothing of some perennially popular projects.

Leadership must also determine whether priorities are feasible before they move ahead with them. This becomes mainly a question of sufficient resources to complete a priority in the allotted time. The archives needs both the tangible resources for the work as well as such intangible ones like staff knowledge and skills, administrative support, or key partnerships. While the university archives' new mission and vision could be well served by the priority of indexing the full run of its alumni magazine (thus supporting services to the alumni and to the campus development office), the work requires additional staffing, space, and computing resources. Lacking these resources, leadership might choose a priority with different, if not equal, strategic value. It could also replace the alumni magazine indexing with a priority for acquiring the resources necessary for doing that work.

It may not be necessary to complete a detailed cost analysis before deciding which priorities the archives should work on. Budgeting can instead be done in the course of preparing to start the work. However, assessing the general resource requirements for the priorities on a short list is vital to avoid impractical or blue-sky projects that will waste any time devoted to them and squander the archives' focus and energy.

Because the constraint of limited resources for nearly all archives means that leadership and staff can choose only a limited number of priorities, they want to make sure that the ones they select move the archives as far as possible in the direction they have committed to. They probably do not have quantitative metrics with which to measure a priority's likely impact, since they have not yet begun to work on it. They can, however, make reasonable if more qualitative projections for a priority's potential effectiveness.

The hypothetical university archives that I'm using as a case for choosing priorities has set a direction toward becoming a program with the infrastructure and resources needed to serve the entire campus community. It has listed several possible ways to start in this direction but must decide which ones have the greatest leverage. Should it reach out to academic schools and departments that are not currently using its services? Could it cultivate even more new users through initiatives with student organizations or with alumni? Would it be better first to forge closer ties to top-level administrative offices? As leaders and staff think through questions like these, they better understand that their options differ in how much impact they can have. They also realize that one or two priorities might actually have the capacity both to widen the archives' circle of users and to bolster its resources—a high level of effectiveness that leaders and staff had never thought possible.

Choosing priorities for strategic work by assessing their potential for incremental progress can lead to exciting breakthroughs in what can seem like a process of steadily limiting options. At my hypothetical university archives, leaders willing to look again at their choices might see that two separately formulated priorities can be merged to create one that has greater power for forward movement than anything else under consideration. Looking at alternative priorities can also be a time for leaders to consider taking risks or beginning bold ventures that previously may not have seemed advisable. A Wisconsin university archives I'm familiar with, which had always had its quarters in the basement of the library, dramatically raised its campus profile by taking advantage of planning for the renovation of a much more visible university space.[7] By getting expanded quarters in this more prominent location, the archives achieved a higher profile on campus. Even in the digital era, when physical location is less important than it previously was, all prospective students and their families now see this archives during their campus visits, and the archives can potentially play a greater role in the university.

Adapting

One certainty about implementing a strategy is that instead of following a straight line of progress, the path toward improvement will commonly zig and zag. One reason that this happens even with the most meticulously chosen priorities and thoroughly developed implementation plans is that their very success can change the environment the archives operates in as well as its own status. Additionally, obstacles or new opportunities always crop up. Leadership might anticipate some of these and make preparations to meet them,[8] but some unforeseen circumstances will also emerge. Obviously these challenges can frustrate and dishearten leadership and staff, but they do not necessarily signal poor planning, nor do they have to threaten continued progress in the archives' chosen direction for improvement.

From the early phases of choosing priorities, leaders and managers can prepare their staff for adaptations and changes. A discouraged staff member once challenged my announcement of a change to planned work by asking, "If we're just going to switch gears and try new approaches, what's the point of doing all the strategizing in the first place?" The question made me realize that I had not anticipated staff's reactions to changes in our strategic work. Indeed, I had not fully anticipated these changes myself.

Leadership makes it easier for staff to adapt to changes in strategic work by maintaining a focus on mission and vision as the most important aspects of the archives' strategy. Keeping these enduring pointers toward the future foremost in staff's minds allows everyone to adapt more flexibly when it becomes necessary to do so. By ensuring that the overall strategic direction stays prominently in view, leaders and managers ensure smoother transitions from one set of tactics to another. If staff can appreciate the importance of the archives' continuing in its strategic direction, it can more easily handle new ways to make progress.

Leaders and managers can avoid the converse of centering strategic work on mission and vision: overcommitting to details of implementing priorities such as budgets, staff assignments, deadlines, and so forth. By overcommitting, I mean devoting inappropriate attention to preparing the many fine points of work plans. Though leadership and staff of course need these in order to work efficiently and to coordinate efforts, they can allocate too much time and energy to working out *in advance* details that likely will change as the archives' work proceeds. This in itself can set the archives up for greater difficulties when the time inevitably comes to alter prepared plans and priorities. Leaders and managers may want to experiment with a just-in-time approach to developing details for implementing priorities, in which they at first define projects generally and wait to flesh out specific procedures, staff responsibilities, and resources until they determine with certainty that the project will proceed.

To see what flexibility in strategic work might look like in practice, we can return to our hypothetical university archives and follow what might happen as it starts work on its priorities. Keeping with its mission to serve the entire campus, staff begin on a priority to work with previously unserved classes. As they start to make progress with this effort, they learn that the African American student union is looking for a new Black History Month program to engage its members. In preliminary discussions with this campus group, the archives' director raises the prospect of introducing all of its members to the archives, in particular to its documents about the earliest African American students on campus. When the students express interest, the director and staff evaluate this new opportunity against their current work with unserved classes and decide to change course to connect with African American students.

Although the archives must give up (for the moment, at least) most of the work with unserved classes, it sees offsetting advantages of pursuing the unanticipated opportunity to cooperate with African American students. Not only does this fresh chance promise to expand as well as diversify the archives' on-campus constituencies, it has the potential to build the archives' understanding of minority students' and faculty's needs and its ability to serve those needs. Seen against the archives' already strong performance as an academic research resource, temporarily setting aside the pursuit of unserved courses looks like a reasonable sacrifice in order to make a significant change.

Let's note several important aspects of this adaptation to a new opportunity. First, it remains true to the archives' strategic direction while changing how it is pursued. Second, seizing the new opportunity could involve increased costs. In the near term, the archives might need to invest resources to increase access to its collections on African American students. In the long term, it could face additional costs in staff time to learn how best to serve African Americans on campus, how to understand their needs, and how to respond to their interests, values, and group identity.

This example of an archives that shifts to take advantage of a new opportunity argues for flexibility in any strategic approach. It also illustrates the value of some opportunism in strategy. No matter how well an archives understands the environment it works in, no matter how clearly it has plotted its forward direction, it will deal with unexpected developments. Strategy lies in adapting to take advantage of some surprises rather than keeping doggedly to the originally plotted course. The crucial qualification here is that the archives maintains the strategic approach and the overall direction established by its mission, values, and vision.[9]

Measuring and evaluating

Resourceful leadership might make steady progress on a strategy without measuring or evaluating its work, but it would need considerable luck to do so. Leaders who build measurements into their strategic work stand better odds of success. This kind of leadership improves by taking results from evaluations and feeding them back into the archives' processes and priorities. While this approach also keeps leadership strategies flexible, it does so in a more rigorous and systematic way than one-off adjustments to new opportunities and unexpected setbacks.

Evaluation of institutional programs—even just those in the information and cultural heritage fields—is too broad a subject for me to deal with adequately in this chapter.[10] My focus here is on evaluation in a strategic context, where leadership looks at intended changes in the archives.[11] Measuring and evaluating tell leaders, managers, staff, and stakeholders whether (and to what degree) their strategic work is progressing. These actions enhance accountability and transparency in a strategy and accordingly become important leadership responsibilities as well as constructive leadership tools.

An archives measures its work when it gathers quantitative or qualitative data about its program activities: terabytes of data accessioned over a period of time; pages of documents digitized and uploaded to a website; users' answers to survey questions about satisfaction with reference services. It evaluates its work by applying specific criteria to the measurements, in order to judge how effective work has been.[12]

The essence of measuring and evaluating in a strategic context is that the results being examined are ones planned in advance. Therefore, leadership and staff can define measurements of progress as part of each priority they choose to work on. They can also specify measurements at a later time or revise the measurements that they originally created. Developing measurements can even become a separate priority for the strategic work, equal in importance to other priorities. This priority could work particularly well when the archives has little or no experience measuring progress and wants to devote focused attention on learning and applying methods. Like measuring, evaluating the results of strategic work can use yardsticks developed as part of strategy itself: the criteria of mission, vision, and values of the archives. What the archives accomplishes through its strategic priorities becomes meaningful only when gauged in terms of the program's direction and fundamental commitments.[13]

Our hypothetical university archives' mission is to serve the entire campus community, while its vision is to build the capability to engage a wider range and larger number of users. Among other priorities for moving forward in this strategic direction, it ultimately decides to collaborate with the African American student union, which has expressed an interest in a Black History Month program that can introduce its members to the archives. What kinds of metrics meaningfully reveal whether or not this particular effort yields progress toward the archives' mission and vision?

If the priority aims to increase the number of students using the archives' services, whether in person or virtually, then tallying the number of African American students making transactions with the archives would be the right metric. However, leadership and staff ultimately realize that making more African American students aware of the archives, its holdings, and its services—whether or not they ever use the archives—better captures the essence of both the mission to serve and the priority of working with African American students. This clarification enables the archives to think again about appropriate measurements.

One type of measurement simply counts the number of "products" or outputs achieved through strategic work: the number of archives staff presentations to the African American student group; the number of group visits to the archives; the number of pages of African-American content added to the archives website; the number of visits to these webpages; and so forth. The value of these quantitative measures lies in their clarity, their usefulness for reporting, and the comparative ease of tracking them. Wherever products or outputs reflect a substantive aspect of strategic work, they should be counted and used to measure progress.

Since the archives defines awareness as the goal of its priority, it really needs another type of measurement, in addition to its counts of awareness-building products. Ideally, it seeks measurement of African American students' changing level of knowledge about the archives. For this, the archives could conduct one survey among the students to be engaged through the work and another with those same students once the work has involved them for a period of time. The surveys might try to measure knowledge before and after through determining what percentage of students know the following information:

- that there is an archives on campus
- where the archives is located
- what kinds of materials the archives makes available
- what kinds of services the archives offers.

If conducted with sufficient care to solicit useful data, these surveys can reveal changes in general awareness of the archives and also knowledge about what the archives offers.

In our university archives example, awareness of the archives among African American students represents an outcome, a change in individuals or groups affected by strategic work.[14] Both qualitative and quantitative measures can evaluate outcomes. Outcome-based evaluation has become more prevalent for all types of mission-based and planned work since the 1990s, beginning with a law mandating it for federal government agencies, the essence of which was later adopted by archival grant-funding agencies.[15]

Leadership pays attention to measurement and evaluation for the simple reason that it has the responsibility to monitor the progress of strategic work. The authorities to whom leaders and managers report expect them to show the results a strategy is producing. The better leadership can do this for a successful strategy, the more it improves the archives' case for support and increases its overall standing. Effective leadership in this area requires understanding evaluation principles and methods. It also involves patience and persistence in identifying the right metrics and applying them consistently.

Evaluation as a monitoring activity in strategic work also gives staff and leadership a valuable tool for refining how the work is being done. Suppose that the university archives' data reveal that the African American students who had the closest contact with the archives demonstrate the greatest increase in awareness. Leadership and staff naturally want to know the reason for this, so that they can better understand students' reactions and use effective outreach in the future. By conducting more in-depth interviews with individual students, they learn that meeting archives staff in person and seeing actual documents written by earlier African American students created a stronger, more lasting awareness than learning about the archives through online exhibits, websites, and printed information. When a sufficiently large number of individual interviews bring out this same correlation, the archives can confidently revise its strategic work to include more staff presentations using original documents.

Leadership also invests in evaluation to promote accountability and transparency in strategic work. Whatever evaluation methods leaders and managers use, they can achieve greater transparency by getting staff involved in developing them and by explaining them to stakeholders and especially to administrators and governing authorities. The outcome-based evaluation methodology provides accountability by requiring the definition of performance measures before work is launched and reporting on those measures once work has started. Leadership reinforces accountability by reporting regularly on measurements and evaluations, including all the contextual information that is needed for a well-grounded assessment.

We can also evaluate the strategy itself and not just its component priorities and projects. Although certain measurements might help in such a broad assessment, we are mostly considering outcomes and consequently need qualitative information. More specifically, this evaluation often compares results of strategic work to expectations:

- Is the progress to date taking the archives in the direction it needs to go?
- Is progress well focused, or have too many separate goals defused the effort?
- Is the work staying in alignment with vision, mission, and values?
- Do the vision and mission themselves remain cogent and compelling?

The archives' staff, governing authorities, financial providers, and partner programs can best answer such questions. If leadership forms an oversight or steering committee at the outset of its strategic work, such a group should also play a major role in this evaluation.

For a strategy-level evaluation, leadership can decide whether or not to use the services of a consultant or outside expert to help the archives judge how well it is doing. A consultant who has assisted the archives develop the strategy and who has knowledge and skills in evaluation might provide important perspectives on the work that has been accomplished. If leadership decides that a fresh vantage on the progress of a strategy is essential, then it should bring in an experienced consultant with no history with the archives. The consultant should talk to all the archives' stake-holders and particularly to the staff before writing and submitting a report.

Evaluations obviously do not become ends in themselves. They do not simply provide an opportunity to step back and reflect on how the plan is going. They not only support monitoring, reporting, and accountability but also provide information for decisions about future work and adjustments to the strategy. Once leadership and staff see a quantitative measure of results, they ask themselves if the numbers indicate a need to alter the planned work. When all who are working on the plan express their feelings and opinions about how things are going, they next decide if what they are voicing should be reflected in a plan revision. Separating assessments and the results of assessments in this way makes it possible to feed back into the plan the most careful measurements and deliberate decisions possible.

Leadership can schedule evaluations on the whole strategy on a regular basis, but they can also choose logical times for evaluations, according to the progress in the work. The completion of important priorities or a major transition from one phase of the strategy to the next can provide good times for scheduling evaluations. Clearly, leaders should follow the conclusion of the final work on the strategy with both a celebration and an evaluation. However, new and unanticipated obstacles to progress furnish equally important chances to pause and take stock of how the strategy is working. Whether evaluations take place on a set timetable or according to progress or setbacks, most importantly they become integral parts of the strategy and strengthen the archives by suggesting changes that lead to better work and improved outcomes.

Leaders' and Managers' Roles in Pursuing Strategy

So far, I have highlighted key aspects of strategic work and discussed leadership's contributions to them. While managers participate in all these phases of strategic work, their particular roles include directing the work on priorities, coordinating concurrent priorities, compiling and analyzing measurements, and facilitating staff discussions about strategy. Archival leaders' key contributions come in setting direction, in selecting a limited number of high-leverage priorities, and in preparing staff to adapt the strategy as it is implemented.[16] Leaders also ensure that the strategy demonstrates accountability and transparency, through the use of appropriate measurement, evaluation, and reporting. Leaders have two other more general responsibilities for any strategic effort: gathering support for the strategy from important stakeholders and maintaining staff's focus and morale. Marshaling support begins even before the development of the strategy, while encouragement for staff continues as long as work on the strategy does.

A leader takes primary responsibility for building and maintaining support for strategy. She does this because in some cases, the archives' parent institution assigns the part to her, and in other cases, because she initiates the planning herself. She takes the part also because she has the best position from which to communicate the whys and wherefores of taking a strategic approach to the archives' work. Moreover, by what she says and how she acts, she also has the greatest ability to influence attitudes toward the project, including those held by the archives staff as well as those held by others in the parent organization.

Since many archives function within larger organizations, the leader's work to win backing often includes the task of gaining institutional sponsorship for the effort to create a strategy. Especially when the leader anticipates difficult challenges in this work, she must ensure support from the parent organization administrators and governing board. Ideally, she also gains understanding and cooperation from other programs and colleagues within the organization, with whose work the archives might coordinate as the strategy evolves. Even if the leader initiates more limited changes, she reduces potential obstacles and builds understanding of the archives program by seeking this executive sponsorship. In some situations, the institutional support for a strategy can take the form of a coalition of key people within the archives, its parent organization, and external partners and supporters. This might be a formal group, like a strategy steering committee, with functions defined by an administrator to whom the archives reports or by a governing board. It could equally well be a less structured group of interested supporters. An astute leader makes sure that the form and roles of any such help maintain the focus on and support for pursuing a strategic approach in the archives.

A leader's second general responsibility for strategic work comes in supporting and encouraging staff. An empathic and creative leader finds many ways to meet this responsibility. She opens as much decision-making as possible to staff, invites new ideas and initiatives from all quarters, points out where there is latitude for making changes, recognizes individual and group accomplishments, and celebrates successes. These measures help increase interest in and build stronger commitment to the strategy among staff.

A crucial way that a leader can encourage staff is by helping them get through the setbacks that inevitably slow down progress. A leader might underestimate the effect on staff morale of delays, false starts, and failed initiatives. In addition to the constant challenge of strengthening and improving work, these problems can cause staff to lose heart and erode their commitment to a strategic approach. These are situations where an effective leader stays in close touch with staff. She does not dismiss or glibly minimize the missteps but also does not overreact to them by making sudden, sharp changes in the archives' course.

For a serious problem, a leader can pause work on the archives' strategy and invite staff to join her in assessing the obstacles or mistakes. If she presents this not as an emergency but as a natural time to take stock, identify flaws, and find ways to resume progress, she can reassure discouraged staff. For lesser issues, a leader can invite staff to propose any adjustments in the original plans that they believe will overcome the problem and to persist. A leader can also help staff put setbacks and disappointments into the overall context of improvements the archives has accomplished. As long as this kind of encouragement does not descend into patronizing treatment or superficial "happy talk," it can go some way toward maintaining staff's spirits and resolve.

Another important though less obvious way that a leader encourages staff is by providing the long-range view of the archives and its strategy. This view takes in all parts of the archives program. It includes the archives' function and responsibilities within a parent institution and its links to partner organizations. This big picture also embraces relationships with donors and with friends groups. It can contain as well the professional ethics and standards to which the archives holds itself accountable and how the archives compares with other archival programs of similar type and size. The leader constructs this broad view partly through the work of creating the strategy itself and partly through daily contacts with stakeholders and with professional archival networks.

A leader can use this broad view to support staff's work on a strategy. This happened for one archives when staff debated part of a priority to improve the ways it managed collections. Staff had used one particular approach for such a long time that they assumed it had developed from a formal policy at some point in the past. After looking thoroughly through all the archives' administrative decisions and mandated procedures, the leader could find no such basis for the method. She reported what she had learned to the staff and suggested that, since the established way of working in fact had no official status, they had the latitude to adopt a different method.

In this instance, the leader used the broad view of the archives in two ways to help the staff. First, she looked for ways to help staff see possibilities for change where they had not perceived them before. She understood the logic behind the staff's perspective on time-honored work. Rather than just exercise her authority and mandate new procedures, the leader presented the way things had always been done in a new light, one in which staff could differentiate between policy-based methods and ones that had grown organically, with no official basis. Second, she encouraged staff to see that they themselves had the ability to change the existing procedures, with the possibility of doing the work better. Using the perspective from the archives' big picture, she put the issue in a larger frame and thus strengthened the case for change and improvement.

A leader also supports the staff's efforts in strategic work by maintaining their focus on the direction for change and improvement. She never loses sight of the fundamental orientation the program has taken. She repeats to everyone as often as necessary that the archives' essential work is the strategic approach, and vice versa. She looks tirelessly and broadly for ways to work more effectively toward the vision and does not permit her staff to get sidetracked.

A leader does better at helping staff focus if she avoids becoming too literal or reductionist about the strategy. It is important for her to recognize that some necessary work in the archives must continue outside the strategy framework. For example, staff must keep up the physical security and integrity of collections whether or not the strategic work specifically covers that area of responsibility. By giving the strategy its proper status as the engine driving progress and improvement, the leader prevents it from becoming the false deity that provides all solutions the archives may ever need. In this way, she helps give the strategy greater credence and makes the focus on it feel appropriate to the staff.

Taken together, the leader's roles make her the champion of pursuing a strategic approach. She is the prime mover and constant promoter of the complex process that enables progress. Her vision provides the initial version of a desired future, and her steady communications to staff and stakeholders strengthen commitment to the whole effort and buoy spirits when the inevitable challenges arise. She ensures that evaluations and adjustments steadily hone the strategy.[17]

The manager's role comes to the fore in implementing the plans that set a strategy in motion. In general, this role is to ensure that the archives makes progress from month to month in pursuit of the strategy. It directs the activities that fulfill goals in a strategic plan. Its functions resemble those of the head of a multifaceted project: plotting out the phases of work; acquiring the necessary spaces, tools, and supplies; designating responsibilities; scheduling and overseeing tasks; handling budgets; and ensuring that statistics on completed work are recorded, compiled, and reported. The role also includes making sure that kinks in procedures and work processes get smoothed out quickly. More generally, the manager becomes the on-call problem solver, whether assuring that staff themselves address obstacles or resolving issues himself.

Coordination of the many related parts in a plan is another crucial managerial role. Maintaining close links among different phases of work takes on greater importance when sequenced phases of work build on each other. In such cases, managers take responsibility for smooth transitions, for keeping work on schedule, and for sharing information among staff to maximize understanding of how one person's assignments in the plan relate to those of others.

In a large archives program, the manager can also assume the role of a link between the leader position and frontline staff. The effective leader in a bigger and more bureaucratic organization must speak directly with as many staff as possible. Realistically, however, the manager can maintain more regular communications with staff. He conveys information from the leader to staff and reports about staff's work and attitudes to the leader.

The limited size of most archives means that a director or program head often plays both leader and manager roles in pursuing strategy. To balance these different functions, a director should keep in mind several principles:

- The leader's role is indispensable.
- The manager's role counts the most once work on priorities begins.
- Scaling a strategy to the archives' capabilities can create focus and simplify leadership.

These principles can help a director who has to juggle both leader and manager roles from getting bogged down or overtaxed in trying to do too much.

The head of a small archives cannot simply ignore the leader's role. Such a director should always try to devote a portion of each week to working on those roles, even if doing this means scheduling hours for it and making sure some of the work gets done outside the archives' premises with stakeholders in the parent institution and in other organizations. Because the pressure of daily tasks and frequent deadlines can easily squeeze the leader's work off the calendar, the director must remain aware of how he allots his time and remind himself that no one else can pick up this slack for him.

If it proves impossible to spend some hours each week on the leader's work, the archives director can focus mostly on that work in the direction-setting phase of strategy formulation and step back from it in later phases. In complementary fashion, the director can later shift largely to the manager's role to implement goals and action steps. Apportioning emphasis this way is not ideal because both roles require attention at other points in the process. Still, shifting attention from leader to manager roles as the archives pursues its strategic work makes combining the two more feasible.

The head of a small archives can also handle leader and manager roles more easily by focusing on one strategic opportunity at a time and not preparing the fuller menu of priorities and projects found in most strategies. For smaller archives, strategic opportunities often arise from the parent institution's priorities. A common one comes through an important anniversary, such as the centennial of the institution's founding, as Jennifer Johnson describes in chapter 8 on corporate archives. Others emerge from a major acquisition that requires archival skills and knowledge to manage. Samantha Norling provides an example of such an opportunity in chapter 10 on museum archives. Devoting the small archives' resources to these high-leverage projects one at a time can foster growth and improvement without burdening a director with a broader strategy. If work on discrete projects fulfills a smaller archives' mission and moves toward its vision, it also represents strategic progress.

Like many other organizations, today's archives use strategy and planning to improve their work. Both leaders and managers succeed with strategic work to the extent that they communicate effectively, as shown in chapter 1. More than in some other leadership endeavors, however, strategy requires distinct contributions of both leaders and managers. The broad, forward-looking perspective of the former and the assimilating, balancing focus of the latter combine to produce sustained growth and improvement. The interplay between these roles involves an appreciation of how each complements the other—a particular challenge when one person enacts both roles. There is as much art as engineering in how archival leadership pursues strategy, and there is no master blueprint that works for all archives. Persistence and learning from missteps are more important than any other keys to progress.

Does a strategic approach to archival work, with its agenda for change and improvement, necessarily require a larger budget? We would say no, and as David Carmicheal explains in the next chapter, "Resources and Budgets," deployment of existing funds and resources can be highly strategic. He also discusses what leadership needs to do when the archives needs more resources, emphasizing that leaders and managers who focus on relationships with key stakeholders and funders have the greatest chances for success.

NOTES

[1]　An excellent general treatment useful to most archives is John M. Bryson, *Strategic Planning for Public and Nonprofit Organizations*, 4th ed. (San Francisco: John Wiley and Sons, 2011), 43–66. Particularly useful explanations of strategic planning specifically for archives include Michael J. Kurtz, *Managing Archival and Manuscript Repositories* (Chicago: Society of American Archivists, 2004), 71–75; Bruce W. Dearstyne, *Leading the Historical Enterprise: Strategic Creativity, Planning and Advocacy for the Digital Age* (Lanham, MD: Rowman and Littlefield, 2015), 131–49; Bruce W. Dearstyne, *Planning for Archival Programs: An Introduction* (Mid-Atlantic Regional Archives Conference, Technical Leaflet Series no. 3, 1989), 1–8; Mark A. Greene, "Useful and Painless Strategic Planning: 'Make a New Plan, Stan,'" in *Management: Innovative Practices for Archives and Special Collections*, ed. Kate Theimer (Lanham, MD: Rowman and Littlefield, 2014), 183–97.

[2]　On the distinction between planning and strategy, see Linda A. Hill and Kent Lineback, *Being the Boss: The Three Imperatives for Becoming a Great Leader* (Boston: Harvard Business Review Press, 2011), 146–47; Larry Hackman, "Ways and Means: Thinking and Acting to Strengthen the Infrastructure of Archival Programs," in *Leadership and Administration of Successful Archival Programs*, ed. Bruce W. Dearstyne (Westport, CT: Greenwood Press, 2001), 40–41; Greene, "Useful and Painless Strategic Planning," 185.

[3]　Dearstyne, *Leading the Historical Enterprise*, 26.

[4]　Jamie Grady, *A Simple Statement: A Guide to Nonprofit Arts Management & Leadership* (Portsmouth, NH: Heinemann, 2006), 4–8; Dearstyne, *Planning for Archival Programs*, 3–4. For examples of mission, values, and vision statements, see these organizations' websites: Massachusetts Historical Society: https://www.masshist.org/mission, captured at https://perma.cc/D4B5-EF58; Texas State Library and Archives: https://www.tsl.texas.gov/agency/mission.html, captured at https://perma.cc/XLT6-RGHP; Clemson University Archives: https://library.clemson.edu/depts/specialcollections/using-special-collections/, captured at https://perma.cc/89UQ-8PZV; Library of Virginia: http://www.lva.virginia.gov/about/default.asp, captured at https://perma.cc/9Q6E-HH2X.

[5]　Bruce W. Dearstyne, "Leadership, Advocacy, and Program Development: Transforming New York's Local Government Records Program, 1981–1995," in *Many Happy Returns: Advocacy and the Development of Archives*, ed. Larry J. Hackman (Chicago: Society of American Archivists, 2011), 141–42.

[6]　James Phills, *Integrating Mission and Strategy for Nonprofit Organizations* (New York: Oxford University Press, 2005), 17, 48.

[7]　"Ullsvik Hall Ribbon Cutting Draws in UWP and Friends," University of Wisconsin-Platteville, May 21, 2008, https://www.uwplatt.edu/news/ullsvik-hall-ribbon-cutting-draws-uwp-and-friends, captured at https://perma.cc/8HDV-UCFT.

8 Larry Hackman suggests that an archives should create an "opportunity agenda" of needs that lie beyond the scope of its current strategy and should be prepared to work on components of the agenda, when possible. Hackman, *Many Happy Returns*, 12–14.

9 Dearstyne, *Leading the Historical Enterprise*, 38.

10 A useful overview of evaluation concepts and methods for nonprofit programs is Andrea Meier and Charles L. Usher, "New Approaches to Program Evaluation," in *Skills for Effective Management of Nonprofit Organizations*, ed. Richard L. Edwards, John A. Yankey, and Mary A. Altpeter (Washington, DC: National Association of Social Workers, 1998), 382–93.

11 This is a different approach from a general program assessment, which uses performance or programmatic standards to measure archival soundness. An early version of archival assessment is SAA's *Evaluation of Archival Institutions: Services, Principles and a Guide to Self-Study* (Chicago: Society of American Archivists, 1982). Jessica Lacher-Feldman offers an example of a museum exhibits assessment framework developed by the American Alliance of Museums in her *Exhibits in Archives and Special Collections Libraries* (Chicago: Society of American Archivists, 2013), 119–20. Jennifer Johnson's chapter in this book also includes a list of standards or criteria for assessing the health of corporate archives programs; see page 123.

12 These definitions of measurement and evaluation follow those in Thomas A. Childers and Nancy A. Van House, *What's Good: Describing Your Public Library's Effectiveness* (Chicago: American Library Association, 1993), 9. For a useful introduction to qualitative research and evaluation, see Michael Quinn Patton, *Qualitative Research & Evaluation Methods*, 4th ed. (Los Angeles: Sage, 2015), 3–13.

13 Childers and Van House, *What's Good*, 18–19, 68.

14 A good explanation of the concept of outcomes is in Rhea Joyce Rubin, *Demonstrating Results: Using Outcome Measurement in Your Library* (Chicago: American Library Association, 2006), 2.

15 Congress passed the Government Performance and Results Act in 1993. As modified by a new version of the law in 2010, federal programs must not only make strategic plans but also adopt performance standards for those plans. These laws also require annual performance reports. Institute for Museum and Library Services, *Perspectives for Outcome-Based Evaluation for Libraries and Museums* (Washington, DC: n.d.), 2–3. National Endowment for the Humanities, Performance Reporting Requirements, https://www.neh.gov/grants/manage/performance-reporting-requirements, captured at perma.cc/4DPY-9S9C.

16 Delmus E. Williams, Janine Golden, and Jennifer K. Sweeney, eds., *Advances in Library Administration and Organization*, Vol. 33 (Bingley, UK: Emerald Publishing, 2015), 13–14.

17 Bryson, *Strategic Planning*, 364–67.

3

Resources and Budgets

David W. Carmicheal

Leadership means aligning your existing resources to support your vision and values, diversifying your resource streams to minimize dependence on a single income source, and casting a vision of how you might use increased resources in a way that is compelling to potential funders. Standard budgeting tools can help managers achieve the best use of existing revenues, but expanding the archives' resources will require determined leadership. This chapter will explore the resources your repository already has, potential sources of additional resources, and how you might tap into them. Information about accounting for resources, which is widely available and not unique to archives, will not be addressed here.

Sources of Existing Resources

Your archives already has resources, and managers and leaders need to have a good understanding of what those resources are and how they can be used most effectively. It's a good idea to take stock of your resources on a regular basis, at least every year or two. Resources encompass many different things—not just money—and you may be surprised that your inventory reveals more sources than you had expected. You may want to make and annually update a written inventory or chart of your resources (using separate columns for each year) so that you can analyze trends. If you are creating such an inventory for the first time, you may need to maintain it for several years before you are able to discern whether individual resources are trending in a positive or a negative direction. Your inventory might include many types of resources.

Money

When people think about assets, they tend to think of money first. This is hardly surprising since the stability and future aspirations of the archives depend largely on a stable source of consistent funding. Your archives probably derives the largest portion of its budget from a single source, and it is important to know the scope of that support and to analyze its stability over time. While the bulk of your money may come from a single source, your repository may have many other sources of income, and it is important to inventory these as well.

- *Primary source.* Typically an archives receives the bulk of its annual operating funds from a parent organization, legislature, board of directors, or members.
- *Grants.* Grants are an important source of funding for any archives. Even though these are generally restricted to a specific project, you should track them carefully as one indicator of the financial health of the archives over time.
- *Gifts.* Does your archives receive bequests or other direct financial contributions? Are there sources of random donations of money—for example, through a donations box?
- *Endowments.* The projected income from any endowments should be included in your inventory, even if the funds are restricted to specific uses.
- *Memberships.* Does your archives offer formal membership with specific benefits? For now, inventory the income from the members. Later you'll need to calculate the costs associated with the group.
- *Friends group and foundation income.* If you are fortunate enough to have a friends group or a foundation, include its projected income in your inventory.
- *Interest income.* Investments—and even simple bank accounts—yield interest over time, and this income should be accounted for and managed.
- *Sales.* Include projected sales of books, magazines, images, and other income from sales and rentals, such as facility rentals.
- *Reference fees.* Fees for conducting research or providing copies are often a significant source of archival income.

Search carefully for sources of income, and get feedback from all the staff. A recent inventory at one archives revealed twelve sources of funding, including general operating budget, fees, grants, agency chargebacks, donations of money, and many others.

As you inventory the sources of your money, don't be discouraged if the archives does not have full discretion over how it spends the money from each source. Gifts and endowments, and even reference income, are often restricted to certain uses. The purpose of the inventory is to get a clear picture of how much money comes in and where it comes from. Knowing this will allow you to deploy your money more strategically, taking into account the sources over which you have little or no discretion.

People

Once you have accounted for money, you can begin to broaden your inventory of assets. It is popular for companies to say that "our people are our greatest asset"—so much so, in fact, that the statement is often greeted with a certain level of cynicism. But nowhere is this statement truer than in an archives, where knowledge about the collections themselves and the history surrounding them, as well as mediation between the records and those who use them, still depends heavily on people. Be sure to account for people as part of your resources inventory and, if possible, calculate their contributions.

- *Staff.* According to Mike Markovits (onetime head of global leadership at IBM and then head of leadership and executive development at GE), "for-profit organizations have been strategically managing their talent for years," but the idea has been slower to catch on in the not-for-profit world. "Even more so than in for-profits," says Markovits, "where there are hard assets like plants and equipment, a nonprofit really only has staff who are working towards its mission, which is all the more reason to focus on [human capital management]."[1] Ironically, archives often fret over their hard assets, like money and buildings, to a far greater extent than over their soft assets, like people and knowledge. Much professional energy is expended to achieve facilities with optimal environments or systems capable of preserving digital records for centuries; viewing staff as assets might lead us to expend similar energy on staff development and support.

  The archives generates value through the collective knowledge and competence of its staff. In fact, their knowledge is probably the archives' greatest resource, and your inventory of resources will be inaccurate if you do not include them. How? Conduct an inventory of skills (what each person knows) and competencies (how well they perform what they know).[2] Knowing the breadth and depth of staff knowledge and skills will help you determine how to deploy your human resources, and it will reveal gaps that may need to be bridged through hiring and training.

- *Volunteers.* Volunteer help may be a significant resource in your repository, and it is a resource to which a dollar figure can be attached. Each year the leadership network for nonprofits and foundations, Independent Sector, reports on the value of a volunteer hour in the United States and in specific states.[3] The calculation is widely respected and provides an easy and relatively objective way to calculate the value of volunteer hours. Since most archives maintain a total of volunteer hours as part of their normal weekly or monthly statistics, this figure should be easy to add to your resource inventory.

- *Interns.* Intern labor, like volunteer assistance, can be calculated in financial terms, but interns may bring more specialized skills to the archives than the average volunteer. The Independent Sector calculation cited above can be applied to interns, but that calculation is based on average wages for nonmanagement, nonagricultural workers, so you may need to adjust the figures if your interns are highly skilled professionals (information technology students performing specialized programming work, for example).

- *Partners.* Be sure to include the value of any partnership your archives maintains. One archives calculated the value of scanning work performed by Ancestry.com (basing the calculation on the typical cost of outsourcing such work) and discovered that the value ran to more than $2 million over several years. Similar calculations can be made whenever students perform scanning or indexing as part of a class project or whenever someone provides work that can be compared to a commercially available service or pays for work to be done on behalf of the archives.

Facilities

The archives facilities may be a major and highly visible resource or a liability that impedes efficient operations. Either way, taking stock of your facility as a resource is an important step toward using it effectively or increasing its utility. Simply taking stock of your facility regularly will give you a better idea of how to capitalize on its strengths and address its weaknesses. What are its strengths and weaknesses? How does it enhance or detract from public appreciation or perception of the archives? Some aspects that could be inventoried include the following:

- Location
- Size
- Public accessibility and convenience
- Functionality (including layout, adjacencies, adequacy of staff and public spaces)
- Stability (structurally, environmentally)
- Security
- Expandability

The facility inventory could be done in a general way—listing strengths and weaknesses, for example—or it might be done very specifically: How does the amount of storage space compare to comparable archives? How does its accessibility and convenience compare to that of a comparable local library? How closely does the environment align with national standards for archival repositories? How many square feet of space are typically available to each researcher? Over time, an inventory of this type might indicate trends before they become apparent to staff and users. If, for example, on-site patron use is diminishing because the repository is increasingly providing records online, the square feet-to-researcher ratio might increase year by year. Eventually this data might suggest that some of the research room space should be repurposed for more pressing uses. Or perhaps the square feet-to-employee space allocated to digitizing is diminishing because scanners and digitizing staff are being added. The inventory could reveal such trends in time to address them before they become critical.

Services

Shared or in-kind resources may make up a significant portion of your resources. Does your archives share or receive services from another institution such as a parent organization? I worked in one archives that shared a facility with a local historical society; I worked in another that was adjacent to a museum with which it shared a garage and loading dock and from which it received maintenance and security services. The latter became especially important when the archives planned a new building that would eliminate those valuable museum services. As in this instance, the dollar value of shared resources often can be calculated.

In-kind contributions may come from other sources as well. A trained conservator who is contracted to perform work that might be impossible (or costly) in house could be considered an asset. I once had a conservator who did private work in my archives lab in exchange for work on the archives' own collections.[4] In other instances, a state library or university may provide an online repository for distributing the archives' digital images online or provide cataloging services, thereby absorbing a cost that would otherwise fall to the archives itself. In all of these cases, it is likely that a dollar value can be placed on the in-kind contribution and specified in the resource inventory.

Goodwill

Your repository may have intangible resources as well, though these may be more difficult to quantify. In a commercial transaction, for example, goodwill is the difference between the price paid for a company and the value of its tangible assets. Goodwill is the intangible part of the company that someone placed a value on by paying for it. In the nonprofit world, the concept of goodwill is more often expressed as reputation. Although no dollar figure can be placed on reputation, and measuring it in any tangible way may be impossible, an archives leader could benefit from making an annual assessment of the repository's reputation. This could be as simple as writing down the leader's own sense of how the archives' reputation stands; as elaborate as surveys of users, funders, and other communities; or something in between. From this inventory, the leadership can make assessments about how the current reputation was earned, whether its trend is positive or negative, and how it might be enhanced. Depending on its situation, the archives will want to gauge its reputation among different audiences:

- the general community
- parent organization or funding authority (board, legislator, parent agency, etc.)
- users
- faculty and students
- employees
- news media

Armed with an inventory of resources, the archives leadership is ready to analyze how their resources are being used.

Deploying Existing Resources

The true priorities of an archival repository can be gauged to a great extent by how their current resources are deployed. Over time, the leadership's highest priorities will attract the bulk of the archives' resources.[5] Now that you have an inventory of your resources, you can analyze how they are deployed throughout the organization. Use a spreadsheet and make simple pie charts if it helps you understand the allocations. The distribution may surprise you because it may not reflect your stated priorities.

Analyzing distribution through expense categories

The simplest way to analyze how your financial resources are deployed may be to use expense categories because your budget probably already breaks your expenditures into salaries, facility maintenance, supplies, travel, and similar categories. Your task may be as simple as adding together expenses that share a category but are accounted for in different places. In one archives, for example, archival supplies may be purchased using funds from the general operating budget or from a dedicated preservation fund. In such a case, you would add together the amount spent for archival supplies, regardless of their source, to get a complete picture of resources that are deployed in the archival supplies category.

The expense categories you use to do this analysis are up to you. Though almost every archives will share certain general expense categories, such as salaries and utilities, the number of categories you define and use to do your analysis will depend on your own situation. You can analyze in detail or very broadly,[6] but the goal of the exercise is to determine what is consuming your money—to get beyond gut feelings and instinct. You should analyze the distribution of resources in categories that help you meet this goal.

As you categorize the way your resources are deployed, you may want to distinguish between discretionary, semidiscretionary, and fixed expenses. Fixed expenses are the least flexible, though even these can often be negotiated if they prove too burdensome. Debt can sometimes be restructured or rent adjusted, and large archives sometimes consume enough fuel to warrant negotiated pricing. Often, though, your fixed expenses are nonnegotiable, and that fact is helpful to know as you look at resource deployment. Semidiscretionary expenses (my own term) are those that are generally fixed but that can be influenced by changes in behavior, technology, or other factors. The cost of a kilowatt of electricity may be fixed, for example, but staff efforts at conservation, or the installation of new technology, might reduce usage and its corresponding costs. This too is helpful to note as you consider how your resources are deployed. Discretionary expenses—a luxury in most archives!—are the most flexible expenses. Since discretionary funds are the ones that enable new or expanded programs and initiatives, these funds are the most critical for advancing a vision.

The importance of analyzing resource deployment through expense categories was borne out during a recent analysis at one archives, which revealed that one expense—a program to store microfilm for local governments—was consuming more than 15 percent of all the discretionary resources of the agency. The program initially recovered all of its costs through fees, but as the program grew, it quietly ceased to be cost neutral. Managing the program was not burdensome to staff, so its impact on resources went largely unnoticed even as its costs crept upward year by year. Armed with the facts, the archives was able to make changes to the program to manage its costs and reduce its drain on scarce discretionary funds.

Analyzing distribution through program categories

Analyzing resource deployment based on expense categories is helpful, but knowing how resources are deployed across program categories is often more helpful still. Armed with such knowledge, the leadership gets a clear picture of how the work of the archives is being prioritized (regardless of *stated* priorities) and how the resources might need to be redistributed to achieve stated goals.

Program categories (as used here) are the various functions the archives performs. A typical archives might deploy its resources in program functions such as reference, arrangement and description, education, digitizing, and similar programs. Some archives will include program categories for fund-raising or membership development. You should define the categories and make them as broad or as narrow as necessary to fit your repository. You may have narrower categories to account for a fully functioning education program and separate programs for recruiting members and soliciting donors, each of which warrant a program category in your analysis. Or you may have one broad program category of "outreach" that includes the resources you deploy to reach out to the public, whether you are educating them, soliciting their money, or mounting exhibits for their benefit.

The goal of analyzing how your resources are deployed programmatically is to determine whether that distribution is balanced in the way that leadership desires and also to provide data that can be used to predict what might happen if the resources were redeployed. For this reason, you may need to analyze this deployment in multiple ways. You might, for example, analyze it from the point of view of money: calculate what percentage of your money is spent on education, what percentage on reference, and so on, regardless of whether the money was spent on supplies or publications or salaries and such. Certain expenses may be difficult to categorize programmatically (it is probably not possible to determine how much electricity the education program used as opposed to the reference program), so you may address those by grouping such expenses into a "program support" category.

While counting dollars is an obvious way to analyze your use of resources, money is not the only way to analyze programmatically. A simple headcount—or a full-time equivalent count, if you include volunteers, interns, and other human resources—can provide a good picture of how the archives is deploying its resources. A recent study at an archives revealed the following staffing distributions, for example:

Reference (on-site and remote)	44 percent
State and local government agency assistance	16 percent
Arrangement and description	25 percent
Digital content creation and access	4 percent
Digital archives development	11 percent

Armed with this data and a desire to increase resources devoted to digital records and access, the archives laid plans to redeploy the staffing over a five-year period (through immediate reorganization and longer term redistribution of future vacancies) in hopes of achieving a distribution of staffing resources closer to this:

Reference (on-site and remote)	20 percent
State and local government agency assistance	25 percent
Arrangement and description	12 percent
Digital content creation and access	23 percent
Digital archives development	20 percent

Increased resources in one program area did not necessarily come at the expense of another. Some of the resource increase in the digital content creation and access program area, for example, was achieved by incorporating certain digital access functions into the work process of the arrangement and description staff while reducing the effort devoted to traditional print finding aids. In addition, one goal of increasing digital content creation and access was to increase the ability of patrons to self-serve, thereby allowing a reduction in resources devoted to reference.

Whether you view your resources through the lens of expense categories or program categories, it is important to account for all of your resources, including staff, volunteers, interns, and supplies. Account, too, for investments if your repository or your friends group has them. Taking stock of cash investments, for example, is the precursor to determining whether they are deployed productively (in interest-bearing accounts) or not. So, too, with programmatic investments, such as friends or members groups. What resources are deployed to build such programs and maintain them? Only with that information in hand can you determine whether you are achieving an adequate return to justify the investment. Much less tangible, but no less important to consider, is the question of how your goodwill is deployed. Is the repository's reputation being leveraged to increase dollars for the program or to achieve greater public visibility? Knowing this—even if it cannot be measured precisely—is a step toward deciding whether it is being put to the very best use.

If you know how your current resources are being used, and if you have a vision for the future, you can think about how your existing resources might be used more effectively.

Realigning Resources

Archival leaders create a vision and define values for their repository. Now that you understand the extent of your resources and how they are deployed, it is time to ask how they might be deployed to more effectively realize the vision and values of the archives' leadership.

Setting priorities

Formulating and communicating clear vision and priorities for the archival repository is among the leader's most important tasks. As Peter points out in chapter 2, it is the leader's *strategy* that focuses the resources of the archives. Ultimately, the leader's vision for the archives is communicated and achieved through the deliberate deployment of resources. It is natural to imagine what you might achieve if given additional resources, but it is equally important to consider how your existing resources might be redeployed to better align with your stated vision.

Realigning resources

The illustration earlier—in which staff and work processes were redeployed to achieve a different distribution of resources—demonstrates some of the ways that existing resources can be realigned. Reorganizing the existing staff is often an effective first step toward realigning resources to meet priority goals.

- *Reorganize staff.* Since you've taken stock of your human resources—your staff's knowledge and skills—you should be able to determine whether it is possible to achieve repository goals by reorganizing the existing staff (if your situation allows you to alter job duties, either immediately or as vacancies occur). Archivists are often professional generalists, able to transition from reference to education to digital content, particularly if they have a hand in planning such transitions and are given proper training. Use that fact to your advantage. If existing staff lack the requisite education but have the capacity to learn, create a plan to educate the staff so that they can be redeployed to the program areas that must be strengthened to achieve your vision. Even if the plan requires several years to implement, you will be on your way to realigning your existing resources in a more productive manner.

- **Reassign vacancies.** If reassigning existing staff proves too disruptive or politically sensitive, it may be possible to redeploy vacancies as they occur. In most archival repositories, staff vacancies occur regularly as a normal part of business. Moving a vacant position from one program area to another is often a relatively painless way to redistribute resources over time. Such a tactic is especially helpful if the repository needs to acquire skills not found among the existing staff. A vacant position in reference, for example, might be reinvented as a digital archivist position in order to launch a digital archives program.

- **Redesign business processes.** It is often possible to realign staff without moving them on the organization chart by redesigning business processes. Perhaps the leadership of a university archives determines that they need to be more proactive about transferring records from university offices and tracking the gaps that occur when records are not transferred as scheduled. A revised business process might institute annual outreach to each university office on a scheduled basis, document the interaction in a standardized way, and provide a vehicle for follow-up. The accessioning process might be redesigned to dovetail with the arrangement and description process to reveal gaps in the collection.

  A more dramatic redesign of business processes would be the elimination of all transfers of paper (or all paper from selected offices) in favor of entirely digital accessions, perhaps coupled with a streamlined process to quickly provide online access to the records.

  Many archives reengineered their business processes in the wake of Dennis Meissner and Mark Greene's seminal article, "More Product, Less Process."[7] In doing so, archivists demonstrated a ready ability and willingness to redesign business processes whenever the benefit is clearly demonstrated. You are likely to find similar value in redesigning selected business processes within your own repository.

- **Redistribute knowledge.** If, as stated earlier, the archives generates value through the collective knowledge and competence of its staff, the archives can redistribute that resource as well. In fact, "compared to physical labor, human capital includes expandable, self-generating, transportable, and shareable characteristics."[8] In other words, while you cannot expand or share your physical strength with another worker, you can share your knowledge and experience with another and, in what amounts to a human capital miracle, expand—not deplete—the stock of knowledge of both people in the process.

  Staff knowledge can be redistributed (i.e., shared) through training, mentoring, and other ways. One repository maintains an internal knowledge base wiki where staff record information about collections and recurring reference questions that other staff can then access and use. In fact, the repository requires regular additions to the knowledge base as part of each employee's performance standards. Over time, such a tool captures employee knowledge that might otherwise be lost through staff attrition, and it provides a relatively painless way to transfer knowledge from one employee to all others.

Paring back

Finally, as you think about how you might redeploy existing resources, it is important to consider activities that might be scaled back or discontinued altogether. The phrase *doing more with less* has become a mantra of modern government and business, but simple logic—and the experience of thousands of archivists—demonstrates that, eventually, less begets less. Serious efforts to achieve a vision are likely to involve jettisoning activities that do not contribute significantly to that vision.

Leaders should look at each repository program and activity as objectively as possible and ask how each contributes to the long-range vision of the leadership. Is the effort to secure grants causing the repository to lose focus? (It is tempting to accept grants even if the project itself does not align with the long-term goals of the archives.) Or perhaps the time required to provide reference to remote users is detracting from efforts to better serve patrons in the research room itself. The reduction or elimination of such services requires careful planning followed by good communication with staff, patrons, and superiors to explain how the change supports the vision of the archives.

Not every analysis will result in the elimination of service. One archives discovered that the digitization of specific genealogical records resulted in a dramatic reduction of on-site reference traffic, thereby reducing the amount of resources required for reference activity. That experience suggests that it may be worthwhile to temporarily reduce services—even highly visible services that are valued by our patrons—in order to devote those resources to another activity that will provide long-term benefit to the repository and its users. In such cases, leaders will be careful to keep their public fully informed about the rationale and future benefits that led to the decision.

Ultimately, the resources of the archives are finite and must be deployed in a way that best supports the vision of the archives' leadership. Imagining how your resources might be deployed may reveal that some simple changes will further the leader's vision. It also sets the stage for imagining how you might use increased resources.

Increasing Resources

As with almost everything in archival leadership, the effort to increase resources begins with a vision. How would you use more money or people or space if you had them? Knowing this will help you identify potential sources of increased revenue and provide the basis for crafting the necessary business case or solicitation message required to secure them. If you have already defined a clear vision for the archives, you probably already know how you would use greater resources. If not, you can still brainstorm about increased resources. Ask questions of yourself and others:

- *What is our biggest need?* This question may be easy to answer. Perhaps you need a new facility because your current building leaks or has run out of storage space. Maybe you need scanning equipment or more staff to address the flood of reference requests you receive. You may find some less obvious answers if you rephrase the question to shift the emphasis, as shown in the next two questions.

- *What is our patrons' biggest need?* Looking at needs from the point of view of your customers helps get your attention away from the more obvious "archival" needs that stare us in the face every day. How does the archives function from users' perspectives, and what needs do they face when they attempt to use your resources? Is the public computer network slow and cranky, or is the furniture wobbly and uncomfortable? Looking at problems this way also offers insights into how you might engage others to expand resources. It is more compelling to make the argument to administrators or potential donors that local high school students need online access to more of your records than it is to argue that the archives needs a new scanner and someone to operate it. The result may be the same, but the perspective of the former is more customer focused than the latter, and it's more likely to capture the imagination of would-be funders.

- ***What is the biggest need of the people who provide the bulk of our resources?*** What do the people who provide your funding lie awake at night worrying about? Is there a way to meet those needs (or reduce their anxiety about them) while securing additional resources for the archives? Perhaps your archives is part of a corporation where profit and loss loom large in the CEO's nightmares. Can the archives' collections be used to support marketing to new customers or brand loyalty for existing customers? There may be an opportunity for the archives to receive increased funding to support such an initiative; if nothing else, the suggestion might put the archives on the CEO's radar in a positive light. Maybe you're part of a university library in which the dean worries about visibility and funding for library programs. Again, if you can create a vision of how to use the resources of the archives to address that concern, you may be able to secure additional resources.

- ***What is our biggest aspiration?*** As you imagine what you might do with additional resources, don't limit yourself to obvious needs; think about your largest aspirations for the archives. If you had no resource limitations, what would the archives look like? What would its outreach programs be, and who would its collections serve? Large goals, such as new or upgraded facilities, often take many years of persistent effort to achieve. The sooner you identify them and begin that effort, the better chance you have of realizing the goal.

    Maybe your greatest aspiration is less tangible. I once worked in an archives where the parent agency set a goal to be "the most customer-friendly agency in state government." Cynics might say the bar is set pretty low, but, in fact, it was a highly aspirational goal. The most important resource required to achieve the goal was time—for training and focused discussions—to create greater awareness among staff about how patrons might perceive their interactions and how to improve communication. Although the goal was not as tangible as, say, a new facility, it required the same thinking: if I had the proper resources (time and training), what could I achieve (more satisfying patron interactions)?

Imagining how you might use increased resources is an important step toward securing them because it begins to tie resources to a vision for the archives. That vision will be key as you take steps to increase resources.

Strategies to Increase Resources

The effort required to secure new resources depends, to a great extent, on the type of resources you need. It may be helpful to consider the possibilities in terms of the types of resources mentioned at the beginning of this chapter: money, people, facilities, services (which will be combined with people, below), and goodwill.

Money

It goes without saying that increasing the flow of money is the most effective way to advance the mission and vision of the archives. Doing so, however, requires patience, persistent effort, and a great deal of luck. There are many sources of money, as you may have found in the process of inventorying your current resources, but tapping these sources requires thoughtful effort.

- *Donations.* Many archives are well positioned to solicit donations from interested people and corporations. Often the archives has or can readily obtain 501(c)3 status, so that donors receive a tax benefit from gifts to the archives. If the archives itself is unable to secure such status, it can often establish a separate friends group that can do so. In addition, it is often easy to make the case to potential donors that what the archives does is valuable and worth supporting. Donors often respond well to requests to fund specific projects rather than to general solicitations for money. For example, someone who loves railroads—or even a local group of railroad modelers—might fund the conservation or processing of a collection of railroad records. Organizations such as the Daughters of the American Revolution, the local Rotary club, or similar civic-minded groups will sometimes fund specific projects that relate to their mission.

  Before you solicit money, of course, it is essential to determine whether there are any legal restrictions prohibiting you from doing so. Once again, a friends group is often the answer to such restrictions.

- *Grants.* Grants have long been a source of funding for specific archival projects. While national grant programs are highly competitive and increasingly underfunded, local organizations may provide targeted grants to accomplish a project related to their mission.

- *Shared expenses.* Sharing expenses is one way to stretch a few dollars into many. Early in my career, I needed to find money to conserve a very fragile eighteenth-century map, but my tiny budget could support barely half the cost of the treatment. I approached the elected officials of the town depicted on the map, and they agreed to cover half of the treatment cost in exchange for an opportunity to briefly exhibit the map in the town hall. Their donation made the conservation treatment possible, and the exhibit also attracted very positive press attention—a bonus!

  Chances are good that an archives across town is just as anxious as you are to bring in that renowned digital archives expert to provide staff training. Split the costs and save money for both repositories. If the speaker agrees, increase the number of attendees and split the costs among every repository in town!

  A more dramatic example of shared expenses occurred when the county archives I directed constructed new archives space in its facility for the county historical society. The combination of the two collections in one space (though still managed as separate entities) resulted in a shared research room, shared programs, better service for archives and historical society patrons, and enhanced goodwill in the community. Sharing resources among independent entities is not without its risks and costs, however, so these should be weighed against the benefits. Success in such a venture demands strong leadership and good communication, but the advantages can be significant.

- ***Redistribution.*** Redistribution of funds, while not technically an increase in resources, can have a similar result. Think about whether you can move funds from one area to another in order to focus on higher priorities. You probably identified some possibilities as you considered how you want to realign resources. And while moving funds from one area to another is sometimes difficult (especially in government accounting systems), it can normally be accomplished given sufficient time and patience.

  Even restricted funds may be potential sources for redistribution: you may be able to argue for a relaxation of the restrictions, or you may be able to argue that the way you *want* to use the funds actually aligns with the spirit of the restriction. I once argued successfully that a sizeable fund that was restricted to publishing should be used to scan records and publish them online. The new source of funds permitted the archives to generate tens of thousands of online records that would have been impossible otherwise.

- ***Increased annual allocation.*** The most satisfying and dependable increase in money resources comes when the archives secures an increase in its regular annual operating budget. Securing such an increase often results from the archives leader's persistent efforts to build relationships with the people who influence the archives' budget allocation; not only decision-makers but budget analysts and influential staff as well. At such times, as Samantha Norling points out in chapter 10, it is important for archivists to be able to speak the language of those who manage the finances of the organization.

  The archives is more likely to see an increase in its budget allocation if it can demonstrate—through hard data—both the need and the benefit that will accrue from an increased budget. If you have considered what you would do with increased resources—and if you have crafted your ideas in terms of how the increases will benefit people the archives serves rather than in terms of how the archives itself will benefit—then you have a good foundation for advocating for increased resources. (Chapter 1, "Communication," explores this topic more fully.) Phil Mooney has pointed out that the people who allocate resources to archives "are seldom influenced by reports on reference requests serviced, cubic feet of processed collections, and numbers of finding aids created. Of greater impact is how the collections positively impact the business, its customers, and public opinion."[9]

  An additional advantage of stating your needs in terms of how it may benefit others is this: if people outside the archives believe that an increase in archives resources will benefit them, they may become advocates for an increase in the archives' budget allocation. Suppose, for example, that a state agency comes to believe that a digital archives would protect them from significant legal liability in the years ahead. Such an agency is very likely to advocate on behalf of the archives out of self-interest, and advocacy from outside the archives is often the most effective advocacy.

People and services

Money, of course, is just one of the important resources in an archives. People comprise a significant part of the repository's resources, and saying that a repository needs people is another way of saying that it needs a certain level of labor or skills to accomplish some goal. If money does not exist to procure such labor or skills, they may sometimes be obtained through in-kind contributions. Obtaining such resources often requires creative thinking on the part of the archives leadership.

Friends groups can be a ready source of in-kind assistance, particularly when simple labor is required. Friends and members might donate a few hours or a day to rehouse a collection or perform other tedious labor that becomes more palatable when performed in a compressed time frame in the company of a companionable group. Such projects might also be performed by an outside group on a periodic or one-time basis. One archives' entire collection was moved to temporary storage (in an adjoining building) by a troop of Boy Scouts as part of an Eagle Scout project. The entire project cost the archivists only ten pizzas (and a few gray hairs). A local garden club might be a source of volunteers for maintaining flower beds around the archives. Matching projects to the interests of potential volunteers is an excellent way to secure increased people resources. As with any donation the archives might consider, leaders must assess the investment of resources required versus the anticipated payoff. Friends groups, memberships, and volunteers are not "free"; they require an investment of time and money, but the rewards can be significant.

The need for more skilled assistance may require the archives to look to interns or others who have the specialized training required by the archives, but such skills don't always require trained archivists. When the Council of State Archivists required special skills to produce recorded webinars for their Intergovernmental Preparedness for Essential Records (IPER) courses, Georgia Public Broadcasting provided its recording facilities, and the Georgia Emergency Management Agency provided a former radio announcer as the narrator, all without charge.

Facilities

Money and people are often obvious and immediate needs; increased facilities resources, on the other hand, are almost always a very long-term goal that must be pursued with persistence. The inventory of facility strengths and weaknesses, discussed above, is a starting point for building the case for a new or improved facility. As with other advocacy related to resources, the best case is one that emphasizes the benefits to archives customers rather than to the archives itself. Yes, a new archives facility would better protect the archives' priceless collections, but how does the facility translate into benefits for others? Perhaps a new facility will allow the archives to better serve a local community or schoolchildren or tourists. Perhaps it will save significant operating costs through more energy-efficient operations. No single argument is likely to carry the day, but leaders should think carefully about how to make a case that appeals to audiences beyond the repository and its staff.

The case must be built from many different angles and with many different audiences in mind, and even then the funding required for new facilities is often the result of sheer luck. Still, as Seneca is reputed to have said, "Luck is what happens when preparation meets opportunity." Funding for a new or improved facility may require a perfect storm of advantageous circumstances, but the archives that has consistently collected and shared data related to its needs will have a better chance of taking advantage of that storm than one that has not.

Remember, too, that it is sometimes appropriate to make the case for a new facility in conjunction with others. An environmentally controlled storage facility shared by the university archives and library may be easier to justify than a stand-alone building for each. Recently, a state historical society worked with its state's veterans' museum to plan a joint storage facility. The State Building Commission appropriated nearly $50 million for construction, to include high-density storage for books and archival collections as well as specialized storage for artifacts, archaeological materials, and films. The building will also house an isolation and treatment suite for pest management and a conservation lab.

Don't simply assume that you need to go it alone.

Goodwill

While the emphasis to this point has been on tangible resources, intangible resources are important as well. Every archives requires a continually increasing store of goodwill, but too often leaders fail to develop that resource consciously and deliberately. Goodwill results when those outside the archives respect it as a valuable resource. Such value may derive from the archives' reputation for excellent customer service or as a source of trustworthy information. Ideally, parent organizations and funding sources will regard the archives as an excellent return on investment, a prospect that requires diligent effort on the part of archives leaders who must understand what those audiences value and then demonstrate that an investment in the archives returns that value.

Conclusion

In most archives, there is a core revenue stream from which the archives derives the majority of its support and a secondary stream of additional revenue and support. Leaders should analyze both streams and then realign them as necessary to support their vision and values. Look beyond money to other types of resources, and make sure that all of them are aligning to your vision of the future. Only then are you in a position to expand and diversify your resources.

Expanding resources, no matter their type or source, depend on a clear vision for the archives and a strategy to make that vision attractive to potential funders and donors (whether of money or services). The job of the archival leader is to craft a vision for the future and then align it to the goals of potential funders or service providers in a way that they find compelling enough to support.

> *If the management of resources requires daily attention from leaders and managers, transformational changes and crises by their nature happen only intermittently. As Peter Gottlieb shows in the next chapter, "Leadership in Transformative Change and Crisis," deep alterations and disruptions can—and do—emerge from basic needs or unanticipated events in many archives. Guiding programs through challenging times tests leadership's capacity for self-management, skill in communication, and ability to use even unwanted change for programmatic improvement.*

NOTES

[1]   "Human Capital Management: Don't Reinvent the Wheel," http://www.bridgespan.org/Publications-and-Tools/Career-Professional-Development/Develop-My-Staff/Human-Capital-Management.aspx#.VyUe1Kuc8st., captured at https://perma.cc/KH9A-94V7.

[2]   Much has been written about the differences between knowledge, skills, competency, and experience, and companies often attempt to inventory staff in each area (though few agree on the definitions of the terms). It is beneficial for the archives leadership to understand the specific strengths that each employee brings to the archives operation, however those are labeled or categorized.

[3]   Recently calculated at $24.14 per hour. See "The Value of Volunteer Time—Independent Sector," Independent Sector, https://www.independentsector.org/volunteer_time, captured at https://perma.cc/8E8H-WPJU.

[4]   The conservator supplied her own materials but used the archives' lab equipment. For every ten hours of work she performed for a client, the archives was "paid" with four hours of work on our own collections. Her work was a measurable asset.

[5]   It is true, of course, that many archival leaders have little discretion over key budgetary factors (how much the staff get paid, for example), but over time, the leader may focus the budget on priorities by taking advantage of vacancies and other regular occurrences, which are discussed in more detail below.

[6]   Businesses sometime analyze expenditures in broad terms—for example, core services, ancillary services, and research and development. For an archives, this might translate to core services (such as reference), ancillary services (such as certain public programs), and research and development (digital archives development, perhaps).

[7]   Mark Greene and Dennis Meissner, "More Product, Less Process," *American Archivist* 68, no. 2 (2005): 208–63.

[8]   "Human Capital and Its Measurement," Dr. Kwan Dae-Bong, 3rd OECD World Forum on "Statistics, Knowledge and Policy" (October 27–30, 2009), http://www.oecd.org/site/progresskorea/44111355.pdf, captured at https://perma.cc/SKP4-QJNW.

[9]   Philip F. Mooney, "Stranger in a Strange Land: The Archivist and the Corporation," in *Leading and Managing Archives and Records Programs: Strategies for Success,* ed. Bruce W. Dearstyne (New York: Neal-Schuman, 2008), 190.

4

Leadership in Transformative Change and Crisis

Peter Gottlieb

Introduction

Some changes in archival programs have a comparatively limited impact while the effects of others lead to fundamental shifts. Between these ends of the spectrum naturally come those at every other level of intensity, and rather than each one clearly differing from another, they overlap and merge at their boundaries. Still, we can conceptually distinguish between limited changes (those making a difference mainly in program operations) and transformative changes (those altering not just the operations but also the policies, identity, or culture of an archives).[1]

In this chapter, I use two different scenarios to look at how leaders and managers can guide archival programs through transformative change. I conclude with an examination of crises as specific kinds of change and challenge for leadership. I discuss strategy separately in chapter 2. I recognize the obvious fact that strategic work and transformative change can and often do overlap. I choose to treat them separately because they do not always begin at the same source, nor do they develop the same way and because, from a leadership perspective, each requires its own focus.

Staff in an archives often exercise leadership by proposing and implementing changes, without necessarily engaging a program director or manager. They may decide to alter the schedule of public services, create digital access to a new part of the collections, or update their cataloging standards. In larger programs, a manager might get involved to ensure smooth implementation for these kinds of initiatives. But since they do not necessarily imply changes in policies, relationships with other institutions, or the basic mission of the archives, they hardly seem to call for a leader's role. Transformative change, on the other hand, draws in leaders and managers as well as staff in adopting a new course for the archives. The following scenarios illuminate leader and manager roles.

Scenarios of Transformative Change

Our first scenario of an archives facing transformative change centers on financial issues. The primary funding source for the archives has fallen chronically short of the amount required to support essential activities, and filling the recurring gap with discretionary monies no longer compensates for the shortfall. In consultation with directors of the parent institution, the archives' head decides that the best available solution is to augment the program budget with earned revenue—income from charging fees for products or services. The head archivist sees promise in increasing sales of copies from the archives' well-known and very popular photograph collection, most of which users can already find in digital format through a website. In the past, user fees for duplicate images only covered the costs of providing the copies, but the envisioned change anticipates earning net income above costs and eventually devoting that income to the support of some staff positions and to some ongoing operations, including continual upgrading of the online user interface. If successful, the earned revenue initiative would be expanded from photographs to other types of collections.

This archives faces different kinds of changes in its plan to expand its funding sources. It has to grapple with new operational demands such as determining intellectual property rights and commercial rights, developing and refining accounting procedures, making new staffing assignments, and even advertising. But the archives must also confront the deeper change of becoming entrepreneurial in its thinking and budget planning. This change requires developing a new outlook on the work in the archives, or at least in one or more program areas of the archives. It shifts the way archives staff think about visitors and users, stressing the importance of turning first-time visitors into customers and then into repeat customers. The change also makes staff look at its collections and services in a new light, heightening the importance of continually offering new value and increased utility. Budgetary issues can provide the impetus for constructing an earned-revenue program, but like the widening circles in the pond that start from a pebble's splash, the resulting ripples of change can eventually spread far.

In contrast to how this archives initiated a profit center, transformative change often starts at times and in circumstances that leadership does not choose. In our second scenario, a county government decides to merge two archives that it has supported for many years, one in a historical society and the other in a sports hall of fame that celebrates local professional and semiprofessional teams. The retirement of the director of the hall of fame in part prompts the county's merger decision, since it removes the need to eliminate one of the two director positions. The historical society's archives holds family and personal manuscripts and records of well-known local businesses. The hall of fame includes a sports history collection of secondary sources, photographs, posters, and ephemera. In requiring the merger of the programs, the county board seeks to economize on expenditures while improving services.

The complexities facing the leader of the combined historical society and sports collections may loom even larger than those confronting the leadership of the earned-revenue program. Even if she focuses just on the first goal of unifying visitor services and waits until later to tackle other objectives, she still must meld physical as well as virtual spaces in addition to retooling reference procedures. As challenging as those alterations appear, they represent only the beginning of the deeper process to change the two collections' separate identities into a new, unified program. The leader's task becomes still more difficult when she understands that the new identity should not lose the strengths and attractions of the two original collections. The historical society's users include scholars, writers, local historians, genealogists, and university graduate students. The hall of fame also serves some researchers but gets many more visits and contacts from fans, hobbyists, collectors, journalists, and K–12 classes.

Whatever specific alterations they involve, transformative changes like the ones in these scenarios invite leadership contributions from all personnel levels. Because leaders are the ones always looking for opportunities to improve and preparing their organizations to seize such chances when they appear, they, more so than managers, play the crucial roles in the beginning phases of profound change. They have the responsibility to grasp the possibilities and the liabilities for their programs, to develop a new vision, to direct every resource toward successful change, and to remove obstacles. Managers' responsibilities for continuity and stability necessarily diminish when an archives program begins changes of such magnitude, though they come more to the fore when the implementation stages begin. Staff also contribute in important ways to successful change processes and have opportunities to exert leadership from their positions in the archives.

The Roles of Planning and Communication

The two key leadership responsibilities in transformational change are ones that are required in other contexts: planning and communication. The leaders who launch changes to their programs without careful and deliberate attention to these tasks invite failure, not to mention the possibility of lasting repercussions of a poorly executed effort. If the archives has a well-crafted strategic approach, within which leaders and managers have already discussed the impending change, some of the preparatory groundwork of communication and planning need not be repeated. But all cases of wide-ranging change require program heads to plan specifically how to carry them out, how to overcome foreseeable obstacles, and how to enlist and maintain the support of archives staff and stakeholders through good communication.

If communications are the essential element for good leadership in most settings, as David shows in chapter 1, they are the very lifeblood of a change process. Effective leader communications in this context should address these needs:

- creating a sense of urgency
- providing a picture of future possibilities
- defining new expectations for staff
- listening to staff's concerns and adopting staff's ideas for change
- establishing the limits of debate about change and the archives' future

No worthy leader of an archives program launches a change project without thorough communication with the parent organization, with constituents like users and donors, with archives staff, and even with the public. Transformational change requires most staff of an archives program to adopt new roles and new outlooks, and they are unlikely to do so successfully unless leaders convey in compelling terms the reasons—positive and negative—for everyone to engage wholeheartedly. Through both words and actions, leaders of change projects must communicate the sense of urgency, the possibilities, and the new expectations for staff. Since good communication always moves in two directions, leaders must also seek feedback from stakeholders and staff and listen to it carefully. Finally, in some cases, leaders have to explain clearly when the time for discussion has ended and when the time to move forward with change has come.[2] We can put these communication imperatives into context through our change scenarios.

The archives leader who starts the earned-revenue program has a strong platform for fostering a sense of urgency because authorities in the larger organization as well as staff can easily see the threats from funding shortages. Since the recurrent budget problem stems from systemic causes and not from a temporary shortage of funds, its current effects are clear to everyone and its future threats easily understood. The archives leader in this situation might focus more on the positive reasons for the earned-revenue venture as a way to maintain the sense of urgency for change. However, some staff may continue preferring other funding remedies, even when those have been shown to be unworkable. The adept leader keeps a sharp edge on the sense of urgency by reminding everyone of the consequences of continuing to spend time and effort on unfeasible solutions.

The leader of the merging archives faces a tougher challenge in making the change feel urgent to staff. The staff in each of the programs may sense that they are doing fine, that long-established processes work well, and that their programs are successful (the leader may initially share this outlook). The leader's task is to explain the county officials' decision to consolidate, economize, and streamline. No matter how objectionable it may be to each archives, that decision is irrevocable. The leader elevates the sense of urgency by stressing the consequences for the archives of resisting what the future is bringing and from failing to embrace the greater role for the combined archives that the merger holds out. Equally, the leader must point out the improved services and collections access envisioned by the change.

As with all leaders' communications about transformative changes, building and maintaining a sense of urgency about the process must be done honestly and with integrity. Staff's readiness to grapple with all the problems inherent in making deep changes can suffer deeply if it perceives leaders manipulating messages about urgency. Rather than trying to convince doubting staff about the urgency for change by inflating threats or inventing causes, leaders should always base their descriptions on facts, on experiences staff have shared, and on examples from other institutions in similar situations. Wise leaders build and maintain the understanding that the time for change is at hand by making a credible case based on facts.[3]

Talking to staff, stakeholders, and the public about future possibilities can also foster the impetus for change in an archives. In any organization, some people by nature take an optimistic view of what lies ahead. They do not necessarily wear rose-colored glasses, but they definitely differ from those colleagues who tend to see the future darkly, particularly when change gets underway. In their communications, leaders try to win over the pessimists and change-averse staff members and to find ways to amplify the voices of staff who have greater comfort with change and incline to brighter views of the future. In describing the future to users, donors, volunteers, friends groups, and the public, the leader avoids going beyond well-grounded projections supported by the county board. For the same reasons that leaders take care not to dissemble about the pressing needs for change, they strictly avoid glibly upbeat descriptions and baselessly happy predictions about what change will bring.

The archives setting out to strengthen its resources with earned revenue has several ways to communicate future possibilities. The most obvious is to recount the reasons to expect success in raising fees from sales of duplicate images. The archives knows—from staff-led studies of potential customers, costs of operating the sales service, and projected revenue—that it can realize meaningful net income within two years. All other things remaining equal, the archives can anticipate using its new earnings to start rebuilding its finances within that period. These details are not promises, but they are reasonable projections based on the investigations that the leader can point out to staff. The better possibilities might require a different portrayal for staff who perceive the danger of commercialism in the earned-revenue project and fear that a profit motive and balance-sheet mentality will compromise the archives' values. The leader can respectfully and genuinely address these reservations by pointing out that the archives remains steadfast in its commitment never to charge fees for access to its holdings and dedicated to the goal of making its collections increasingly available to all users.

Communicating to the archives' users about the new earned-revenue program, though obviously related to addressing staff concerns, represents a separate challenge. Accustomed to the former cost-recovery fee schedule for copies, users—especially regular users—are likely to question rate increases. Here leaders and staff can benefit from studying the marketing profession's concepts of brand communications that include the idea of promising something of value.[4] Leaders can explain how users can benefit in the near future from having more digitized images to select, from a better web interface, and from faster delivery of copies. Making and delivering on such offers better communicates users' stakes in the proposed change than describing the likely alternative that continued funding shortfalls will bring about.

The point for the leader in making the arguments for urgency and for brighter possibilities is not to make all staff and stakeholders equally enthusiastic about change. Rather, the first objective is to deepen the resolve for change as widely as possible throughout the archives and its core supporters. The more they feel the pressing need to move forward with change, and the better the possible future that they look for from transformation, the more resiliently they can deal with the inevitable difficulties that change involves. The second objective is to keep the larger rationale for change in front of staff and stakeholders and to discourage them from fixating on specific obstacles and potential problems. This second aim becomes particularly hard, if not impossible, when change in an archives means loss or severe disruption for staff.

Some staff in the two archives that must merge operations clearly foresee the end of their current routines, their work groups, and even their job assignments. The reference staff members especially fear these losses and also perceive that their futures involve dealing with unfamiliar kinds of users, understanding different kinds of collections, and mastering new public service procedures. Some staff look forward to the challenge of learning all this, but others deeply regret giving up work that makes them feel competent and forsaking the camaraderie they enjoy with their coworkers. They may react angrily to these prospects and may focus negative feelings on the merged archives' leader. Any kind of change can trigger similarly resistant responses, including change that leadership might view as relatively easy and uncontroversial.[5]

Leaders therefore must carefully prepare to communicate with staff who do not go along with change. If they regularly talk to and listen to staff, in most cases they can anticipate which ones are likely to resist change. When transformations move from general ideas and rationales to actual proposals, when staff have more opportunity to assume leadership in the process from their own positions, those who never before voiced an opinion can start to show their opposition. The reference archivist in the historical society, for example, abruptly objects to the merger when it becomes evident that the combined reading room will gradually de-emphasize expert guidance for researchers seeking particular documents. That criticism joins ones raised by employees in the sports history collection who oppose new security arrangements, including surveillance cameras, lockers for researchers' personal items, and withdrawal of employees' building access keys.

Whether or not these staff try to win colleagues over to their point of view, leaders need to pay particular attention to them, without immediately categorizing them as opponents. Instead, at the outset of communicating about change, leaders should listen closely to questioning staff and genuinely consider their reservations and criticisms. In fact, enabling these staff to reshape proposals for change can improve the project blueprint and model how leadership stands ready to engage constructively with all staff members. Progress in this approach requires earnest efforts from both staff and leaders.[6]

When leaders find that they cannot gain support for change through a process of openness, reasonableness, and give-and-take, they need to take other steps. They can, for example, assign resistant staff to work teams composed mostly of others who support the change project. In such groups, oppositional staff can both help improve a project and can ultimately be convinced of the necessity for change.

Although good leadership communications in all circumstances are always sincere and forthright, in episodes of deep change, they must be particularly so. Should no other measure prove successful in bringing resisters around, leaders must speak with staff opponents of change clearly, honestly, and without rancor. They must explain that in the end, the change to the program will proceed and that they need all staff to be willing to help it succeed. They clarify in a straightforward way the choice the resisters face: constructively support the change or find a position in another organization. The bottom line in the communication is that resisters do not have to love the change ahead but they do have to work with all other staff to implement it.

To make this difficult communication effective, it is critical for leaders to say and to show (both in their general conduct and in such stressful situations) that they are not acting out of any personal bias toward the resister. Rather, they are carrying out what is ultimately and unavoidably the leader's responsibility to make a final decision and to explain it forthrightly. In taking that responsibility, they are, at the same time, clarifying where the resister's responsibility lies: giving up resistance (though not constructive criticisms of change) to remain with the archives program or pursuing other career options where they will more likely find job satisfaction.

Stressing a leader's need to engage with staff resisters again emphasizes the importance of building support for the change process. Another way to do this is through good planning—leadership's second major role in directing change. Unlike the situation with communication, however, leaders can share the planning role with managers and staff. In small repositories where the head of the archives bears the responsibilities of leader and manager, starting to plan can involve shifting gears from one type of responsibility to the other, from the conceptualizing, visioning, and promoting to the plotting of step-by-step processes. The leader role transitions to oversight and ultimate direction that ensures that change stays on track.

Managers may need either basic or refresher training in project management skills before they can expect to handle the many phases of work. While every change involves its own specific mix of phases, in general terms, requirements must be spelled out, processes and tasks plotted in a logical sequence, staff teams appointed and organized, and quality reviews and reporting scheduled. When change involves construction of new facilities or major renovations, an additional planning phase can include project team meetings with engineers, architects, construction supervisors, contractors, and members of construction crews. Once planning starts, leaders and managers continue to communicate with staff, seeking their perceptions and reactions to progress and addressing their reservations.

Transformative change in an archives may begin from the top down, but it cannot take hold and progress unless staff get directly involved.[7] Supervisors and nonsupervisory staff belong on planning teams, according to their knowledge, skills, and experience. Wherever possible, in fact, they should lead these committees. Leaders and managers select committee heads and members with an eye to individual expertise and interpersonal and communication abilities. The manager gives the committees their charges, assigns deadlines for interim and final reports, and provides funding, if necessary. The manager or leader may sit in on committee meetings from time to time but delegates to the staff members the authority to research, investigate, discuss, and recommend plans. How does planning by staff committee look in one of the change scenarios?

The head of the merging archives appoints a joint staff team to plan webpages for the combined reference services. Each archives has had its own collections access webpages, so the leadership designates co-chairs representing both programs. They also appoint reference staff from each archives and a website manager while contracting with a web designer to work with the committee. The committee's charge includes proposing a series of webpages where the public gets general collection information, access policies, reference service information, access to online collection descriptions, and links to digital images of documents. The committee does not have to produce prototype webpages, but it does have to specify the content and how each page links to others in the access section and other parts of the larger archives website. In addition to a final deadline, the manager also schedules several interim updates as well as meetings among the chairs of all the planning committees, open to the entire staff so that everyone can track progress and comment on planning developments.

Leaders and managers monitor the work of their planning committees and make any necessary changes to keep the work on track. They balance the importance of staff responsibility and initiative by always assuming leadership's responsibility of reaching the right outcomes. Because they understand that change does not always progress in a linear fashion, they sacrifice staying on preset schedules in order to realize optimum results. For example, if the joint committee on reference service webpages bogs down on how to maintain the identities of the two formerly separate collections, leadership may revise the committee's charge and specify a new set of deadlines. On the other hand, it may reshuffle the committee's co-chairing arrangement, if necessary, to get around personal antagonisms that prevent resolutions on issues. In some cases, leadership may even have to decide whether to abolish a staff committee that proves entirely dysfunctional and assemble a new committee or shift planning responsibilities to a different vehicle altogether.

Assembling committee plans into the master blueprint for change and then implementing the change process again call on both the manager and the leader to play their parts. The leader ensures that the discrete planning recommendations fit together and that, in sum, they amount to the envisioned change. The manager's role at the conclusion of the planning tests the recommendations for feasibility and sustainability. During implementation the manager supervises the rollout of new processes and routines in a logical pattern and smoothes out kinks as they occur. When leadership successfully carries out both roles, staff improve steadily in new assignments, and the archives gradually leaves the husk of its former program and begins to embody its new identity.

Though transformational change draws in efforts from all personnel in an archives, leaders' and managers' roles are decisive in at least one respect. They are the ones who see to it that the whole change exceeds the sum of its components. Transformation in archives requires many changes in policies, processes, professional practices, and technology, yet as we close the examination of the two scenarios, we can see that it amounts to more than these. Deep change in archives brings about new ways of thinking about stewardship, users, donors, funders, and governing authorities. It forges new program identities and new values. It shifts emphases and goals, requiring new metrics for performance. This is why the archives that is adding earned revenue into its long-term finances needs more than just good accounting procedures and marketing plans; even more essential will be an entrepreneurial mind-set. It is also why the archives that are merging need not only seamless reference services but also a new view of all their users as one public that they can serve better than they ever did as separate programs.

Leadership in Crises

On the one hand, crises test archival leaders, managers, and staff in unique ways. On the other hand, they also call for some roles involved in transformative change. For example, communication during crises—both to everyone connected to the archives and to external audiences—becomes just as important as it is for processes of change. But unlike most episodes of profound change, crises demand quick and decisive responses from leadership, often without complete information about all the contributing factors. The similarities in leadership roles in a crisis and in a deep change indicate at least one relationship between the two. Because they disrupt established patterns and procedures, crises can lead into transformative changes. Leadership's first responses to a crisis might well be efforts to restore the previous modes of operation or to make incremental improvements. However, leaders may ultimately decide to use the rupture caused by the crisis as an opportunity for change.

Crises often erupt as sudden, short-term events that threaten human life and safety as well as archives' core stewardship responsibilities. Natural disasters like floods, tornadoes, hurricanes, and earthquakes can quickly destroy public facilities and collection storage locations. Wildfires ignited by lightning strikes or by embers from open fires can also endanger lives and collections, but it is fires started by human accident in archival facilities that more often destroy documents and cause severe smoke damage. Mechanical system failures can cause major water leaks or shut off environmental control systems, and, in addition to water damage to collections, they can lead to sharp fluctuations in storage area temperatures and humidity levels that speed up deterioration of fragile materials. Except when there is extensive damage to facilities or infrastructure, conditions in the archives can be stabilized relatively quickly, though restoration of collections can continue for a long time.

Other kinds of crises develop out of long-term problems that can seriously compromise the integrity of archival programs. Such crises may come to light abruptly even though their underlying causes have festered for months or years. Lax collection security, for example, represents one such insidious archival problem. Inadequate security can enable theft from the collections—a direct attack on an archives' fundamental purpose that undermines its credibility with every important constituency. Persistent poor management of archives operations can cause deterioration and lack of access to collections, poor donor relations, or negative user experiences—any of which can create crises. Addressing the roots of such crises can require months or even years of work.

Leaders' and managers' roles in short-term crises are similar. If each of these roles belongs to two different individuals in an archives, the leader may take a more publicly visible part than the manager (providing information to the media, for example) and may assume primary responsibility for communications. Both leaders and managers, however, focus on tasks that return the archives to normal operations as quickly as possible: protecting individual health and safety; stopping the source of the threat; limiting damage to facilities and collections; restoration and preservation of damaged collections; communicating with staff, supervisors, stakeholders, and the public.

Festering crises represent a twofold challenge for leaders and managers that differs from the difficulties of handling a shorter-term crisis. First, while leadership must take immediate steps in the face of the crisis, it also needs time to address the underlying conditions that built up to the rupture. Second, the crisis can damage perceptions of the leader's and manager's competence and make it difficult, if not impossible, for them to direct the recovery from the crisis. It can fall to new leadership to cope with the aftermath of a crisis and to eradicating its roots. Even when such a mandate is accompanied with an expanded authority for action, it can be an unenviable leadership responsibility to deal with the aftereffects of a crisis.

Short-term crises by their nature remove control for some period of time from the hands of leaders, managers, and staff. From the shocking revelation of the threat through the initial coping reactions, leadership must first think and act as clearly and calmly as possible. Avoiding panic and overreaction not only increases the chance for addressing dangers thoughtfully and in the proper sequence but also models for staff the best way to respond to frightening circumstances. The second challenge is to gather as quickly as possible the most accurate available information about the nature of the threat to people and to the archives and the extent of the damage. A rapid assessment gives leadership some ability to determine initial responses to the crisis and also provides information to communicate to governing authorities, stakeholders, and, if necessary, to the public.

Because responses to sudden threats do not allow for methodical planning, advance planning for dealing with a disaster or crisis becomes one key task for leaders and managers. Ever since the devastation caused by Hurricane Katrina in 2005, cultural heritage institutions throughout the United States have better appreciated the importance of disaster planning. In the archives field, government archivists in particular studied their repositories' readiness to cope with natural disasters and then conducted a nationwide project to improve their preparedness.[8]

Leaders and managers work with their staffs to compile such plans and train their staff on how to use them. Particularly in the stressful early phases of a crisis, the disaster plan provides an indispensable framework of practical steps for protecting human health and safety, safeguarding collections, communicating with emergency responders, and conducting the first cleanup processes. Among other things, the plan identifies evacuation procedures, assigns staff responsibilities for certain tasks, shows the location of equipment and supplies, and provides contact information for essential service providers.[9]

Every crisis response unfolds differently, and even the best disaster response plan leaves leaders and managers facing urgent demands. Of all these, timely and accurate communication is perhaps the most essential. Unless leaders and managers immediately begin to direct action and coordinate the various phases of work, threats of confusion, wasted effort, and disinformation pile on top of the threats to lives and collections. Prompt communications to staff in these pressured situations clarify priorities and coordinate different tasks, including the job of reporting to leadership on changing conditions as the response to the crisis progresses.

During any crisis response, leadership must also inform the archives' parent institution and external groups. This particular responsibility best belongs to the leader, who represents the entire archives program to the larger organization of which it is a part. Whenever conditions change during the response or substantive new information emerges, the leader provides an update to the organization and answers questions. The leader's diligence and care in these communications reflects the importance of the archives to the parent institution and that institution's capability to assist the archives in dealing with the crisis.

For communications to other authorities and stakeholders, the parent institution may delegate responsibility to the archives' leader, share it between the head of the organization and the leader, or place it in the hands of another designated spokesperson, such as the public information officer. The president and members of a governing board, a friends group, the representatives of the archives' key partners in other institutions, and user constituencies share responsibilities for the archives, and therefore have definite needs to know about the crisis response. The parent institution's director decides when and how to communicate with these groups, especially the governing board, but depends on the archives' leader's information to do so.

Communication with the general public is also important. As soon as possible during the crisis, the parent institution must assign responsibility for responding to media inquiries and make that assignment known to everyone. Although the media receives information from many sources during a crisis, the archives and its parent institution have a vested interest in clear communications to the public. Rumors and conflicting information can damage institutional credibility and complicate recovery from the crisis. In coordination with the parent institution, the archives shares information about the crisis and response through social media. As the crisis response progresses and recovery phases begin, communications with the general public focus increasingly on resumption of normal archives operations, including resumed hours of public access and rescheduling of public programs.

Recovering from a crisis that is symptomatic of deeply rooted operational weaknesses can take a long time and require new thinking. When existing leadership manages the recovery, it must be able to challenge its own and the staff's assumptions about the proper functioning of the archives. It must closely examine the archives' operations and reacquaint itself with current professional standards and best practices. It may have to adopt new performance measures and new evaluation methods. Leaders, managers, and staff can learn how to strengthen their program by talking to repositories that overcame similar problems. Ultimately, this review and reconstruction phase of recovery can convince leadership that safeguarding against a similar crisis requires deep change in the archives.

Theft from an archives' collections by a staff member can be a particularly disruptive type of slow-forming crisis that brings the challenges of such episodes dramatically into focus. The discovery of one or more thefts raises alarms within the archives and can force leadership and staff to suspend some normal functions in order to investigate. As the investigation proceeds, archives leadership and staff may need to deal with law enforcement and criminal justice systems.[10] By its nature, this kind of crisis also involves complex communication issues, including the choice whether or not to share information with external audiences once the details about the thefts are known.[11]

Should evidence prove that a staff member in the archives or the parent institution has stolen from the collections, the crisis reaches a new level. Leadership not only faces the immediate need to bolster collections security, it may also confront a breakdown in the trust among colleagues that every organization depends on to a greater or lesser extent. In archives, that mutual trust and shared understanding of the repository's mission intangibly but vitally sustain the program. If staff work together side by side for many years, they can easily assume that everyone has the same dedication to their jobs. Insider theft can betray this understanding and weaken the foundation on which staff cooperate daily to do the archives' work.[12] In cases like this, leadership realizes it must deal with several kinds of damage.

The thought process for an innovative and empathic leader in this situation might go something like this: "We are facing two longer-term issues: compromised security and damaged staff morale. Due diligence requires that we use every conventional tool we have available to improve collection security, including better collection management processes. We can help staff by giving them opportunities to talk through their feelings of betrayal and even use professional counseling services in the process. But how can we *both* make a quantum improvement in security *and* restore trusting work relationships? Not even the best security devices provide fail-safe solutions against theft, and we want at all costs to avoid putting staff on guard against each other."

A leader thinking along these lines might decide that there can be no way to recover from insider theft without making a transformational change. For example, she might begin a conversation with staff and the administrators to whom she reports about making collection security a much higher institution-wide priority than it has been, with implications for collections access policies as well as many practical consequences for budgeting, staff training, staff assignments, facilities upgrades, and renovations. She might, on the other hand, initiate changes in the way staff carry out their responsibilities (including those involving collection security) to move away from individually defined jobs and independent accountability and toward teamwork and group accountability.

We can only speculate about what deep changes the leader would implement and how they could address the dual challenges of improving collection security and restoring healthy working relationships. The main point here is that overcoming certain crises can push leaders and managers to undertake major changes. It does so because leadership cannot easily solve the problems left in the wake of the crisis, nor can it quickly patch up the weaknesses in the archives that the crisis reveals. Everyone realizes that there can be no return to the former state of affairs. Stabilizing the archives in the short term simply means continuing vital operations (with attention to improving collection security), pending the communications and planning for change.

Crises test the abilities of archival leaders and managers precisely because they often occur with little or no warning and because they threaten archives' core missions. Like transformational changes, crises also provide opportunities for leaders to develop particular skills and qualities and thus to further the cycle of leadership development that David examines in Chapter 6. Leadership should do advance planning for responding to crises and disasters and should make sure that staff are well prepared to play their parts. Yet in important ways, leadership reveals its true character by the way it conducts its own roles, both in the heat of a crisis and in its aftermath. Those who quickly gather available information and then act calmly but decisively earn the trust of staff and superiors. Effective leaders also understand the wisdom of the popular admonition "never waste a crisis." Amid the anxiety and pressure of coping with crises come opportunities to improve preparations for the next one and, in some circumstances, even to initiate a transformative change that can inoculate the archives against recurrence.

Leadership of transformational change highlights the importance of vision and communication. Even more, however, it reveals that the essential work of leadership concerns relationships. Just as a fundamental reordering of an archival program takes place through interactions among staff, users, donors, partners, financial supporters, and governing authorities, so healthy relationships among these groups sustain repositories. In the next chapter, "Building Relationships within and beyond the Archives," Peter Gottlieb examines how archival leadership cultivates these vital connections.

NOTES

1   For a similar distinction between types of change, see Petra Düren, *Leadership in Academic and Public Libraries: A Time of Change*, Chandos Information Professional Series (Philadelphia: Chandos Publishing, 2013), 9. See also Kotter, *John P. Kotter on What Leaders Really Do* (Boston: Harvard Business School Press, 1999), 55.

2   Düren, *Leadership in Academic and Public Libraries*, 141–44, 157–60; Kotter, *John P. Kotter on What Leaders Really Do*, 76–79.

3   John P. Kotter and Dan Cohen, *The Heart of Change: Real-Life Stories of How People Change Their Organizations* (Boston: Harvard Business Review Press, 2002), 83–95.

4   See, for example, Neil Kotler and Philip Kotler, *Museum Strategy and Marketing* (San Francisco: Jossey-Bass, 1998), 219.

5   Fynette Eaton, "Managing Organizational Change in Archives: Taking Control," in *Management: Innovative Practices for Archives and Special Collections*, ed. Kate Theimer (Lanham, MD: Rowman and Littlefield, 2014), 109–10.

6   Düren, *Leadership in Academic and Public Libraries*, 131–33; Eaton, "Managing Organizational Change in Archives," 110; Kotter, *John P. Kotter on What Leaders Really Do*, 38–39.

7   Eaton, "Managing Organizational Change in Archives," 108.

8   The study of government archives' readiness to deal with disasters was published as *Safeguarding a Nation's Identity* (Iowa City: Council of State Archivists, 2007). The Federal Emergency Management Administration funded the project (named Intergovernmental Preparedness for Essential Records) to help government archivists improve their disaster preparedness. See https://thehep.files.wordpress.com/2013/04/iper.pdf, captured as https://perma.cc/5FA4-8EB4.

9   Johanna Wellheiser and Jude Scott, *An Ounce of Prevention: Integrated Disaster Planning for Archives, Libraries and Record Centres*, 2nd ed. (Lanham, MD: Scarecrow Press, 2002), 15–22, 85–105, 114–18; Emma Dadson, *Emergency Planning and Response for Libraries, Archives and Museums* (Lanham, MD: Scarecrow Press, 2012), 212–17.

10   Mary Jo Pugh, *Providing Reference Services for Archives and Manuscripts* (Chicago: Society of American Archivists, 2005), 184; Christopher J. Anderson, "Special Collections, Archives and Insider Theft: A Thief in Our Midst," in Theimer, *Management*, 47, 49. For descriptions of thefts from archives, rare books libraries, and special collections that involved institutional security personnel, law enforcement from multiple jurisdictions, state and federal justice officials, attorneys for plaintiffs and defendants, and expert witnesses, see Miles Harvey, *The Island of Lost Maps* (New York: Random House, 2000), 82–84, 88, 89–94, 133, 175–77, 281–82, 313–15; Travis McDade, *The Book Thief: The True Crimes of Daniel Spiegelman* (Westport, CT: Praeger, 2006), 42–43, 88–91, 125–34, 164.

11   The archives profession and related professions in museums and libraries debate the proper steps to take. In practice, many cultural institutions keep information about thefts to themselves, fearing damage to their reputations from publicizing losses. Others send information to law enforcement agencies, repositories with similar collections, and networks of book and manuscript dealers in hopes of alerting all these to possible threats and to attempts to sell stolen items. An archives that chooses to share information about a theft from its collections not only raises awareness of a threat to cultural heritage but also encourages other institutions and agencies to reciprocate should they become victims of thefts. Vincent Totka Jr., "Preventing Patron Theft in the Archives: Legal Perspectives and Problems," *American Archivist* 56, no. 4 (1993): 670; Anderson, "Special Collections, Archives, and Insider Theft," 58; Susan M. Allen, "Theft in Libraries and Archives: What to Do in the Aftermath of a Theft," *Journal of Library Administration* 25, no. 1–2, 6–9, https://doi.org/10.1300/J111v25n01_02, captured as https://perma.cc/J4CR-UDNK; see also McDade, *Book Thief*, 28–32, 42–44.

12   Anderson, "Special Collections, Archives, and Insider Theft," 45, 54. For an indication of the insidious effect of insider theft on working relationships, see Gregor Trinkaus-Randall's list of behavioral indicators that an employee might be stealing from collections in Trinkaus-Randall, *Protecting Your Collections: A Manual of Security* (Chicago: Society of American Archivists, 1995), 63–64. McDade also discusses the damage to trust among colleagues at institutions that have suffered from insider theft in *Book Thief*, 23–27, 43.

5

Building Relationships
within and beyond
the Archives

Peter Gottlieb

More so than most other areas of archival program development, fostering healthy working relationships among the staff of an archives and between an archival program and other organizations allows for contributions from all quarters. Program directors, managers, and staff can all play leadership roles in cultivating the relationships that sustain archives, and they all bear responsibility for doing so. In this chapter, I discuss how leaders as well as others build strong bonds among archives staff, between the archives and other programs in the same parent institution, and with partner organizations.

The reason such relationships matter to archives and why leadership must focus on these relationships springs from the reality that archives are inherently both people-oriented programs and, in most settings at least, collective enterprises. Contrary to some stereotypes of lone archivists performing their skilled tasks in isolation from other staff or members of the public, much archival work depends on close, daily cooperation among several people and nearly continuous interactions with users, visitors, donors, supporters, and colleagues from other departments of the parent institution or from other organizations. Like many other professionals, archivists spend some of their time working alone on their individual responsibilities and projects, but this fact does not alter the predominantly group effort that characterizes most of their work. How archivists work together makes a significant difference to what their programs accomplish and to the quality of their work.

Leadership itself must fulfill two general types of responsibility for promoting healthy working relationships. The first is to set expectations for working relationships and communicate these to staff and partners. In almost all archives, regardless of staff size or program complexity, it falls to the leaders and managers to establish and uphold standards for staff interactions and for relationships with other programs. The second responsibility of leaders is to gain self-awareness not only of their strengths and weaknesses, as David discusses in chapter 6, but also of their own temperaments and personalities:

- Do they tend toward the introverted or extroverted end of the spectrum?
- Are they good listeners?
- How adept are they at handling conflict and sharp disagreement?
- How comfortable do they feel talking with archives staff about non-work-related or personal matters?
- In certain situations, are they prepared to temporarily give up their status and authority in the interest of strengthening bonds among staff or collaborators?

These and similar questions about individual temperamental and emotional dispositions point to factors that come into play for leadership's roles in developing good working relationships. Different personalities bring their own strengths to this work, and no one temperament or set of people skills holds the key to success.[1] The only certain obstacles to progress are lack of self-awareness and refusal to gain greater self-understanding.

Working Relationships within the Archives

Good working relationships among the staff of an archives make for versatile, resilient programs that progress and strengthen over time. Trust, respect, open communications, and cooperation form the foundation for these relationships that enable staff to share the work, cooperate on teams to accomplish important projects, rely on each other's individual contributions, and grow professionally while working toward the archives' goals. Leaders, managers, and staff foster such relationships and discourage negative interactions through every decision they make, from defining job descriptions, to recruiting and hiring staff, to modeling collegial interactions in their own behavior. For leaders, creating and reinforcing supportive relationships requires their constant attention, including an awareness of their own attitudes and actions.

Encouraging trust among all staff leads to working relationships that support strong archives. Trust results from recognizing that each staff member is equally committed to the archives' mission, has the capability to carry out her responsibilities (with the necessary support), and stands ready to support her colleagues' work. When leaders and managers have confidence about these aspects of their staff's orientation, they share more information, delegate more responsibility, and permit staff to take wider initiative. Because they demonstrate trust, these steps in turn can encourage trust among staff and lead to a reinforcing cycle of supportive relationships throughout the archives. But where and how does leadership begin to instill trust and lay the groundwork for productive staff relationships?

Few leaders and managers have the opportunity to start an archives from scratch and employ a completely new staff. The great majority of them move into established programs developed by others, facing the need to become acquainted with staff, to find out the archives' assets and liabilities, and to formulate their own sense of where the archives should head.[2] Among this majority, the more fortunate ones discover solid relationships among staff that mostly need encouragement and strengthening. Clearly, in worse situations, the staff relationships cannot change overnight or simply through the new leader's edict. From the beginning of his tenure, however, the leader can nudge them in a positive direction through his own actions: communicating frequently with staff, individually and as a group; listening carefully and asking questions; showing respect for their opinions, knowledge, and expertise; and honestly discussing his differences with staff on important issues.

No incremental step for building trust among staff counts more than sharing information. From his first day in a new position, the leader or manager can choose to provide the staff with as much information as possible about the program. While he must understand and observe the exclusions to this open approach (personnel and some legal matters, for example), he can affirmatively adopt a pattern of reducing barriers between his position and other staff, as well as among staff, by maintaining a steady flow of information. Pursuing this approach signals a leader's trust in his staff and the attitude that everyone in the archives program shares the same interest in its success. It can nourish the staff's trust in the leader, reduce staff's turf-guarding behavior, and reinforce relationships of mutuality, cooperation, and staff cohesion.[3]

Broadly sharing information with the archives staff is not as easy as it may look. In addition to minding the legal and ethical limits on what information he can pass along, the leader or manager confronts other factors and circumstances mitigating against an open policy. The archives' parent institution may have a relatively restrictive approach that constrains the archives leader's readiness to share information. With resistance from the institution's directors or governing authorities, he, at the very least, has to hedge his inclination to inform the archives staff or else damage his own standing with his superiors and indirectly jeopardize the archives. The exercise of authority is another factor a leader has to consider. Because who does and does not have information delineates power in any organization, a leader must judge when giving up his power through sharing information works in the archives' best interest. He must also feel prepared for the potential for reducing his own authority by making the archives staff more equal in their possession of information. These various influences make clear that when, where, and how a leader passes along information can be just as important as what details he shares.

I once worked as an archives director for a parent institution that withheld information practically as its default mode of operation. This produced constant competition among departments for influence and resources. It also gave rise to endless rumors about the administration's plans and pending decisions. I even got into a heated argument with a valued colleague from another department over a minor resource issue, just because neither of us knew that an administrator had already decided the issue himself but had not informed us. While, in this instance, my colleague and I quickly repaired our rupture, the administrator could have prevented it in the first place simply by sharing some details about his decision. More significantly, the work of the whole institution could have proceeded much more smoothly and efficiently with the steady, judicious sharing of information throughout all levels.

Productive staff relationships also take root in a setting where leaders encourage all archivists to view their work as part of a unified enterprise rather than as a series of discrete programs or individual projects. Leaders promote this view by consistently emphasizing to their staff the archives' mission, vision, and major goals. They look for ways to reduce barriers between staff, even altering floor plans where possible to combine work spaces and break rooms. These leaders also seek opportunities for staff to work together on project teams and to delegate as much responsibility as possible to the teams for the results of their work.

Archival leaders and managers, no less than the leadership in any other contemporary institution, need the skills to direct today's diverse work groups. Individual identities arise from an increasing number of social and demographic factors, like race, ethnicity, culture, education, religion, and language. For some individuals, other bases for personal identity, such as gender and sexual orientation, are fluid rather than fixed. If all members of an archives staff regard themselves in some sense as archivists, they also definitely think of themselves in terms of other attributes, affiliations, and identities. Leadership that nurtures healthy working relationships recognizes and respects all these varied dimensions of their individual staff's status. As one of my own staff once said to me, "When you employ someone, you employ the whole person."

The trusting and cooperative work relationships that support strong archives do not admit any hierarchy of identities among staff members. The same respect and dignity that leaders and managers accord to their individual staff should also be exchanged among everyone in the work group. Leadership encourages this inclusivity by supporting diversity not only of backgrounds and identities but also, as David reminds us in his discussion of developing leaders, of values, opinions, perspectives, and temperaments. A policy of inclusion goes hand in hand with a very clear set of standards and expectations for each individual staff member.

The most important expectation for building relationships based on trust, mutuality, and cooperation is for each staff member to understand his role in terms of the same overall program goals. Whatever their identities, job titles, or expertise, staff members must give priority to making progress toward those goals and to supporting their colleagues' efforts toward the same ends. Their professional rewards come from developing their mastery of some specific archival knowledge and skills, not only as accomplishments in themselves but also as contributions to the success of the archives. They pride themselves not on owning some valuable territory within the program but on their and their colleagues' ability to make the archives ever more valuable to more users.

Clearly, no leader or manager ever fully creates such consistently sustaining relationships. Archivists, like all other humans, resist inducements to work together respectfully and supportively just as often as they embrace them. Leaders and managers themselves miss opportunities and fail to maintain standards and models of behavior. Rather than advocating some perfect situation where ideal leaders and angelic archivists realize an organizational state of grace, I want to emphasize the importance of consistent attention to working relationships in an archives and consistent efforts toward making those trusting, supportive, and cooperative relationships the strong foundation of a successful program.

Scenario: Fostering healthy working relationships

What might this kind of leadership look like in practice? Let's imagine a new leader at a small archives making some progress in her effort to break down the barriers among the staff. During her first year, she has accomplished the following things:

- discussed a strategic direction with her staff in order to bring program-wide goals into focus
- redefined job responsibilities to foster greater cooperation among staff
- initiated a rotation of staff on public service functions to spread knowledge about users among all staff
- regularly shared information with staff and encouraged their feedback

Just as she is looking back with some satisfaction at the progress being made, she observes a particularly serious lapse by her staff.

Though a staff member sees that a visitor to the archives has approached the reference desk when no one is there to offer help, the staff member just walks past without stopping to assist. Observing this obvious breach in the archives' priority on user services, the leader goes to check on the reason for it. She overhears the staff member explaining to a colleague how he knew assisting the visitor is the norm, regardless of job assignments, and saying, "But if you start doing other staff's work, they'll just keep giving you more stuff to do, until you're running around like crazy."

Careful not to call him out in front of colleagues, the leader invites the archivist to her office and opens a conversation about the incident. She takes time to inquire about the circumstances facing the archivist when he walked past the visitor, knowing that he could have perceived valid reasons for continuing his own tasks and not helping someone at the reference desk. She then points out that improving services for visitors ranks first among the archives' major goals, reminding him that this means all staff share responsibility for progress on it, regardless of other duties. Finally, she asks the archivist to expand on his concern about taking on new assignments and pays close attention to his responses to make sure she has not ignored problems created by her efforts to integrate program functions. She assures him that she would be concerned if staff were overworked and wants to hear whenever archivists feel burdened. She ends the conversation by re-emphasizing the salience of all staff cooperating to achieve program-wide goals, and the archivist gives her his commitment to support them.

We can take away two important points from this scenario. The first is that progress toward healthy working relationships usually goes in fits and starts. Leaders cannot simply put the right pieces in place and expect optimum results from then on. Even when the archives staff achieves a mode of open and mutually supportive relationships, any number of internal and external factors can start to unravel them. Leaders can only keep working with their staff toward the goal of genuine collegiality and watch out for missteps and malign influences.

The second point comes through in the opportunity that the leader grasped. She took advantage of the staff member's egregious behavior to underscore the link between mutuality among the staff and progress toward the archives' goals. Rather than presuming that she knows enough about the incident to simply correct her staff member, she also uses the incident to check on her own information and understanding of her staff's views. When serious problems with working relationships come to light, they can open a window on underlying issues a leader must address. They also make it possible for staff to understand in new ways the benefits of good working relationships.

What if we reverse the respective roles of leader and staff in this scenario? What if a leader takes little interest in the program's working relationships, and staff members take the initiative to improve them? Since much of the interactions take place among staff, they have plenty of scope to bring about change.[4] Perhaps a new archivist joins the staff, bringing her experience in collaboration and teamwork from another repository. Or a long-term archives employee, seeing how another department in the same parent organization shares information and achieves progress on cooperative goals, suggests to his colleagues that they try to do the same. They themselves rally their colleagues to take on more flexible work assignments and to extend cooperation in order to improve customer satisfaction. These and any number of other first steps can easily lead to wider conversations and efforts among staff to improve their working relationships. In a larger, more complex archival program, the initiative could well come from a manager. They all represent "leading from the middle," since staff itself starts to strengthen the archives and point the way toward lasting improvement.

For this staff-led impetus to improve working relationships in the archives, staff members must eventually bring the leader on board. Without her active support, staff at best face a struggle to make mutuality and cooperation the accepted approach to work, and at worst, they can expect to clash with her over priorities, job assignments, and the whole direction of the program. Staff may continuously have to fight for more information from a leader who instinctively protects her authority and organizational turf. Staff who are leading from the middle may best avoid friction with leadership by pointing out how better working relationships lead to improvements in the archives. They can show evidence that these relationships overcome compartmentalized information, overlapping or duplicative functions, and intrastaff competition, while at the same time speeding the completion of key projects. They can invite the leader to help define ambitious and creative new goals that take advantage of the new working relationships and the archives' greater potential. Most leaders can come to see the advantages of these improvements for the archives, for themselves, and for the archives' parent organization.

Relationships beyond the Archives: The Parent Institution

Strong working relationships among the staff of an archives strengthen the entire program, just as such relationships between the archives and external parties augment a program's capabilities. As we have noted, most archives exist within a larger organization. The connections between the archives and its parent institution can vary significantly in intensity, with some archives strongly integrated into the organization's work and others operating more independently. Whatever the ties between the two, however, the relationship with the parent institution usually ranks as the most important external one for the leadership of the archives.[5]

The reasons for this may appear obvious. Resources for the archives, wholly or in part, flow through the parent institution. Such resources include both funds and physical spaces, security systems, storage environments and controls, information technology, and public information. Even when the archives independently controls some of its funds, it frequently relies on the larger organization for critical infrastructure. Beyond such resources, the archives may also depend on staff expertise from other departments, from legal or financial knowledge to web design, exhibits, or preservation. The parent institution may also support the archives through the work of education specialists, fund-raisers, and brand managers.[6]

A less obvious reason that the relationship with the parent institution holds pride of place for archives stems from the value of earning goodwill or credibility. This can happen in more complex bureaucratic organizations where the archives reports to one department but serves several other programs in the bigger institution. When the archives' services impress a powerful office, its reputation within the organization grows, and consequently its value to its own department rises. Good standing within a bureaucracy can translate into greater resources for the archives, but it can also bring such vital benefits as a larger voice in decision-making, recognition of value to the organization, and opportunities to serve other influential parts of the institution.

Developing strong working relationships with the parent organization begins with clearly understanding what the organization expects from the archives. An effective archives leader keeps these expectations constantly in mind and orients her program's goals to them. She ensures that her staff also realizes the expectations, and she encourages staff members to think of new ways to fulfill them. Meeting the expectations seldom becomes a challenge for the archives, unless those expectations definitely fall outside legal, ethical, or professional boundaries. When the parent institution looks to the archives for something that violates these fundamental obligations, it often does so in ignorance. Staff and leadership can show how the larger organization can obtain the same or equally valuable outcomes through legitimate means.

More often, the challenge for leadership becomes figuring out how to exceed expectations. While delivering on what the organization wants from the archives should be the primary objective, seeking new, unanticipated opportunities to further the organization's mission can bring about much greater gains. Directors of the parent institution often take a comparatively narrow view of the archives' functions and services, while adroit archival leaders look broadly for possible ways their programs can support the organization. A corporation might see its archives' work related solely to trademark and patent concerns, while the archives leader and staff know that they can also contribute in the area of public relations. A university administrator might think of the campus archives as a research resource primarily for faculty and graduate students, though the head of the archives realizes that his staff also has the knowledge and skills to help the university with its records management obligations.

Seeking to exceed its institution's expectations can require the archives leader to balance potential gains and losses. She needs to avoid pursuing those projects that, however valuable to the institution, divert too much staff time from the archives' priority projects, let alone those that carry the archives far from its core mission and responsibilities. No amount of credibility, goodwill, or new resources for her program justifies ventures that jeopardize collections or seriously compromise users' access. On the other hand, leader and staff should remain attuned to the area where the archives' work and the institution's goals overlap and never fear committing to projects in that space—even unprecedented, experimental ones.

In many instances, the archives has room to negotiate in order to hit the sweet spot between its primary function and the institution's priorities. Leadership lies in maneuvering toward the place where the archives' role and the larger organization's needs meet. For a December event recognizing donors to the institution, should the archives allow a traditional Christmas tree with lit candles in its reading room? *Definitely not*, though it should suggest the alternative of using its historical holiday cards for a very attractive exhibition in the reading room's gallery. Should the archives contribute original items from its collections to an institutional initiative in which curators from the museum program do trunk shows for young students in elementary school classrooms? *Certainly*, as long as the archives can give curatorial staff a few pointers on secure transportation and safe handling of the originals.

What is worth emphasizing here is the need for leadership to remain alert and flexible regarding the possibilities for collaboration and mutual benefit when working with other organizations. Positive outcomes reinforce healthy relationships that help the archives to extend its reach. Within its parent institution, the archives may have so many such possibilities that its leadership must pick and choose among the best of them. Additional possibilities for cooperative work lie beyond the archives' home institution, with other organizations. Some of these possibilities can be fundamentally strategic for the archives, so leadership comes through looking for opportunities to work with partner institutions on significant projects.

Relationships beyond the Archives: Coalitions, Partnerships, and Collaborations

Many archives discover opportunities for improvement and growth through working with other organizations beyond their parent institution. Whether the opportunities deal with documentation projects, digitizing collections, or joint advocacy for improving archives, making ties with other institutions enables archives to accomplish more in combination than they could do on their own. A leader's role in building productive relationships with other organizations becomes one of finding the best opportunities, of forging effective collaborations, and of fostering the personal and professional relationships that sustain inter-institutional efforts.[7]

Interinstitutional work among archives has taken many forms, perhaps because meager budgets for most programs make it advantageous for them to pool their resources. State archives across the country have allied with both local governments and with local historical societies to improve the stewardship of historical records. Granting agencies have offered incentives for joint work among multiple funding applicants, particularly for electronic records management, archival training, and preservation projects. As long ago as the 1950s, archives started building state and regional networks to collect, house, and provide access to documents.[8] Other archives have joined together to mount public campaigns both against institution-threatening budget cuts and for path-breaking legislation.[9] Since the 1990s, the Internet has strengthened the logic for archives to work with each other and with other institutions, so cultivating relationships beyond the parent organization seems certain to remain a part of many leaders' work.[10]

When a new leader takes the reins in a participating archives, he takes time to learn and understand how the collaboration works. Much like his initial steps in acquainting himself with his own staff, the leader gets to know the perspectives and priorities of his fellow participants in the joint work and also begins to relate to them on a personal basis. He discusses the collaboration with the heads of his parent institution in order to appreciate their take on it and gain more information about its history. He seeks the views of his staff on the joint work and how it affects the archives. Unless confronted by a pressing problem or an imminent change in the interinstitutional effort, the leader has time to size it up and decide how best to represent his own archives or decide whether continuing to participate at all remains advantageous.

Should a leader receive an invitation to join a group of cooperating organizations, he must decide if it makes sense for the archives to join. He should first consider the decision strategically, particularly because many possibilities can present themselves, with various inducements: grant funding, increasing the archives' visibility, professional networking, staff training, and so forth. Though these and other opportunities can all benefit the archives, he must assess them against the archives' plans. How do the collaborative opportunities map to the archives' strategic priorities? In what specific ways can they meet the archives' mission?[11] Are the expected benefits for participating worth the required resources? In addition to these primary considerations, the leader can also look at the prospects for joint work in terms of the ties to other organizations. What can the archives contribute to the work with other institutions? Are there costs or liabilities to withdrawing from the collaboration?

A careful appraisal, applying questions like these, avoids a decision to participate based on the belief that collaboration is a good thing in itself. When leaders start by examining an opportunity for joint work through a strategic lens, they help make the ultimate decision a conscious, deliberate one and not simply an intuitive step. If they conclude that, on balance, the joint work looks like an attractive opportunity, they present the case for participation to their staff. They carefully point out where collaborating with other organizations changes work assignments for staff and how it affects existing expectations and priorities. Leaders may not feel it necessary to have their staff's full support for joint work, but they should make a final decision on participation only when they have the benefit of staff's perspective on the impact it will have on the archives. By the same token, they should explain their final decision to the staff. Effective leaders also make sure they have support from their superiors in the parent institution. New issues can emerge from reviewing pros and cons with higher officials, and leaders must take these issues into account before having a firm basis for a decision.

Whether or not to participate formally with other organizations is properly a leader's decision. If the decision does not ultimately rest in his hands, he must at least seek a major voice in it. A parent institution may direct the archives to participate (or not), or make a very strong recommendation. Staff may lobby for or against him signing on, for any number of reasons. Professional peers might seek to persuade him that joint work holds out attractive programmatic and career opportunities. Yet the leader must keep his own council on whether or not to bring the archives into ongoing efforts with other programs, based on everything he knows and learns from others. He never makes a mistake by taking advice from those the decision impacts and those he trusts, but he cannot rightly allow anyone else to decide, at least not without first hearing him out.

Joint work with other organizations may require a written agreement that sets out each partner's responsibilities and contributions, and capable leaders scrutinize the details of these documents before approving them. The longer the time over which a proposed collaboration extends, and the greater the resources from each participant it requires, the more detailed and formal an agreement can become. Leaders can seek legal advice about an agreement's provisions in order to proceed confidently in launching joint work. Whenever the archives operates within a larger institution, the leader consults early and often with the institution's directors to prepare the agreement for final approval and implementation.

Whether or not written agreements govern joint work among archives, good working relationships among organizations ultimately depend to a significant degree on personal interactions, and a leader's own involvement with his counterparts among participating programs often becomes his critical contribution to cooperative work. The leader should assume the chief responsibility for cultivating healthy, productive relationships with the heads of other cooperating institutions. In many cases, he can delegate to his staff the actual tasks required from the archives while he attends formal meetings with the representatives of the other institutions and works collegially to reach decisions on the course of the joint work. He cultivates collegial bonds with liaisons from other institutions by making appointments to meet with them or by looking for social occasions to talk informally with these representatives, both about the collaborative work or about other shared interests. He also stays in touch with them by email and by telephone, especially when there are scant opportunities for face-to-face communication.

For this same reason, good working relationships in joint work with other institutions call for many of the elements of good working relationships among the staff of an archives: openness, trust, mutuality, flexibility. How much these count toward success varies with the duration and intensity of a partnership. A three-year cooperative project among several archives to digitize the papers of a historical figure may involve only limited, clearly defined contributions from each participant while an ongoing collaboration between two institutions to support a regional archives office requires more open-ended commitments that evolve and change over time. Coalitions to secure legislation on behalf of a group of archives can call for heavy investments of time over one or two years, but an alliance to share disaster response resources on the state or local level might mean relatively modest resources for much longer periods. The deeper the archives' engagement in a joint enterprise, the more that success depends on the qualities of a solid relationship.

The greatest leadership challenge in interinstitutional cooperation can come when joint work brings together archives from different cultural, ethnic, or religious communities. Before these efforts can advance the participants' archival objectives, they must comprehend the meanings, values, and sometimes even the language surrounding the organizations' stewardship of documentary heritage. Power dynamics among different cultural communities further complicate such collaborations, particularly when repositories developed by mainstream or elite institutions seek to engage with archives created by local organizations or by dispossessed or marginalized groups. The smaller organizations may recognize the professional expertise of the mainstream institution, but they often closely guard their own stewardship rights and prerogatives against any signs of influence or encroachment. Instances of cross-cultural cooperation among archives are not unusual, despite the many challenges they face. The work of many larger, well-established repositories such as state historical societies and state archives (through affiliated State Historical Records Advisory Boards) commonly includes assistance to diverse communities that wish to start or to strengthen their own archives.[12]

In the last twenty years, the growing importance of community archives has shaped joint work among archives from different cultures and has redefined leadership roles in such cooperation. While seeking assistance from archives outside their own communities, minority ethnic, racial, and cultural groups have insisted that their developing programs embody their own traditions and values and not just institutionalize the principles of mainstream repositories.[13] Professional archival associations have recognized the importance of these claims and have devoted discussions to them at their annual meetings and in their journals and newsletters.[14] As a result of this significant shift, cross-cultural institutional cooperation among archives in recent decades has involved less tutoring by mainstream archives and more real collaboration—efforts to translate the participants' traditions into useable terms and operations and to apply those to each archives' needs.

In order to lay groundwork for successful cooperation, leaders of mainstream archives approaching joint work with community archives need to understand and prepare for these interinstitutional dynamics. They can initially coach their own staff and their parent institution in what to expect from the engagement, even including training in cultural literacy. Even before meeting with members of the minority community, they can commit time to learning and understanding the cultural traditions that shape its approaches to stewardship and documentary heritage. Most important, leaders of mainstream archives can recognize and accept the essential need to listen to the perspectives from the minority community, to compare and discuss different approaches to archival work, and to understand what the community wants from its archives. Only after this lengthy process, during which little actual archival work gets done, can the joint undertaking move on to subsequent steps of defining cooperative goals and beginning to work toward them.[15]

These pointers emerge from research on cross-cultural collaborations. Elizabeth Joffrion and Natalia Fernandez surveyed Native American tribes and their nontribal partners in archival joint ventures to find ingredients for success. Their main conclusions clearly indicate the importance of understanding, respect, openness, patience, and flexibility from all the partners: " . . . we have identified several fundamental elements essential to building ethical and trusting relationships. These include respect for and an openness to learn from differing cultural perspectives, recognition of historical differences in power and privilege, establishment of reciprocal partnerships where knowledge and expertise is equally valued and shared, and acknowledgment that relationship building is an ongoing process and the responsibility of all partnering communities."[16]

Some of Joffrion and Fernandez's respondents make an observation about cross-cultural collaborations that we might apply to archives' joint work with all other organizations, whether from minority communities or not. They underline the importance of the relationship itself. While leaders of mainstream archives tend to measure success in collaborations by the outcomes they produce, the relationships from which the outcomes arise are equally valuable accomplishments.[17]

Among the many responsibilities that archival leaders shoulder, they cannot minimize the importance of the working relationships that sustain vibrant programs. Leaders model and shape the relationships among their staff, and their daily interactions count just as much in small repositories with very little hierarchy as they do in a large, bureaucratic program with many organizational gradients. Staff can join leaders to propose and even carry out measures to improve working relationships. Capable leaders, in fact, empower their staff to do so. Beyond the archives itself, leaders play the primary parts in developing cooperative goals, mutuality, and reciprocity with partner organizations and collaborators. Though they may not include this work on résumés or send notices about it to professional publications, their success in building good working relationships should take its rightful place among any leader's noteworthy achievements.

Whether we are discussing communications, strategy, or relationships, our view is that archivists improve in their roles as leaders and managers through a combination of new knowledge, practical experience, and reflection. Nowhere is this truer than in the work of developing new leaders, which David W. Carmicheal discusses in the next chapter, "Developing Leaders." He shows that there really is no such thing as an accidental leader and that, on the contrary, leadership is very much intentional.

NOTES

1. Michael J. Kurtz, *Managing Archival and Manuscript Repositories* (Chicago: Society of American Archivists, 2004), 26–27.

2. Similar tasks also confront those leaders who move into their positions from previous jobs in the same archives. They may know many staff and have a grasp of the program, but in their new status as leader, they have to gain the perspective that comes with that wider responsibility.

3. Bruce W. Dearstyne, *Leading the Historical Enterprise: Strategic Creativity, Planning and Advocacy for the Digital Age* (Lanham, MD: Rowman and Littlefield, 2015), 35.

4. John P. Kotter and Dan S. Cohen, *The Heart of Change: Real-Life Stories of How People Change Their Organizations* (Boston: Harvard Business Review Press, 2002), 28–30.

5. It could be debated whether the relationship with the parent institution is an "external" one, particularly for those cases where the archives is closely integrated into the work of the larger organization. When we use the term *external* here, we simply mean beyond the scope of the archives program itself.

6. Frank Burke, "The Art of the Possible: The Archivist as Administrator," in *Leadership and Administration of Successful Archives Programs*, ed. Bruce Dearstyne (Westport, CT: Greenwood Press, 2001), 28–29.

7. Kurtz, *Managing Archives and Manuscript Repositories*, 43–44; Dearstyne, *Leading the Historical Enterprise*, 40.

8. Richard Erney, "Wisconsin's Area Research Centers, *American Archivist* 29, no. 1 (1966): 11–22.

9. For information on the 2012 statewide effort to restore funding for the Georgia State Archives, see Society of American Archivists, *Archival Outlook* (November/December 2016): 7, 28.

10. Robert S. Martin, "Cooperation and Change: Archives, Libraries and Museums in the United States" (presented at the 69th World Library and Information Congress, Berlin, August 2003), 3–5, https://archive.ifla.org/IV/ifla69/papers/066e-Martin.pdf, captured at https://perma.cc/4HWE-LAU5; Juris Dilevko and Lisa Gottlieb, *The Evolution of Library and Museum Partnerships: Historical Antecedents, Contemporary Manifestations, and Future Directions* (Westport, CT: Libraries Unlimited, 2004), 45–46. Although the title of this work does not refer to archives, the authors clearly subsume archives under libraries as one of the cooperating institutions they study.

11. Larry Hackman, "Ways and Means: Thinking and Acting to Strengthen the Infrastructure of Archival Programs," in Dearstyne, *Leadership and Administration of Successful Archival Programs*, 45.

12. One example is the Oregon Historical Society, which explains on its website that it "practices and promotes inclusiveness. We honor the diverse strengths, needs, voices, and backgrounds of all members of our community and are committed to the equitable treatment of all people and the elimination of discrimination in all its forms." See http://www.ohs.org/about-us/, captured at https://perma.cc/67TG-M955. See also New York State Historical Records Advisory Board, "Mission and Vision," http://www.archives.nysed.gov/shrab/vision-mission, captured at https://perma.cc/ZV6T-X7B4; Minnesota Historical Society, "Mission, Values, Vision and Strategic Priorities," http://www.mnhs.org/about/mission, captured at https://perma.cc/S9UE-BAPD.

13. Of these, the best known in the United States is the "Protocols for Native American Archival Material," first formulated in 2006 by nineteen Native American and other cultural heritage professionals. See http://www2.nau.edu/libnap-p/protocols.html, captured at https://perma.cc/D8JW-W7HV. For an in-depth discussion of the issues for archives raised by the protocols and similar documents, see Jeffrey Mifflin, "Regarding Indigenous Knowledge in Archives," in Mary Caldera and Kathryn Neal, *Through the Archival Looking Glass: A Reader on Diversity and Inclusion* (Chicago: Society of American Archivists, 2014), 61–89.

14. "Native American Protocols Forum (August 12, 2010). Minutes from Forum," http://www2.archivists.org/groups/diversity-committee/native-american-protocols-forum-august-12-2010, captured at https://perma.cc/RK5N-5G3B.

15. Tracy Grimm and Chon Noriega emphasize the importance of devoting time to relationship building in their discussion of a project to document Latino arts and culture, "Documenting Regional Latino Arts and Culture: Case Studies for a Collaborative, Community-Oriented Approach," *American Archivist* 76, no. 1 (2013): 101. On archivists and special collections staff working with Latino communities generally, see Patricia Montiel-Overall, Annabelle Villaescusa Nuñez, and Veronica Reyes-Escudero, *Latinos in Libraries, Museums and Archives* (Lanham, MD: Rowman and Littlefield, 2016), 175–205.

16. Elizabeth Joffrion and Natalia Fernandez, "Collaborations between Tribal and Nontribal Organizations: Suggested Best Practices for Sharing Expertise, Cultural Resources, and Knowledge," *American Archivist* 78, no. 1 (2015): 219.

17. Joffrion and Fernandez, "Collaborations between Tribal and Nontribal Organizations," 215.

6

Developing Leaders

David W. Carmicheal

Can you be a leader? Yes, if you decide to be. In books or movies, the hero is often chosen by some outside source (a god or a prophecy) and then ordained to lead. But in real life, leaders are more often self-chosen, imperfect people; they may be driven by a vision or a passion, or they may simply find satisfaction in accomplishing things through collective action.[1] So while it is true that many people who become great leaders are born with innate qualities that accelerate their path to leadership, those same qualities can be learned by archivists who set themselves the task. In fact, even established leaders must continue to *become* good leaders, because no leader is ever done growing. Each generation of leadership development involves continued growth for recognized leaders and intentional shaping of new, upcoming leaders. Leadership development requires intentionality and strategy, resilience and insight; it means being mentored while also mentoring and empowering others; and it means building trust and knowing when to pass the baton of leadership to a new generation.

Building Your Own Leadership Capacity

Leaders—whether well established or emerging—build their capacity for leadership. They are not afraid to critically assess their own strengths and weaknesses or even to recruit others to do so. They build on their strengths and mitigate their weaknesses through self-improvement and diverse team building. And, as they grow, leaders look for opportunities to expand their sphere of influence in small and large ways.

Building self-awareness

Good leaders are highly self-aware. If you want to become a leader, or become a better one, you must be willing to view your own skills and weaknesses with a critical eye. Regularly conducting a personal SWOT (strengths, weaknesses, opportunities, and threats) analysis can reveal how you can best lead others by capitalizing on your strengths, and how your leadership can be improved through personal development and education. Personal analysis can take many forms.

- *Self-assessment.* Most of us don't regularly devote an hour to writing down our strengths and weaknesses as objectively as possible, but conducting this simple exercise in self-assessment even once a year can help you enhance your leadership skills. Jennifer Johnson (in chapter 8), for example, was self-aware enough to identify gaps in her own skills that kept her from being as effective a leader as she might otherwise be. In her case, communicating effectively and strategic planning were skills that needed to be strengthened. Your own gaps may be different. Is your archival knowledge current? Professional thought evolves over time, sometimes very rapidly, and being familiar with how the archival profession is thinking about new technologies and old practices keeps your leadership relevant and nimble. Are you communicating effectively, both verbally and in writing? Accurate communication is essential to good leadership. If you find it difficult to communicate thoughts in writing, or if you freeze at the thought of speaking in front of a large group of people, these are places you might build strength. Even if you communicate well, the tools of communication evolve constantly, and leaders should be ready to adapt to new technologies when appropriate. Not every leader needs to know how to tweet effectively, but every leader needs to be aware of new technologies since their followers are probably adopting them as rapidly as they appear on the market. Do you listen to and empathize with others? Strong leaders risk becoming isolated, particularly from unpleasant or unwelcome information, and many longtime leaders come to believe in their own infallibility, often unconsciously. Regularly assessing your own ability and willingness to listen to others and to place yourself in their shoes is an important exercise. If you want to become a leader, learning to listen well is an essential skill.

  These are just a few of the qualities you might assess, and regular self-assessment is healthy in leaders and would be leaders. As you assess yourself, be as honest as possible; if you make a list, no one needs to see what you write down. Celebrate your strengths and expose your weaknesses (to yourself, at least), and then make an intentional effort to benefit from the knowledge. Self-assessment can be as simple as spending time in quiet reflection, but if you want a more structured method of conducting such an analysis, search for an online self-assessment tool and use it to focus your thinking. Online tools range from general leadership self-assessments to very specific tools that measure cultural competence or specific management skills.[2] Try a variety of tools, and see how much you can learn about yourself.

- *Performance evaluations.* Self-assessment can carry you only so far; assessment by others is critical to building your leadership capacity. Performance reviews offer an opportunity to assess your performance through the eyes of the person (or people) who oversees that performance. Even top leaders often receive such an evaluation, from a board member or an executive committee, for example. If you do not receive such an evaluation regularly, you might want to request one. Ask the person who evaluates you to be honest. Even if their evaluation is flawed by some bias (against you or in your favor), you may glean valuable insight into how others see you.

- **Trusted peers.** A less formal way to review your own performance is to request feedback from trusted peers. Professional peers who have the requisite knowledge can be a source of objective observations about your own performance. The most helpful information will come from peers who have observed you in professional situations and have enough knowledge to appreciate the context of your work environment. You will want to find people you trust and who are likely to be honest with you, even if their assessment includes negative observations. Although it is tempting, it is probably better not to "trade" evaluations with a peer (you evaluate me, I evaluate you) since each may downplay criticism to discourage negative feedback in return. Those who are newer to the profession may want to seek out a more experienced mentor to provide this feedback.
- **The people you lead.** Peer-to-peer reviewing can be supplemented by feedback from the people you lead. Multisource (or 360-degree) feedback is a standard evaluation tool that gathers input from supervisors, peers, and subordinates, but even if your workplace does not use 360-degree assessments, gathering feedback from the people you lead can help you identify strengths and weaknesses. Such feedback, of course, is unlikely to be highly objective; subordinates may be afraid to speak honestly or may see it as an opportunity to curry favor (two reactions that may say much about your leadership style). Still, it may be possible for you to gather feedback anonymously (through an anonymous survey or by asking a peer to gather and anonymize the responses, for instance) to increase the chances of objective comments. It requires humility for a leader to sincerely accept the feedback of subordinates, but humility is an excellent quality for leaders (and would-be leaders) to cultivate.

Building skills

As you gain a better understanding of your own personality and knowledge, you will almost certainly discover gaps or lapses in your skills. If you are already a leader, you will probably have little difficulty identifying such gaps (though you may find it difficult to admit them, even to yourself). If you are just beginning your efforts to become a leader, you may feel overwhelmed by the sheer number of gaps in your knowledge. In that case, focus on just a few to start. Given the broad scope of skills appropriate to leadership—budgeting, planning, communication, and many others addressed throughout this book—you might ask a mentor or a friend to help you prioritize, but your priorities will almost certainly include one or more of these key leadership skills:

- **Professional expertise.** The very first requirement of the archival leader is professional expertise. The professional archivists you are attempting to lead will hardly respect a leader who is not well versed in their profession. This does not suggest that your expertise must exceed or even equal that of the people you lead, but it implies that you have sufficient knowledge to appreciate the scope of their work and the skills they bring to it. It also implies that your knowledge is sufficient to understand when the work is not being done as effectively as it should be. Here is where leaders benefit from having firsthand knowledge of a broad range of archival work. I once met with the senior staff of an archives that I had directed for only a few days. As the staff members described their work, I asked questions that I hoped would show a reasonable grasp of their specialty, whether at the reference desk or in the conservation lab. I wanted them to know that I understood the challenges of their particular aspect of archival work, often from personal experience. At the same time (I admit), I wanted them to understand that they couldn't deceive me; I had enough knowledge to hold them accountable. Leaders who experience a wide range of archival work will find it easier to lead other archivists throughout their career.

- **Communication.** Every archival leader I know—and every staff person I've ever seen become a leader among their peers—has communicated effectively verbally and in writing. Identify gaps you may have in this skill; then follow an intentional plan to close them. Communication courses are readily available at most colleges, and there are many available online. If you are a creative type, writing fiction may improve your ability to communicate even in your nonfiction writing. Plain language, a tool developed by the federal government, is easily learned and can dramatically improve your business communication. An online search will identify manuals and examples to help you learn. The best way to develop written and verbal communication skills, though, is to practice them: write for a blog or a professional newsletter; volunteer to speak at a conference or to present an update about your work to your colleagues in the office. Ask a trusted friend to provide feedback; then use it to improve your future efforts. Above all, keep trying. Practice doesn't always make perfect, but it is the path to incremental improvement.

- **Listening skills.** Learning to listen to others is a vital skill for leaders, but doing so requires conscious effort. How engaged are you when others are speaking? Are you already formulating your response or, worse yet, talking over others before they've finished speaking? Are you alert to nonverbal communication coming from the speaker as well as that being communicated by your own body language? Leaders (and emerging leaders) are often confident about their own ideas and plans, and this may make it difficult for them to value what another person is communicating. Study your own performance in this area or, as suggested elsewhere, ask a trusted friend to pay attention to your behavior and provide feedback.

- **Teamwork skills.** Just as with good listening skills, good teamwork skills require the leader to sincerely value the contributions of others, a skill that can be learned like any other. No one achieves leadership success in a vacuum; you are dependent on others. Good leaders gather information and advice from other people and lead most often by example and persuasion rather than by decree. This is why it is possible to lead from the middle; leadership does not derive from an official designation but from an ability to focus the energies of a group toward a common purpose, something you can practice from any level of the organization, not just from the top.

Leaders should learn to value the insight and skills of others, even others who are new to the profession or who think differently from the leader or who lack the social skills to assimilate readily into the group. Encourage team members to express ideas and opinions, then monitor your own thoughts and behaviors to see whether you are being dismissive of contrary opinions or unorthodox suggestions. Even negative opinions and radical ideas may yield a kernel of truth to those who take the time to dig it out; even if they don't, your reaction to such ideas will signal to the team whether it is safe to advance suggestions in the future.

Watch yourself, too, to see whether you are giving greater weight to the opinions of certain people on your team—probably the people who share your viewpoint or your sense of humor or other personality traits. Such people are easy to listen to. Make an intentional effort to engage people whose company, perhaps, you find difficult to enjoy, particularly people who may be socially awkward but who may have insight that benefits the team. Through intentional effort, you can learn to value and recognize the contributions of others.

Some leadership skills are easily acquired through formal education.[3] In particular, gaps in your professional skills can be filled through online courses, books, journals, and workshops. Other gaps may require more personal interaction. For emerging leaders, a mentorship—usually with an older person who represents the kind of professional you hope to become—is a proven method of developing interpersonal and professional skills. Such a relationship, though, requires trust and a certain vulnerability on the part of both individuals, so invest the time required to find the right mentor.

If you are an established leader, you may acquire a surprising number of skills by offering to mentor or teach others. I once taught an archival appraisal course as an adjunct professor and discovered, as I prepared my lesson plans, that I had fallen behind in my professional reading as it related to this topic. The course offered me an opportunity to catch up on thinking that had evolved considerably while I was busy practicing my profession, and the interaction with the graduate students helped me sharpen my thoughts over the course of many weeks. Later, I discussed this with a colleague, a recognized leader in our profession, who admitted to a similar experience. We had both discovered that teaching others is an excellent way to keep our own skills current.

Building resilience

As you develop your skills as a leader, you should try to build your own resilience—the ability to rebound in the face of setbacks. The business and political worlds are full of examples of leaders who isolated themselves from contrary opinions and bad news, with predictably disastrous consequences. Archival leaders are hardly immune from the same danger. Leaders can easily come to believe that they alone are responsible for their success (forgetting the workers, peers, and role models who were integral to their achievement), or they may unconsciously come to see themselves as the smartest person in the room, developing an ego that resists the ideas and opinions of others. Good leaders resist the drift toward isolation and the deceptive safety it offers. Leaders accept hard truths and build the resilience necessary to pursue their vision despite setbacks, and they expand their own vision by embracing the vision of others.

- *Keep your vision clear.* Resilience depends on a clear vision that remains foremost in the leader's mind, regardless of circumstances. Resilience depends on staying focused on relatively stable long-term goals, even as the leader's vision for the archival repository may flex and adapt in light of new information, new circumstances, or new advice from diverse sources. The leader who concentrates on the big goal is less likely to be overwhelmed by obstacles, opposition, and delays. Setbacks that do not entirely upend the long-term goal can be viewed as temporary distractions rather than catastrophes. More importantly, the leader who keeps an eye on larger goals is more likely to value the contributions of others. If leaders cast a clear vision and reiterate it until it becomes part of the repository culture, new ideas and diverse opinions are likely to be seen less as threats to the leadership and more as valuable contributions toward a common goal.

- *Ask hard questions.* Leaders who have the tenacity to carry on in the face of setbacks are not afraid to ask hard questions about themselves. If you bristle at the slightest criticism, you're probably not asking hard enough questions about your own leadership qualities. As mentioned above, good leaders are highly self-aware, and self-awareness always exposes flaws and gaps. Strong leaders do not shy away from such awareness; rather, they embrace it as an opportunity to improve their ability to lead.

Good leaders are not afraid to ask hard questions about the institution they lead even if the answers—in the short term, at least—are discouraging. What value does your archives add for the people it serves? Until recently, the archival profession has been reticent to discuss its work in terms of return on investment. "That's a business concept," archivists might say, "and we are here to serve a higher public good." But I have led archives that are supported by millions of dollars in public funds each year, and the taxpayers who support such institutions have every right to ask what return they are getting for their investment. In the same way, archives at universities or corporations, or at small historical societies supported by voluntary contributions, should be able to explain what value they return for the dollars invested. This is not to suggest that the return on that investment will always be in monetary profits (though, in a corporate archives, it might very well be). You may add value by educating students, or by attracting tourists to the region (with tourism's attendant financial benefits), or by protecting the legal rights of citizens, or in any of dozens of other ways. It is the responsibility of leaders, though, to face hard questions such as these and devise satisfactory answers that can be relayed through hard data and compelling stories.

In the same way, the archival profession has a long tradition of reporting its value in terms of use rather than impact. While use statistics—number of researchers served or records accessioned—may be helpful data for the archivist to know, they say nothing about the impact of the archives on the people who use the records. How were the records used in ways that were meaningful to the user or the community? Records in my archives were once used to ensure the public's access to a river that a small group of people wanted to reserve for their own private use. Records have been used to right historic injustices or to restore and beautify historic places, to solve boundary disputes and to hold public officials accountable. Admittedly, it is often difficult to trace the result of archival research, but leaders are not afraid to face the hard truth that impact is more compelling than use, and leaders try to incorporate such thinking into their repositories.

Hard questions sometimes yield uncomfortable answers: maybe people are not using our records in meaningful ways; maybe our impact is less than we would like it to be. In such cases, a good leader does not shy away from the truth but sets about making changes that will deliver more positive outcomes. At one archives, the leadership team concluded that researchers were not using records in meaningful ways because the archives was not consistently identifying and accessioning meaningful records. The process of transferring records from institutional agencies had quietly slipped into autopilot, and the quality of records had slowly declined. The team devised an intentional plan to systematically iden-tify and procure the records that were most critical to their users. A hard question that yielded a difficult answer led to positive action. When leaders face hard questions about themselves and their institutions, they build resilience, for themselves and for their team.

- ***Embrace new communities and diverse opinions.*** Leaders sometimes fail to ask and face hard questions because they surround themselves with people who think just as they do, so the hard questions never get asked. Sometimes the practice is defended as building a "compatible" team, but diverse people can work together very compatibly if they are well led. When *compatibility* becomes a code word for unwavering conformity, the archives and its leadership are ill served. Leaders who want to build resilience embrace new communi-ties and diverse opinions.

If you are an established leader, you may be comfortable with the team around you; you may find it difficult to invite people into your circle who do not think or talk the way you do, who look different or have physical or mental challenges, or who have belief sys-tems that make you uncomfortable. Work through your discomfort, first by remembering that variety among people is the result of factors that rarely have bearing on professional issues or performance. Turn your reticence into anticipation by recognizing that teams almost always draw exceptional energy and insight from diversity; look forward to the dynamism that will grow as your team diversifies.

Examine your circle of advisers to see whether you have unwittingly created a danger-ous circle of homogeneity. Diversity will not only spice up your life (and your meetings!) but will also encourage innovative thinking and broader relevance. I once held a job where I reported to the company's chief information officer, and all of my peers were informa-tion technology professionals. One day the entire team participated in a daylong exercise to measure and describe our thinking preferences. At one point, the instructor asked us to stand on the color that represented our dominant thinking preference. All of my col-leagues stood together on a single color, while I straddled the remaining three. My tests had shown nearly equal dominance in three areas but almost no inclination toward the fourth area, where all of my colleagues now stood. The instructor pointed at me and said to my colleagues: "He is the person none of you will want to listen to because he doesn't think anything like you do. But he's the one you need in the room when you make a major decision, because he will balance out the groupthink that you're going to fall into." While the instructor's assessment may have been overdramatic, my colleagues (to their credit) accepted her admonition and made a point of inviting me into their deliberations. Over time, I learned a great deal from these people whose way of thinking about problems was very different from my own, and many times they told me that I had seen problems or solutions that had not occurred to them. The experience suggested to me that even a little diversity will open new avenues of thought and increase the chances of success.

It is easy to surround myself with people who think like me, look like me, and have similar educational and socioeconomic backgrounds. As I grow older, I have found yet another pitfall: my most trusted colleagues tend to be close to my own age, a natural outcome of having entered and developed in the profession together. Here is yet another instance in which I must make a conscious effort to seek out the opinions of people whose perspectives are markedly different from my own.

Whether you are an established leader or a developing one, you should remain alert for opportunities to benefit from the ideas of people whose thinking is very different from your own. Such people are certain to annoy you at times, so you probably don't want them to constitute the majority of your advisors, but contrary voices can help you see pitfalls and new possibilities that your own patterns of thought leave unexposed.

If you are someone who wants to become a leader, you may have an additional challenge: the discomfort you may feel when your opinions diverge from those of your peers. After all, "those who get along go along" (so it is widely believed), and you may hesitate to create waves that might hinder your career. It is better, though, to resist the temptation to curry favor by becoming a yes-person, agreeing instantly to any idea suggested by higher-ups. I have worked for several elected officials who wanted instant agreement and conformity from members of their key leadership team; in some cases, disagreement with the official meant instant and intense conflict. But my experience has been that even these people were normally amenable to hearing contrary opinions if their authority was not challenged. One approach was to make it clear that their decision, as the elected official, would be final, but that hearing an honest opinion from someone with expertise in his field might inform that decision in positive ways. For developing leaders, being able to form a considered opinion and defend it is an excellent quality; doing so diplomatically is equally important.

Building influence

Leadership ultimately comes down to influence because the best leaders achieve results by influencing other people rather than commanding them. Here, again, is the reason it is possible to lead from the middle; you do not need to be the CEO to influence your peers, your subordinates, and even the agency executives. In fact, as Samantha Norling points out in chapter 10, it is not unusual for an archivist, particularly in a new program, to have far more knowledge of archival practices than his or her supervisor. In such cases, it becomes essential for the archivist to build influence by "managing up" and influencing the organization's leadership. Whether you are an established leader or a leader in formation, expanding your sphere of influence is critical.

- *Influence begins with integrity.* People are influenced by people they trust. If you show that you are a person of integrity—someone who can be trusted to keep their word, who delivers on promises—people will naturally give weight to your advice and opinions. People gravitate, too, toward those who lead by example, who are not afraid to work, and who value excellence in their own work as well as that of others. Your personal integrity is the foundation of building influence.
- *Hone your skills.* Integrity alone, of course, is not enough to produce influence. Archivists who stay current with professional thinking and who develop essential archival skills are more likely to influence their colleagues than those who stopped learning decades ago. After your archival skills are well in hand, add nonarchival skills to increase your contributions to the repository and its leadership. Many archivists have added web and social media skills to their résumés, but think beyond even these: take a course in marketing or public speaking; learn a language that helps you communicate with emerging populations

in your area, whose members might become patrons and whose records might add richness to your repository's collections; become more proficient in business-related skills or in project management, a skill that is sorely needed—but often lacking—in archives that face complex projects, from arrangement and description to data migration. Widening your professional competence is an excellent way to widen your sphere of influence as people come to depend on you for critical advice and assistance.

- *Put your skills to use.* How can you best use the professional competence you've honed on your way to becoming a leader? Put them to use for others in your organization. Your peers will value your new skills if you use them to advance a team effort. And executives in your organization will value them as well if they are used to solve problems. "The most effective way you can become a trusted advisor for an executive," says one professional publication, "is to take the information given to you [about a problem] and map out a solution."[4] Produce a plan to solve a problem, or determine how to sustain a solution that is already working but may be losing steam. Of course, you should be careful not to intrude on the work of others, but demonstrate that you have learned new skills for the good of the archives, not just for personal fulfillment (though there is nothing wrong with learning skills for that reason). Doing so demonstrates that you are a team player and someone who is invested in the future of the archives—the perfect candidate for progressively more responsible leadership roles.

    Even if your executives decline to put your skills to formal use, you might find ways to use them and build influence. As Mark Greene has written about his own experience, "I inaugurated many changes in the archival program in which my bosses were completely disinterested, but which made a significant difference to the visibility and usability (and use) of the archives." And, as he later notes in the same essay, "ideally, change should occur incrementally in every organization without the top leader being aware of it—if all change has to pass approval by the boss, there is little likelihood of it occurring at all."[5]

- *Be proactive.* Bruce Dearstyne, writing in *Archival Outlook*, points out that leaders should learn to anticipate "changes in stakeholder expectations, information technology shifts, and changing resource levels."[6] Leaders, in other words, should strive to be proactive rather than reactive. Such thinking does not require a crystal ball, but it requires research, thoughtful reading, and some analysis. Do you have a new boss or new appointments to your organization's board of directors? Even a few minutes of online research might reveal helpful information about what their expectations might be or what deeply interests them and occupies their time outside of work.

    Newspapers and magazines (online or in print) can give the archival leader clues about how the economy is trending or what issues are occupying the legislature or the university administrators, and that information can help the leader anticipate changing resource levels or stakeholder expectations. I visited a legislator one day after reading a morning news report that the state's budget gap had risen to $2 billion. I knew what was on his mind, and my discussion about the archives focused almost entirely on how we increase efficiency and save tax dollars. Leaders, or would-be leaders, should read widely. Too often our only response to a problem is to investigate how our archival colleagues have responded to similar problems. It is helpful to learn from the successes of other archives, but other industries may offer more innovative solutions to our problems. Archival leaders can gain much insight simply by reading about what Amazon or Apple are predicting about the future, or what leading museums are doing to excite patrons, or how education is being transformed by new technologies and methodologies. Good leaders don't wait to see what the world may throw their way; they proactively envision the future and their role in it.

- *Ask for a greater sphere of influence.* Building a greater sphere of influence may be as simple as asking for it. If you want to be a leader, find opportunities to lead; then ask for the opportunity. Volunteer to lead a team or to take on more responsibility. Find the thing that few others want to do—such as revising the strategic plan—and volunteer to lead (or participate in) the effort. Offer to guide an intern or oversee volunteers. If opportunities are difficult to find, look outside the archives—in your community, your worship community, your child's school, or any other place that might offer a chance to practice leadership.

The archival profession itself offers ample opportunity to develop leadership skills. National, regional, and statewide professional associations are always looking for volunteers to serve on and lead committees, task forces, or affinity groups. In a small archives, especially, as Lynette Stoudt describes in chapter 9, local and regional archival organizations can provide leadership development opportunities at little cost and in a setting that parent organizations are likely to support. At the same time, such settings offer a relatively safe place to learn to lead among colleagues who share the same profession and purpose. Mentoring is another avenue for budding leaders to learn new skills. Nothing challenges you to think through your philosophy and assumptions better than a less experienced professional asking questions. No matter how new you are, there is someone newer who could use your help. Give back to your profession.

Beyond the archival profession itself, you may be in a position to take advantage of leadership opportunities and training offered by your parent organization. In her efforts to develop leadership skills, Sarah Koonts found opportunities in her parent organization's marketing and public information office (see her description in chapter 7). Such training is widely available in larger organizations, though, in corporate settings particularly (as Jennifer Johnson notes in chapter 8), such opportunities may be reserved for or weighted toward managers willing to move beyond the archives into the wider corporate structure. As you expand your sphere of influence, you may find that you develop a core of influential supporters, perhaps people you met while serving on a dreadful committee, or someone you mentored who went on to achieve professional success. Such people can help you professionally throughout your career, and they can also become close friends and advisers.

Ironically, leadership is really about teamwork, and most often it bears little resemblance to the modern myth of the lonely-at-the-top exceptional individual. While it is true that leaders spend time thinking about themselves and how they can improve their skills and influence, the best leaders spend much time thinking about other people—the people they lead, the role models who can mold them, and even the challenging people who test them. They think too about another group of people: the people they will help nurture and build into the leaders of tomorrow.

Building Leadership Capacity in Others

No one becomes a leader in a vacuum. The people who mentored you, the peers who supported you, and the people who have followed you have all honored you by their contributions to your own development. One of the best things you can do to honor them in return is to nurture new leaders. Growing new leaders requires intentional effort to first identify people with leadership potential and then to support them with the careful exercise of your influence. Promising leaders need to be trained and given opportunities to stretch their skills, but then they need to be empowered to take risks and find their own approach to leading.

Be intentional

Your job description may not say that developing your employees is a core function of your job, but if you are a leader, then it is. Every employee should be given opportunities to learn and grow professionally, but developing the next generation of leaders requires additional effort.

- ***Identify potential leaders in your archives.*** Although you could mentor an emerging leader who does not work for your repository (and you should, through professional organizations and other avenues), your most successful efforts will probably occur closer to home. If your repository is large enough, look for potential leaders right under your nose. Begin by looking for your own successor, the person you think may be capable of performing your functions one day. Even if that person never succeeds you (and often they don't), you will have advanced the prospects of a talented archivist. If you are in a very large organization, urge—or even require—every manager in the organization to look for and develop at least one potential successor. Of course, you must be careful not to show favoritism toward the person you believe may have the potential to rise in the ranks, but this caution should never become an excuse to ignore professional potential in your staff, and if you give every employee opportunities for growth, favoritism should not become a problem.

  As you scan your professional circle for potential leaders, be alert to those who perform well as archivists, but do not assume that a talented professional will make a talented leader. As Robert Bahmer, SAA's president in 1962, noted in his presidential address, "it does not follow that achievement as a professional archivist in all cases fits one for administration or management . . . [I]t is possible that over the years we have blighted the professional careers of a good many archivists by rewarding them with promotion to positions of administrative responsibility."[7] Be alert to professionals who exhibit personal qualities that make a good leader, such as persistence, innovation, and open-mindedness.

  Clearly you will need to identify people who are themselves willing or eager to develop their leadership capacity. It is not unusual for someone to resist your first suggestion that they may have leadership potential—it is difficult for many people to picture themselves as leaders—so some gentle urging may be appropriate initially. Recognize, though, that many people have no taste for greater responsibility, so avoid wasting your time and annoying others by applying undue pressure.

  As you look for potential leaders, be alert for employees whose potential may have been thwarted by attitudes toward members of underrepresented groups. As the National

Archives and Records Administration (NARA) recognized during their efforts to increase diversity, "individual development—or lack of incentive for same—plays a significant role in enabling or disabling diversity across pay grades."[8] Many employees from underrepresented groups may find it difficult to advance beyond entry-level positions, and NARA found that "a lack of 'stretch' positions open to employees in lower-graded positions prevented diversity from increasing within the organization."[9] Leaders can proactively create those stretch opportunities.

- *Identify opportunities for emerging leaders.* Potential leaders need opportunities to assume new responsibilities. Quite often these opportunities come in the form of emerging technologies or theories that need to be explored and analyzed for possible adoption by the archives. Many archivists gained their first leadership experience while exploring and implementing EAD or DACS, or by leading an effort to engage the public through social media, or by testing MPLP.[10] Implementing new technologies and new approaches to archival processes provides opportunities for emerging leaders to make meaningful contributions to the archives while stretching their skills. Monitor such developments in the profession, and watch for opportunities to exercise potential leaders on your staff.

  As a young professional, I worked for a man who was enamored of new technologies, and in the days when videotape was just emerging as a tool for nonprofessionals, he turned to me one day during a staff meeting and asked (with huge excitement), "Have you ever made a video?" I replied, "Um . . . no." (I didn't even know anyone who owned a video camera in those days.) My boss was undeterred. "Do you want to make one?" So I set off to write, film, and narrate a video, *The Information Highway*, explaining why the Internet was going to change the way we created and managed records and information. That summer my staff and I hauled a tent and lots of equipment to a half dozen local fairs and ran the film on a continuous loop. Quite a few people actually stood and watched it, though I doubt any of them experienced an epiphany as a result. Still, the experience was an important one to me, both personally and professionally. A leader I respected had entrusted a project to me that—in his eyes at least—was very important. At the same time, it taught me to be alert to new technologies that might be harnessed to grab the public's attention and tell an important archival story. It was an excellent opportunity for a young, eager professional.

- *Be intentional about outcomes.* As you identify opportunities for emerging leaders, be intentional about the outcomes these opportunities should produce. Is the purpose for them to learn how to organize a team, or to accomplish something outside their comfort zone, or to inspire some less enthusiastic colleagues to greater effort? Help them to take ownership of the opportunity, and don't just send them out to succeed or fail; train them first and then touch base with them often along the way. Hold them accountable for the outcomes because they are ultimately responsible for their own growth, even if you provide assistance.

Use your influence

If you are a leader (or *the* leader) in your archives, you have tremendous influence over others, whether you are aware of it or not. Good leaders use their influence intentionally to build new leaders. Your personal influence can be used both internally, within your organization, and externally.

- *Model good leadership.* Be aware that you are modeling leadership, for good or ill, at all times. New professionals are likely to form their concept of leadership from the leaders in their own archives. Use every opportunity to model good leadership. Be clear about your vision and expectations; show resilience in the face of difficulty; and be fair, not shying away from hard decisions or difficult issues and conflict. While no leader does all of these perfectly, the leaders we most respect are the ones who consistently strive to live up to such values. Most people who are leaders in our profession today probably encountered at least one such individual early in their career and adopted that person (consciously or not) as a role model. In my own case, it was a supervisor early in my career who encouraged me to think big and be willing to take risks if the potential benefit was significant. He was an enthusiastic leader who never lost faith in his staff, even when their attempts sometimes ended in failure. If you want to build leaders, become a role model they can emulate.

- *Create a culture of ownership.* Use your influence to create a culture of ownership within your repository. Every organization has at least one culture, an underlying set of expectations about how people will behave and interact in the organization.[11] In fact, different units of the same organization may have very different cultures. An organization's culture is not written down or taught in a formal way; it develops organically, most often as a reflection of the leadership. The best leaders think about their archive's culture and shape it intentionally through their expectations and their own example.

  All leaders expect certain performance and contributions from their followers, but the organization's culture grows most significantly from the leader's own behavior, from the example the leader sets. As the authors of one report stated from their own experience, "the behavior of the senior leadership team sets the upper limit for what others will contribute."[12] Leaders who want to nurture new leaders create a culture in which the employees "own" the organization: they embrace its vision and purpose, they contribute to its well-being through diligent work and innovative ideas, and they take responsibility for solving its challenges. Such an environment provides ample opportunity for emerging leaders to learn new skills and test the limits of their own skills and talents.

  If you are a leader, you should "take the temperature" of your organization frequently. What kind of culture does your archives exhibit? Do people feel free to suggest new ideas and challenge orthodox ways of thinking and working? Do staff show respect for each other, even when they disagree about methods or outcomes? Are they open to different points of view and willing to listen to diverse ideas and proposals? If, instead, they seem constrained by the ways things have always been done or seem fearful of change or afraid even of suggesting change, they have very likely learned this behavior by observing how the senior leaders work. Look at the leadership team—look at yourself—and ask what message is being sent to, and adopted by, the staff of the repository. Talented leadership is most likely to emerge from a culture where people own their work and are unafraid to contribute their best to its accomplishment.

- ***Be an advocate for rising leaders.*** Within your own institution and within the larger profession, you can use your influence to advocate for the next generation of leaders. If your archives is part of a larger institution, such as a university, use your influence to have potential leaders appointed to committees or become part of a larger project team. In your professional circle, encourage potential leaders to build a network of archival colleagues by introducing them to friends, and help them find a role within archival organizations at the state, regional, or national level. Emerging leaders can practice their skills and contribute to the profession by serving on task forces or standing committees and by presenting at conferences.

     I attended my first regional archives conference after I had been an archivist for only six months. My manager encouraged me to go and then introduced me to many people, including people who had written books and articles I had studied in graduate school (a heady experience for a fledgling archivist). Within a few more months, I was serving on a committee for that regional association, the first step toward active involvement regionally and then nationally. None of that would have happened had my manager not taken the initiative. First she urged me to attend the conference, and then, very importantly, she guided me through it, helping me make connections and begin to build professional relationships. Longtime leaders easily forget how bewildering life can be for newer professionals. As you identify potential leaders, consider how you might open doors for them and help them succeed. Become an intentional advocate for the next generation of leaders.

Train others

New leaders develop when someone intentionally trains them to lead. Even a person with innate skills needs to have those skills cultivated and honed. If you are a leader, look for ways to train future leaders in specific ways. And if you want to become a leader, ask for the guidance and opportunities necessary to develop your potential.

- ***Lay a foundation of self-awareness.*** All leadership begins with self-managing our own behaviors. Some people are able to view their own behavior with detachment, but most of us need help from a trusted observer. One way to help others develop their leadership capabilities is to help them become more self-aware. In planned meetings and impromptu conversations, provide honest feedback based on your own observations.

     People who are becoming more self-aware often fixate on weaknesses rather than strengths. Help such people consider how their weaknesses can be developed into strengths. A person may avoid conflict, for example, because they are highly empathetic toward others. Conflict avoidance can be a weakness in leaders, but empathy can be a tremendous strength. How can the developing leader harness the power of empathy to effectively resolve conflicts? By working through such seeming contradictions, people can develop greater self-awareness while also gaining confidence in their own unique approach to leadership.

- ***Build leadership competence.*** Many potential leaders possess significant professional skills—and such skills should be enhanced and expanded continuously—but leadership demands an array of interpersonal skills that are seldom learned in formal settings. Each of us brings to our profession a personal background shaped by nationality, ethnicity, gender, language, and countless other factors. Effective leaders appreciate and harness the power of such diversity. Present your emerging leader with opportunities to work with people who think and act very differently from them. Be clear about the goal: to develop the interpersonal skills necessary to good leadership. Then make it a point to discuss the experience with them and evaluate their progress as honestly as possible. Discussions such as these can benefit developing leaders greatly. Challenge them to think like a leader: What vision might they imagine for the archives? How should repository leaders be communicating with the staff? What is working, and what might be improved? How would they improve it? Frequent discussions about such questions will help emerging leaders develop a sense of their potential and build confidence in their ability to lead.

- *Hold people accountable.* Finally, part of training potential leaders who are developing new skills is to hold them accountable for their own progress. Help them lay out a development path and define their goals; then (if appropriate) use formal performance reviews to evaluate progress toward these goals. Use informal discussions to encourage or redirect, as needed. People who are mentored by a more seasoned professional enter that relationship voluntarily and often take pride in it. Holding to a high standard of accountability will demonstrate commitment on your part and theirs.

Empower others

Training potential leaders is important, but ultimately they must be empowered. Moving beyond the theory of training to the practice of actually leading requires both the emerging leader and the mentor to stretch.

- *Stretch assignments.* Such opportunities, particularly in the early stages of the leader's development, should stretch the person's abilities while posing only limited risk. A new leader might spearhead an internal project before taking responsibility for a project with more public exposure. Or the person might be assigned to lead a project that includes aspects outside his or her comfort zone. A reference archivist, for example, asked to lead a team that is exploring new online services, might find the digital aspects daunting. The stretch assignment provides an opportunity for the new leader to draw on the skills of colleagues and motivate team members to contribute equally.

  Stretch assignments should be intentional and transparent. Explain why you are providing this particular assignment and what you expect people to learn from it. Then encourage them without stifling their own creative approach to the assignment. Along the way, help them see what has worked and what might be improved in future. Then help them incorporate the lessons learned into their daily work to reinforce the learning experience.

- *Letting go.* Mentoring potential leaders poses a risk for those who do the mentoring. Every stretch assignment introduces the risk of failure. The emerging leader may propose ideas and methods that make the mentor uncomfortable (an opportunity for the mentor to grow, perhaps). But the mentor's biggest challenge comes in letting the new leader go. Figuratively, new leaders must be released to follow their own vision of leadership.

Ironically, the most successful mentoring may produce leaders who are most different from their mentors. (Notably, Theodore Roosevelt carefully groomed William Taft to succeed him as president, only to regret the choice when Taft proved to be a very different type of leader from his mentor.) Those who help leaders develop should remember that the goal is not to produce a clone of the mentor but to produce a person with the vision and capacity to lead in a unique way. You may need to let new leaders go in a literal way as well. Opportunities for them to lead may come from outside your archives, from another archives or from other agencies within the parent organization. In such cases, the mentor should let go and try to take satisfaction in a job well done. Your effort to develop a new leader was successful enough to draw the attention and admiration of others.

Conclusion

Leadership development begins when existing and emerging leaders intentionally build their own capacity for leadership. Self-awareness exposes gaps that are resolved by building new skills and behaviors. As they expand their self-awareness and skills, leaders build resilience and a greater sphere of influence. At the same time, such leaders intentionally use their influence and knowledge to identify and train new leaders whom they then empower to embrace their own unique leadership roles. Ultimately, our goal must be to develop leaders who, in turn, develop others. Like the life cycle of a healthy organism, the process will strengthen individual archives and the archival profession in a never-ending cycle of growth and renewal.

In Part II of this book, five archivists—Sarah Koonts, Jennifer Johnson, Lynette Stoudt, Samantha Norling, and Megan Sniffin-Marinoff—discuss their own efforts to build leadership capacity. Each represents a different type of archival repository, but their experiences demonstrate that leadership is shaped as much by personal uniqueness as by repository distinctiveness. They demonstrate, as well, that leadership can blossom in many settings and circumstances—anywhere there is a person with the ambition and patience to grow. In the final chapter, Rachel Vagts assesses the contributions of the Archival Leadership Institute to the profession's efforts to encourage leadership growth and development.

NOTES

1. TEDtalksDirector, "Dave Meslin: The Antidote to Apathy," YouTube, April 14, 2011, https://www.youtube.com/watch?v=5Knz100ldLM%5D, captured at https://perma.cc/8SBF-VEWK.

2. The *Harvard Business Review*, for example, provides an online test called "The eight-minute test that can reveal your effectiveness as a leader" (https://hbr.org/2013/08/how-effective-a-leader-are-you, captured at https://perma.cc/2TBQ-8MWR). The Kellogg School of Management provides eight self-assessment tests, including "Gaining power and influence" and "How creative are you?" (https://www.kellogg.northwestern.edu/faculty/uzzi/htm/teaching-leadership.htm, captured at https://perma.cc/HBS3-6A7A). Some organizations, such as the National Center for Cultural Competence, provide highly specific online assessment tools (https://nccc.georgetown.edu/assessments/, captured at https://perma.cc/8RUJ-J3L5).

3. The Society of American Archivists (www.archivists.org) provides many educational opportunities for professional archivists at every experience level, as does the University of Virginia Rare Book School (http://rarebookschool.org), to name just two. For more general education in leadership, the Executive Leadership Program at the Harvard Business School (https://www.exed.hbs.edu) is among the most highly respected.

4. Keith Cooke, "Engaging with Executives Is Critical to Your Success," *ESRI News for State & Local Government*, Spring 2016, 3.

5. Mark A. Greene, "Trying to Lead from Good to Great and Some Reflections on Leadership at All Levels," in *Leading and Managing Archives and Records Programs: Strategies for Success*, ed. Bruce W. Dearstyne (New York: Neal-Schuman, 2008), 155.

6. Bruce W. Dearstyne, "Strategies for Leading Archival Programs," *Archival Outlook* (March/April 2015): 11.

7. Robert Bahmer, "Management of Archival Institutions," *American Archivist* 26, no. 1 (1963): 8.

8. Sharon Thibodeau, "Building Diversity inside Archival Institutions," in *Through the Archival Looking Glass: A Reader on Diversity and Inclusion*, ed. Mary A. Caldera and Kathryn M. Neal (Chicago: Society of American Archivists, 2014), 203.

9. Thibodeau.

10. EAD (Encoded Archival Description), DACS (Describing Archives: A Content Standard), and MPLP (More Product, Less Process).

11. "Truth and Courage: Implementing a Coaching Culture," Douglas Riddle, Center for Creative Leadership, https://www.ccl.org/wp-content/uploads/2016/08/coaching.e-1.pdf, captured at https://perma.cc/WZ2H-ALTK.

12. "Truth and Courage," 8.

Part II

7

Embracing the Ambassadorship: Leadership at the State Archives of North Carolina

Sarah Koonts

Introduction

Since its founding as the North Carolina Historical Commission in 1903, the State Archives of North Carolina has collected, preserved, and made available to the public records of state and local government, as well as private manuscript materials.[1] The State Archives operates with sixty-nine staff members managing the acquisition, reference, arrangement and description, digitization, records management, public programming, and education functions you would expect to find in a large state archival agency. Leadership of an organization with an archives and a rigorous records management program requires creativity and the ability to recognize opportunities to advocate, connect, and build both relationships and programmatic capacity. Because state archival programs exist as a function of the state government enterprise serving broad constituencies from multiple user groups to custodians of public records, leadership in this environment requires organizational awareness about the operations of state and local government.[2] That allows the state archivist to best connect the work of the archives to the public records custodians they serve. The state archivist is called upon to market the program to resource allocators and stakeholders, evaluate the efficacy of services, inspire staff to develop innovative programs, and respond to public relations crises all within the framework of the public sector.

The state archivist is in many ways the ambassador for the program, reflecting to the public, media, resource allocators, policy makers, and other stakeholders the importance of the institution, its vision, and its mission. Leadership in a modern state archival institution means seeking allies across the spectrum of government. State archives need to be active in building partnerships to strengthen program fundamentals, in developing new outreach opportunities, and in remaining committed to providing relevant services to all customers. Leading an archival and records management agency at the state level requires skills and competencies to supplement the fundamental archival principles gained in graduate programs and internships.[3] Reflecting on my experiences in state archival leadership, first as a program leader and now as the agency administrator, I recognize the importance of formal and informal opportunities I've seized to expand my skills in critical areas such as advocacy, public relations, management in a state government environment, and the evaluation of our operations within the state's legal framework. These skills and experiences are critical when working to meet deadlines, evaluating agency operations, developing workable solutions to problems, and planning program development under the umbrella of my parent institution.

Beyond the Archival Fundamentals

Leading any major division or program within state government requires acquisition of management skills in several areas for a public management setting. Beyond the standard management training for supervisors in a state agency, seeking out other leadership training or mentorship opportunities grew my public management skills.[4] Our state human resources office offers a variety of midlevel management training programs. Aimed specifically at state government managers, the Certified Public Manager Program (CPM) spans eighteen months to two years of intensive leadership and management training in a government setting, as well as the development of a capstone project designed to produce strategic improvements in the participant's agency operations. My project developed a structured decision-making body for preservation programming at the State Archives. After obtaining CPM certification, I participated in a pilot program called the Leadership Institute for Female Employees offered jointly by state human resources and Bennett College. The program targeted midlevel female managers from across government; program alumni now can be found in senior leadership positions throughout state government, including as the deputy chief information officer for North Carolina.

More than a decade ago, when I managed the preservation and imaging programs within the State Archives, the new state archivist approached me about taking on the role of the budget manager for the state archives. She provided the mentorship and training for me to acquire a fuller understanding of budgeting fundamentals within our parent agency and state government as a whole. Beyond learning how to read and interpret monthly budget printouts, this training offered me the opportunity to understand the larger budgeting process long before I became state archivist. To strategically manage a budget, I had to first understand how budgets are developed in a government context.[5] Unless there is a groundswell of legislative support for program expansion, our resources may remain fairly fixed in the near future. The challenge becomes how to improve the fundamentals of the archival and records management program within a context of a static budget. It may mean shifting resources from one area of the program to another in order to build up aspects of the program that are of the most strategic value. Working with former state archivists as they determined budget cutting and expansion scenarios provided me with a more comprehensive understanding of the budgeting lifecycle. Another state archivist provided mentorship in the areas of legislative operations and the management of boards and commissions. He took me to legislative hearings on both budgetary and programmatic topics. He guided me as I increased my involvement with a variety of boards and associations. As with the formal public management training opportunities, informal mentorships in key aspects of public management serve me today as I seek to fit the budget of the State Archives into the strategic budgetary goals of our agency and state. Informal mentorships also taught me about advocacy to resource allocators and board management skills. My challenge now is to provide adequate mentorship opportunities to ensure that the next generation of leadership acquires these same budgeting fundamentals.

Another place where the resources of our parent agency, the North Carolina Department of Natural and Cultural Resources, have taught me important skills critical to the management of the State Archives can be found in our robust marketing and public information office. This office provides training and skill development in a variety of marketing arenas, including a training session on crisis communication. On the surface, this type of workshop may seem more applicable to our agency divisions with enormous public visitation programs, including state parks and historic sites. Upon completion of the training, I realized that crisis communication skills can be applied to the everyday development of streamlined messaging, including for marketing materials and interactions with policy makers. These skills also help you avoid message creep by demonstrating the importance of concise, consistent, and strong messages. In a state government environment, leadership changes regularly through elections and appointments. In chapter 2, "Communication," David Carmicheal encourages readers to see advocacy as a mind-set to be maintained at all times. This daily advocacy plays out in state government as the faces of agency heads and legislative champions change. Communication platforms and outlets should be seen as engines made to work for your program in conjunction with a unified marketing and advocacy strategy. Plus, when facing a public relations challenge or crisis, as I would shortly after the training, I felt better equipped to handle prolonged questions from the media and the public.[6]

Connect with Larger Projects

The projects that connected our programs to larger communities, both statewide and nationally, stand out as experiences that most afforded me opportunities to develop and enhance leadership skills. Just as you will see in chapter 8, "Cultivating Success: The Business of Archives," seeking connections with stakeholders is a critical activity for a state archivist. Robust and proactive state archival programs recognize the need to actively seek connections with their stakeholders and peers. In 2000 I applied for the State Archives to be a part of a national group beta testing a new datalogger and software. In the short term, this opportunity provided us with some free equipment and software and helped develop our environmental monitoring program. As the project progressed, the developers asked that testers include our facilities staff in training on these new tools. On the surface, this small grant may not appear to offer any leadership opportunities, but it did. It helped me acquire knowledge about facilities and HVAC systems beyond the preservation fundamentals taught in graduate school. In developing a relationship with a stakeholder like the facilities management division, I also recognized the importance of approaching a new partner with a request for input or action, as well as an offer of assistance from our program. This lesson continues to present itself in a multitude of settings.[7] A motivated leader can make a great impact on building strategic partnerships with an agency or stakeholder group. It isn't enough to build relationships on simply sharing some information about the State Archives. If we want real progress and a collaborative approach, I always bring an ask and an offer to the table. It provides a reason to continue discussions and planning beyond the informational stage and lays the foundation for a relationship based on mutual efforts. Leadership in relationship building involves recognizing the value and importance in changing the status quo to the mutual benefit of our agency and the partner organization.

Another time when a larger initiative provided the vehicle with which I was able to enhance our records management program, develop new partnerships with stakeholders, and hone leadership skills came when the Council of State Archivists (CoSA) developed the Intergovernmental Preparedness for Essential Records (IPER) program.[8] For years our agency had been trying, with mixed success, to be more integrated into emergency response activities involving public records. Success came mainly through established relationships with groups such as the North Carolina Association of Registers of Deeds, and less so with emergency management entities on the state and local levels. Emergency management was sporadically interested in what we had to offer by way of public records protection and recovery. During Hurricane Isabel recovery in 2003, State Archives personnel were on-site at a damaged courthouse only because the register of deeds had a long-standing relationship with our agency, and she called my cell phone asking for assistance. (Her requests to local emergency management for help with damaged public records never made it to us through official channels.) At its core, the IPER program aimed to address a challenge such as this by integrating a state's information technology, emergency management, and archives in the delivery of training on the identification and protection of essential records. I recognized that the IPER curriculum provided a vehicle to improve the programming in all three agencies in our state. Having FEMA money and weight behind the program offered a gravitas that resonated with the state emergency management structure. Provided with the message, I took the opportunity to learn all I could about the emergency response and business continuity planning requirements, statutes, and structures in North Carolina. I demonstrated the benefits to be gained from the program and asked for assistance in the customization, marketing, and delivery of the training.[9] In return I offered my leadership in the management of the program and in staffing the training. By the end of the IPER grant, we had delivered eight webinar series online and four in-person sessions, reaching 492 government officials across state and local governments. We have improved relationships with state emergency management and information technology business continuity planners, and our department's disaster response role is defined in the state's emergency response plan. Connecting to a nationally funded project allowed us to leverage the benefits of the program into long-lasting gains for the State Archives.

Sometimes the opportunity to connect to larger projects can be found within the state. The resources of the State Archives have always been used for larger programming initiatives produced by our parent department.[10] Looking beyond the collections of the State Archives as a research resource for other divisions' work, my leadership team took a bold step in 2012 and decided to expand our notion of outreach education and to inform the public about the mission, work, and resources of the State Archives. We wanted to tell our story in a new venue and to new audiences using our collections as the centerpiece. To do so would mean finding a larger space and new platforms to use in this outreach effort. We asked the North Carolina Museum of History to partner with us to create an exhibit specifically about the importance of the State Archives.[11] The museum provided the gallery, a curator and exhibit designer to guide the process, and assistance in marketing and publicity. My staff developed the exhibit story lines, selected supporting collection materials, and wrote the exhibit text. A marketing team planned the budget and called upon our support group to raise funds for the expenses. Working with our departmental marketing department, we produced a companion catalog to supplement the exhibit and provide a lasting, stand-alone resource once the exhibit closed. Two years in the planning, the entire project produced great benefits in public exposure to our work and collections. Additionally, the staff broadened their skills in a number of key areas, including message development, exhibit planning, outreach, and marketing. Defining a coherent theme and story lines for the exhibit and producing a catalog enhanced our ability to tell a concise story about the value of the State Archives to the citizens of our state. We started the process as an institution focused more on basic outreach and programming to groups who approached us with interest or who were established users of our resources. We opened the exhibit with an expanded notion of outreach beyond the walls of our building. We found the excitement for and benefit of actively taking our stories and work to new audiences. The effort stretched our skills, honed our communications, and provided a new way to connect with broader audiences. Our next project is to create a traveling version of the exhibit to be displayed at regional history museums across the state.[12]

While major exhibits take years to plan and execute successfully, we are developing low-cost methods of bringing special exhibits to the people of North Carolina through one-day events hosted by a local historic site, museum, or community college. We travel with a couple of archivists and two or three small cases that fit in our van; these pop-up exhibits bring a small slice of our work into communities that may not know much about the State Archives and what it does. Selection of partners for these one-day events is a key aspect in their success. For example, partnering with Alamance Community College in Burlington, the State Archives brought some documents for a Constitution Day event hosted by the college. We provided the exhibit panels, teacher resource packets, and archivists to talk to the visitors. We gave the college images and feedback on marketing materials. The college provided space and local outreach to the K–12 community, as well as numerous volunteers to assist with the events. The college also designed a poster contest around the exhibit themes and offered prizes to the middle school and high school participants. By the end of the day, the archivists on duty had interacted with 1,900 visitors to this special event. Work with these short-term exhibits demonstrates the value of the State Archivist's interacting with constituents. I take the opportunity, while the kids, teachers, and public are waiting in line, to share information about what they are about to see, what a state archives does, what we collect, and how we impact their lives. A special exhibit may have 1,000 or 100 visitors in a day, but I have learned that it is time well spent to provide visitors with context for the documents and a personal connection to the work of the State Archives. Just as in our work with initiatives such as IPER, this partnership is also built on an ask and an offer. I ask for assistance from the host location and offer to bring them programing and resources to support their event. Our collections are held in trust for all people, and it is a great honor and opportunity to bring these treasures directly to communities when we can.

Accept the Ambassadorship

Exhibits are just one aspect of our increased publicity, promotion, and advocacy work on a formal and informal level. Beyond leading the professional work of the agency, I believe it is an appropriate role of an archivist leading a program to serve as a sort of ambassador for the archives. Accept the appointment and embrace the role.[13] Like many archivists, I had been called upon over the years to provide background for a local print media story, to appear on a cable access program, or to be interviewed for a clip on the evening news. Shortly after my appointment as the state archivist, I was asked to appear in the national television program *Mysteries at the Museum* in an episode focusing on the story of the theft and recovery of North Carolina's original copy of the Bill of Rights. It proved to be an opportunity to grow my skills in and comfort with longer recorded pieces. If a strategic goal of our program is to increase our visibility and promote our work to new audiences, I must be ready to talk to print, online, or television media. This is another area where developing skills and honing messaging can be applied. Understanding the needs of the particular media outlet allows me to tailor responses appropriately. While media interviews are often done in noncrisis situations, the lessons of a crisis management communication workshop may still be used when providing focused, streamlined answers for recorded and print interviews. As the ambassador for a program, I must reflect enthusiasm for my institution's work in all my efforts.

Years ago the only tours of the State Archives were done very infrequently, and usually with a visiting group of professionals. That has changed in my tenure as state archivist. We continue to enlarge our offerings of tours to a variety of groups. In the last year, we provided tours to school groups, legislators, upper-level administrators from state agencies, chambers of commerce, political and genealogy groups, and the weekly rotation of legislative pages. As the public face of our program, I try very hard to lead nearly every tour, particularly if it involves a visit to our vault to see rare state treasures. Beyond waiting for groups to seek us out, I work to ensure that our agency administrators can use these tours in their advocacy work with resource allocators. Tours are not ad hoc, free-flowing conversations. Instead, I have particular messages about our work and programming that I choose from when customizing the tour to the audience. The tours provide a method for visitors to feel connected to our work and collections.

Another important way I've learned to fulfill my duties as the ambassador for the State Archives is to take committee appointments seriously. For example, after a successful National Digital Information Infrastructure Preservation Program grant working on the archiving of geospatial data, our agency was offered a nonvoting seat on the statewide Geographical Information Coordinating Committee (GICC). Comprising representatives from state, federal, and local agencies, as well as industry representatives, the committee provides oversight and direction for geospatial data standards in the state. Our agency's real connection to the active work of the GICC is in the Statewide Mapping Advisory Committee, where metadata standards and archiving protocols are managed. It would be tempting to skip the GICC meetings, particularly when they discuss extremely technical aspects of geospatial data standards that are beyond my skill set with electronic records. It would be easy for the archives to become an afterthought for these agencies, thinking of us only when they occasionally want to transfer data. I make it a point to attend every meeting. Meeting agendas often include presentations on new uses or applications for geospatial data. Data sharing and standards development are discussed. This committee represents a major success story in collaborative data governance and preservation on a statewide level. If I want the State Archives to be an active part of data management discussions for public records in the state, I have to be visible and participate in the committees, forums, and conversations such as those conducted in the GICC. This is part of the subtle and direct advocacy work discussed in chapter 2. I have recognized the opportunity to remain in contact with appropriate agencies and demonstrate the relevance of the State Archives in the management of state data, regardless of format.

Leadership as the face of the archives and records program means that I place an emphasis on the development of strong messaging for outreach opportunities. I am the public face of our program for traveling exhibits, tours, and other outreach opportunities. I purposely grew my skills and comfort level with media interviews on any topic relating to our program. I believe it is my role to represent the archives in positive outreach pieces as well as probing and potentially negative ones. The leader of an archives and records management program should be comfortable in the role of chief advocate and spokesperson to audiences that range from records custodians to the general public to professional colleagues across the state and the country.

Crisis Communications

Just as planned outreach opportunities are critical to the development of program capacity, so, too, can crisis communications impact a program. Records management can be a tricky business to explain succinctly to outside stakeholders. Different groups may find long-term value in just about any record created by a government agency. Why shouldn't it all be saved? Why would we sanction the disposal of any government records? Isn't it our job to save old stuff? The process of records management and tools used in a program can seem complex too. Records retention and disposition schedules seem straightforward, but they have to be understood in conjunction with the methods our agency employs to provide records management services to all 77 agencies and commissions, 100 counties, and 552 municipalities in North Carolina. More often than not, questions involving our operations often lead to questions about records management programming and how the authority to dispose of records flows from our agency to the records creators. How a leader responds to these questions can escalate or diffuse a brewing public relations crisis.

Deep within one county courthouse in North Carolina sat a basement storage room. For decades it had been used to store old records from a variety of offices. In recent years, surplus furniture crowded the entrance, and the records sat undisturbed and slowly rotting from the humidity problems in the room caused by a regular water leak. Interest in the records was awakened when one elected county official and a local heritage society began looking into what had been stored in the basement. In May 2013 a concerned local citizen phoned our main number requesting help recovering the mold-covered court records. Our records analysts initiated contact with the clerk of superior court and arranged a visit to see the room and records in question. Some records in the room were literally disintegrating in the high humidity and moldy environment. Others were quite dirty from years of basement storage. Analysts discovered that despite the condition of the records, some had been recently removed from the room by the local heritage society and relocated to another space. Fearing that the records were close to being out of official custody, if they were not already, the analysts took possession of some civil and criminal files that had been removed from the basement. Following normal procedures, our analysts requested that the county conduct a preliminary inventory of the records in the basement storage area.[14] Additionally, our Administrative Office of the Courts (AOC) plays a role in the management of local court records. The AOC sent its safety and health expert to examine the courthouse environment. Conditions in the courthouse revealed potentially serious mold problems in some rooms, including the basement storage area containing these disintegrating records.

Inventories produced by the county officials revealed records that were scheduled for destruction since the 1963 inventory created by the State Archives.[15] The AOC safety and health assessment of the storage room and courthouse recommended no movement of the records or amateur cleaning of them for fear of contamination of other records and the safety of staff involved. In a joint letter, our office and the AOC outlined our findings for the records custodians. The letter recommended that the remaining records be destroyed. The State Archives had taken into custody the only potentially archival records that could be located in the room. Even those materials required segregation, intensive cleaning, and imaging prior to destruction. Our records analysts reminded county officials that citizens should not be allowed access to confidential records and that all the records on the inventory they provided were eligible for destruction. By late fall 2013, the State Archives was confident that we had provided all that was needed to county officials regarding records retention and disposition procedures. We also felt that we had communicated the process adequately to the local heritage society and area citizens. I soon discovered that we were wrong in that assumption, particularly when the eventual destruction of the records by county officials became a public relations disaster for them and for us.

While the local heritage association still hoped that the county would allow them to retain the records stored in the basement, late one Friday afternoon, county management moved, with no public notice, to have the records removed and sent to an incinerator. Suddenly the situation seemed to local citizens like a scene from *Fahrenheit 451* as records were carted off for burning. Our agency assumed that the county officials would deal with what we saw as a local question. Even when social media and local newspaper stories began to discuss the burning, I assumed that once people understood the nature of the records in the room and their condition, everyone would agree that it was the proper course of action to destroy moldy records of no long-term value. Following a social media and blog post by a member of the heritage society, the story rapidly began taking on an exaggerated aspect and spread nationally. I checked my email one day to find hundreds of angry, uncivil, and at times threatening messages about this destruction, based purely on one social media post that masqueraded as the complete story. Additionally, I found that no other offices involved in the inventory or destruction of the records were making public comments or responding to media inquiries. Suddenly the State Archives was out on a proverbial limb, the sole focus of ire from concerned citizens and professionals from around the country who were unaware of the complex nature of the problem. After more than a century of building a solid records management program, I believed our agency had an obligation to disclose the process behind our decisions and recommendations. I believe in transparency, especially when it comes to our own agency. County officials and the AOC declined to make public comments on the situation. As painful as it is to be the only involved party talking about a crisis, I owed our stakeholders every opportunity to understand the fuller picture of the circumstances and the actions taken in response to them.

In his chapter on leadership in transformational change and crisis, Peter Gottlieb notes that crisis can lead to deep change. I saw this come to pass here as some important leadership lessons came out of this crisis. The situation was my first experience with how information on a social media platform can evolve and morph into the appearance of a factual story. I was slow to recognize that. After more than a hundred years of the State Archives' tirelessly working to preserve and protect the historical records of our state, it was painful to have an opinion piece sabotage the good work and public trust we had earned. The State Archives and departmental administration strategized to create a variety of responses that were used in letters to newspaper editors, in communications with stakeholders, and as talking points in responses to email inquiries.[16] I spent a great deal of time in personal communication with citizens, the local heritage society, and numerous genealogy groups. True disclosure meant standing behind our actions and not blaming any other involved parties for aspects of the situation. It became evident that while my staff had normal communications with a records custodian for this type of situation, we had not done enough to explain to the public the complexities of records management programming in our state. We worked to correct that through our messaging. We actively sought out the major misconceptions in the case, including that we need to save every record created by any government office, and worked to provide a stronger message to the public regarding the benefits and challenges of an active records management program. I realized and understood that I can't simply see records management questions from an insider's perspective. Communications from the State Archives, particularly those about appraisal, must reach a lay audience. Finally, in every professional challenge lie the seeds of programmatic improvement. Talking with genealogists and historical groups about the events in this one county showed me that there was broader advocacy work to be done on this topic too. What can I do to help educate citizens and researchers on the role they can play in ensuring that their local officials take proper care of their records? How can our agency communications better explain how records are managed through our programs? When dealing with complicated records retention questions, how can we better craft communications to meet the needs of the custodians and potential public perspectives about the records in question? My lesson from this incident is to see all situations as advocacy opportunities. Even crises provide the chance to see where communication strategies can be strengthened.

New Directions

With a long-established program, it can be easy to avoid taking a comprehensive look at established procedures and processes. Why fix what isn't broken? Leading a large archival organization has shown me the importance of recognizing opportunities for programmatic evolution or change. Leadership means taking steps to seize these opportunities and to guide staff through the changes. This may also mean listening to tough questions from stakeholders.[17]

This was the situation the State Archives found itself in by early 2013. We have a records retention and disposition structure for state agencies built upon a general schedule for commonly created public records, as well as numerous program-specific schedules that identify records governed by a particular state function or program. The program-specific schedules were developed in close collaboration with individual agencies, and they contain information on the agency structure, providing great detail for an analog-based records scheduling program. In 2011 the sitting governor of the state announced that she would not run for reelection, leaving the seat open for a new administration. The transition proved to be fortuitous for our records management program when the new chief information officer asked me tough questions about the ease of use in applying our existing records management schedules to modern government records. How easy was it for the average state employee to utilize our schedules? Did the schedules address how data is created and managed in all formats? His questions prompted me to work with our government records head and take a hard look at our entire schedule development process.[18] Was it enough to continue modifying our existing processes, or did we need to consider a comprehensive overhaul? Were our analysts spending time strategically, or was their time too occupied with administrative changes to individual retention schedules at agencies' requests? What would happen to our records holdings data if we recast any of the records scheduling system that relied on the assignment of unique item numbers to each series in a records schedule? I understood that management of modern government records poses new challenges and requires our analysts to be part of conversations with agencies at the front end of records creation rather than passively waiting to receive a transfer of paper records. An overhaul of this long-established system would take a great deal of strategic planning, communication, and stakeholder input. Recognizing the opportunity and circumstances, I also saw that I had a manager of our government records operations who was very capable of leading this project. She had some analysts ready for the challenge of moving our schedule development from one based on structure and series to one that approached retention based on core government functions. The human resources were in place to evaluate this existing process and take advantage of the opportunity to effect positive change.

This is an intellectually challenging and complex project requiring close communication among the staff driving the research and development and the administrators of our records management program, as well as our state agency partners and other stakeholders. Such a project cannot be accomplished easily, so I worked with our head of government records and her records analysts leading the project to conceptualize a project plan that included an environmental scan of our existing retention schedules, regular and varied communications with records creators about the project, and research on all legally mandated state agency functions. Project timelines and benchmarks were developed to break this enormous undertaking into manageable pieces and milestones.[19] In many ways, I serve as the chief salesperson for the project, working to promote it to higher state agency administrators, explaining how our program believes strongly in active management of modern records and how we fit into data governance conversations, and demonstrating how we can work collaboratively to better manage our state information regardless of format. Leadership in this situation means providing the environment for staff to explore, develop, and grow bold, new programmatic ideas, as well as projecting to stakeholders my desire to resolve challenging records management issues to benefit all records creators and custodians.

Developing new methods for delivering public services can be challenging and rewarding, but what about leading change for the delivery of established services? Leaders also recognize the opportunity to change existing programs and to improve the archival fundamentals. In a public records context, that means that leaders return to the legal foundation of records access. You may need to explore access service beyond an archival setting and include the legal basis for access rules and procedures. In addition, issues of proper access rules and procedures demonstrate the importance of building relationships with the legal community within the state government environment. Legal review of archival operations may be needed, and I understood the importance of building that community of experts to consult with me.

This was the situation I found myself responding to when I explored how staff referenced some restricted records for patron requests. Many of our finding aids reference access to restricted records upon consent of the state archivist. Early in my tenure, I found this note to be too simplistic. Instead of an outside stakeholder asking tough questions, I found myself in the role of inquisitor. Was there a process in place for systematic review of restricted records and the proper methods for gaining access to them? Was there uniformity in staff response to requests for access to restricted records? What resources had been consulted in making a legal interpretation for access? Was the decision to grant access only mine, or was there a methodology for patrons to appeal my decisions? It seemed to me that uniformity was needed across the reference spectrum for restricted records. What I uncovered, particularly for some of the most litigated records in North Carolina, was far from a standard application of procedures and analysis of legal restrictions on individual records. This seemed particularly critical because at the time, there was no sunshine legislation in North Carolina, and closed records remained closed forever.

Unlike in many other states, prison records are one of the most restricted and litigated series of records in North Carolina. Procedures for access have mainly developed through court rulings. Our holdings of historical prisoner data are not large, and many materials came from sporadic transfers decades ago. There is no systematic transfer of prison registers or prisoner case files to the State Archives. However, the historic records we did hold were becoming increasingly interesting to genealogists and scholars as they researched the history of crime and punishment in the modern United States. As I reviewed how we handled requests for access to these materials, I uncovered a history of uneven reference practices. Some public services staff showed patrons individual register entries; some responded that all the records were closed. Other series of death penalty case files were sporadically released piecemeal to researchers, depending on how the staff member handling the reference interpreted what was restricted in the files. Uniformity of reference provides common access, even if instituting changes upset those who benefited previously from extralegal access. I set about developing a mechanism for review of pertinent legislation and case law regarding prison records. I sought input from the records creators to ensure that our process mirrored theirs for current records. I requested legal review of my decisions by our agency counsel, legal counsel from the creating agency, and the Department of Justice. At times this has meant that restricted records erroneously released previously to researchers are now restricted. I was prepared to communicate to unhappy researchers why the changes took place. One researcher complained loudly and bitterly, taking her complaints to members of the General Assembly. But returning to a legally sound and unified application of reference for restricted records, along with solid legal review of our processes, meant that the only redress is a change to the law governing access to these materials. Developing policies and procedures around reference for restricted records continues to be an ongoing process as I seek to ensure that our fundamental procedures are within the law and applied correctly. Understanding legal issues and authority, specifically surrounding access and a state archival program, is an important part of program leadership. Legal interpretation is more than just the copyright law covered in an occasional seminar or graduate program. Leaders should develop a comprehensive understanding of the laws relating to records and their restrictions within a state environment. Sound fundamental procedures are important and should be reviewed with legal advisors familiar with cultural resources. Review them regularly to spot flaws or inconsistencies. Just as archivists rely on accurate descriptive data and finding aids to ensure access, other foundational activities of the enterprise need review with a critical eye for uniformity in legal grounding and application.

The Importance of Community

State archival institutions may be found within a department headed by an elected or an appointed official. The agency may have cabinet-level status, or it may answer to a governing board. Regardless of where in the state government hierarchy the archival enterprise sits, there are some common aspects: the materials collected, public services provided, and variety of stakeholders served. Over the course of my career, my appreciation for the value of working in community with other state archives has grown.[20] Our similarities are greater than our differences. I first saw this twenty years ago when I began attending the annual Southeastern Archives and Records Conference (SARC). Started more than thirty years ago as an opportunity for the state archives in the Southeast to meet annually and share best practices, the conference features informal roundtable discussions grounded in particular aspects of state archival operations. The attendees share experiences, challenges, and new programming initiatives in areas such as access, records management, and outreach. SARC allows peers in similar institutions the time to dive into deeper discussions about program development, challenges, and successes. The small group settings encourage the building of professional relationships with staff from institutions very similar to our own. I encourage our attendees to bring back ideas and notes from their sessions to inform development of our own programs.

In the last several years, I've been fortunate to have the opportunity to become more involved in the CoSA, both with specific programming initiatives, such as the State Electronic Records Initiative, and also with the board of directors. In both areas, the ability to work with other state archivists and subject specialists to develop tools and programming benefited the community as a whole, as well as North Carolina. In serving the CoSA community, I brought back informal approaches, best practices, sample procedures, and other tools that have proved invaluable when trying to effect positive change within state agency partners. Many years ago, CoSA's Intergovernmental Preparedness for Essential Records (IPER) project demonstrated the importance of building relationships with other state agencies to effectively deliver programs that protect essential records. Modern archival programs are all about community. We have to be in relationship with records creators regularly to ensure that we are effectively providing for the preservation of modern public records. It takes time and attention to develop these relationships within state agencies, and having information on other states' successes and approaches enhances the ability of our program to offer tangible solutions to our records management and preservation challenges.

The challenges to state archives are numerous. We often face static or declining budgets, the press of new technologies and their impact on the management of government records, the transformation of our services for online delivery, and the revolving door of government leadership that comes with each election cycle. Our collections are growing, our facilities aging. Just as I have benefited from training and experiences working with and learning from professionals in the public management, marketing, and legal professions, so, too, have I grown through formal and informal interactions with my colleagues in other state archives. In facing similar challenges, they provide relevant experience that assists me when I seek to improve my program fundamentals, to develop new outreach opportunities, and to serve as the ambassador for the State Archives within my state and beyond.

After more than two decades in the state archival environment, I understand that leadership means more than strong archival management skills. Program leadership means you often do not spend time processing collections or pulling records for patrons. Instead, as the program ambassador, you are translating that work to larger and varied communities and constituencies. Leadership means learning how to communicate concisely and clearly to reach those constituencies. You constantly seek opportunities to advocate for the work of the archives and to connect it to your stakeholders and their needs. You understand that to effectively manage complex, modern public records, you need to build relationships with records creators, information technology providers, and the larger professional community across the country to incorporate the best new ideas to improve your services. Seek out your stakeholders; don't wait for them to approach you. Be ready with that "ask and an offer" upon which to build a stronger relationship. This takes time and the ability to connect your program to foundational activities of state and local agencies. As the way citizens interact with their government evolves and moves from in-person to virtual interactions, so must our notion of service delivery evolve. Beyond the archival fundamentals, there are formal and informal opportunities to connect your program to new audiences, larger projects, and new service delivery. Accept the ambassadorship, and advocate for your program and all the good work it does. The archival ambassador corps can benefit from the next generation of leadership ready to advocate for and build our programs while connecting with new stakeholders.

NOTES

[1] A brief history of the North Carolina Historical Commission can be found at "N.C. Historical Commission," https://www.ncdcr.gov/nchc, captured at https://perma.cc/9N9W-LXBH.

[2] The State Archives of North Carolina is administered by the Department of Natural and Cultural Resources, an executive department of state government run by the appointed secretary. The department includes all historical, arts, and natural science institutions and programs for the state. Its overall mission may be found at "Natural and Cultural Resources, Department of," https://www.nc.gov.agencies/natural-cultural-resources, captured at https://perma.cc/Z4DL-5Y4Y.

[3] In the "Teaching Leadership" portion of the article, Randall Jimerson lists some important leadership skills for archivists beyond the fundamentals taught in graduate programs. George Mariz et al., "Leadership Skills for Archivists," *American Archivist* 74, no. 1 (2011): 118–19.

[4] The importance of mentorships is covered in several places in Anne Ackerson and Joan Baldwin's book on leadership. The interview with Anne Cathcart contains some important advice about taking a little bit of knowledge from every experience and job. Anne W. Ackerson and Joan H. Baldwin, *Leadership Matters* (Lanham, MD: AltaMira, 2014), 94.

[5] A review of financial management in the archival environment can be found in Michael J. Kurtz, *Managing Archival and Manuscript Repositories* (Chicago: Society of American Archivists, 2004), 185–200.

[6] "Good communication is like any other skill. It must be mastered and practiced over and over if performance is to improve." Kurtz, *Managing Archival and Manuscript Repositories*, 145.

[7] The importance of seeking regular partnership opportunities is discussed in Kurtz, *Managing Archival and Manuscript Repositories*, 44–45.

[8] A summary of the IPER curriculum can be found at "Emergency Preparedness," https://www.statearchivists.org/programs/emergency-preparedness/, captured at https://perma.cc/B9JG-MZS2.

[9] In chapter 8, Jennifer Johnson highlights the importance of learning to speak the language of the archives' audiences. In addition, Megan Sniffin-Marinoff discusses the importance of identifying those who may benefit from the work and services of the archives in chapter 11.

[10] Bruce W. Dearstyne, "Leading Archives and Records Programs: Issues and Sources," in *Leading and Managing Archives and Records Programs: Strategies for Success*, ed. Bruce W. Dearstyne (New York: Neal-Schuman, 2008), 292. In the list of essential leadership roles for archivists, Dearstyne says, "Good leaders stand ready to seize opportunities that may enhance their programs and, at the same time, benefit the parent organization."

[11] "Treasures of Carolina: Stories from the State Archives," https://www.ncmuseumofhistory.org/exhibits/treasures-carolina-stories-state-archives, captured at https://perma.cc/3VKF-88WX.

[12] Engagement is a core strategy in leading archival programs. Bruce W. Dearstyne, "Strategies for Leading Archival Programs," *Archival Outlook* (March/April 2015): 11.

[13] "Leaders often symbolize their programs." Bruce W. Dearstyne, *Leading the Historical Enterprise: Strategic Creativity, Planning and Advocacy for the Digital Age* (Lanham, MD: Rowman and Littlefield, 2015), 30.

[14] Before any decisions on the fate of the records could be made, our office required an understanding of the types of records in the basement. As we suspected, the records stored there belonged to a number of local offices, and according to our records management procedures, only the creating office may make determinations with our office as to the disposition of public records.

[15] The list also contained records of minimal to no long-term value, including canceled county checks, as well as records containing confidential information. Even those records with confidential information were preliminary materials used to create a final, archival record, such as a marriage license or delayed birth certificate.

[16] In his chart of archival leadership skills, important items for this situation are numbers 6 and 7, "Leaders see difficult situations not as problems, but as opportunities for seeking solutions," and "Leaders are calm in the face of adversity. When faced with a challenge, they look for solutions rather than scapegoats." Kurtz, *Managing Archival and Manuscript Repositories*, 23. In addition, Mark Greene covers the importance of leadership that makes decisions and takes responsibility in Greene, "Trying to Lead from Good to Great and Some Reflections on Leadership at All Levels," in Dearstyne, *Leading and Managing Archives and Records Programs*, 149.

[17] One leadership lesson I particularly like comes from Anne Ackerson and Joan Baldwin, chapter 6, "The Authentic Leader." One lesson they gleaned from interviewing leaders in the museum world was that "authentic leaders are map makers." Map makers are described as innovators, decision-makers, and experimenters. Being a map maker can be critical as we lead our programs through a process of evolving and updating our services to stakeholders. Ackerson and Baldwin, *Leadership Matters*, 121–22.

[18] "Archival leaders assess their programs constantly, looking at current needs but also future trends. They make difficult decisions that are intended to provide a better foundation for the archival enterprise in the future." Edie Hedlin, "Meeting Leadership Challenges: Lessons from Experience," in Dearstyne, *Leading and Managing Archives and Records Programs*, 178.

[19] A review of project management in the archival environment can be found in Kurtz, *Managing Archival and Manuscript Repositories*, 89–100.

[20] In chapter 9 of this book, Lynette Stoudt offers another important perspective on the importance of community in archival leadership. Active involvement in a professional community can also be seen as a professional development tool.

8

Cultivating Success:
The Business of Archives

Jennifer I. Johnson

Phil Mooney, retired corporate archivist of the Coca-Cola Company, once wrote that business archivists "must be aggressive self-promoters, seeking every opportunity to sell the use of the archival record for business enhancement. To achieve success and financial stability, the archivist must adapt to the business environment and constantly seek new opportunities to market its resources and service to its constituents."[1] Successful business archivists navigate the corporate setting by continually making their knowledge and products useful to their colleagues. The archivist finds ways to support the company's goals, demonstrate the archives' value, and connect coworkers with heritage. The corporate archivist must be flexible with prioritizing on a daily basis, comfortable with change, and also strategic and articulate. It can be challenging to identify the best arguments that persuade business clients of the importance of heritage, particularly if you do not feel that you are naturally aggressive or good at marketing, but leading and developing a thriving archives in this arena requires effective and creative promotion to corporate leaders. A successful corporate archives leader builds relationships and develops new abilities to build recognition of the archives and the corporate heritage.

One of the most challenging tasks in a corporate environment is that the archivist has the responsibility to lead others to heritage. The archivists are the experts and often the interpreters of the corporation's past. Historical events may be misunderstood or misinterpreted by colleagues in order to make a better story or to uphold a particular marketing endeavor. Business archivists must verify the stories and myths that arise[2] when people think they understand the corporate history, and "accurately preserve the integrity of the corporate memory, that often hazy body of knowledge that combines what really happened with what people thought was happening."[3] Even the word *history* can turn people off if they have a negative connotation from a high school class they once took. At Cargill, the archivists refer to corporate heritage rather than corporate history.

The term "heritage" is more encompassing of corporate culture and values, better articulates the historical interpretation the archivists provide, and is more engaging than *history*. Heritage may be found throughout the corporation if one knows where to look, with brand legacies, historical buildings, management practices, and business partnerships, to name a few examples. It is up to the archivist to connect colleagues to heritage and to make heritage interesting and relevant to their daily activities.

Many business archives strive to serve both their colleagues and members of the public. The opportunities at Cargill are different from many companies because all of the archives' stakeholders are internal. Cargill is one of the world's largest global, privately held, family-owned companies, with a rich history dating back to 1865. The majority shareholders are also family owners, so there is a family legacy to preserve and protect. Cargill's business is mainly serving other businesses, so its primary customers are other companies and not consumers. With a history in commodity trading and businesses in food, feed production, and food ingredients, Cargill has few branded products. These may not be familiar to the public, unless one happens to purchase animal feed[4] or nonsugar sweetener;[5] even then, it may not be obvious that the product is made by Cargill. Though the company website features a section on the company history, it does not reference the archives. The corporate affairs team is equipped to answer the most frequently asked questions about Cargill history and refers only the most complex inquiries to the two corporate archivists, so the archivists' contact with the public is minimal. The archivists are focused entirely on providing services and value to the employees of Cargill, so that they, in turn, may better serve Cargill's customers.

The Cargill Corporate Archives opened in 1988, with the first full-time professional archivist hired in 2000, followed by a second in 2007. While some activities are undertaken by part-time and short-term employees, at Cargill the archives is run by a core team of two people. In other organizations, leadership responsibilities may fall solely on the corporate archives director. The Cargill archivists have found that advocating for the archives and expanding their network of stake-holders falls to each archivist, not just the one in the position of manager. Certainly the corporate archives director retains important decision-making accountability and serves as the primary face of the archives, but each archivist must take on leadership roles in spite of where that position falls in the managerial hierarchy. In a business archives, because of the necessity of continual outreach to colleagues, it is difficult to remain shielded from these responsibilities. Leading in a business archives means being prepared to face the institutional realities of corporations while serving in any position. For this reason, the focus of this chapter covers both a general discussion of strategies for overcoming challenges archivists face in developing an effective business archives, and thoughts on the specific leadership qualities individuals must foster to be successful in this environment. When advocating for heritage in a business, it is important to have leaders at all levels in the archives in order to contribute value to the corporation for years to come.

Demonstrating Strategic Value

To understand how archivists contribute value to their company, it is first important to understand what is valuable to the organization. Every corporation wants to earn a profit, and good profit margins and sales are keys to a successful business. "Ultimately, corporate archives are responsible to the shareholders, and the primary interest of shareholders is to increase their investment."[6]

Companies prize success, but there are other values that underpin why the company started doing business in the first place—its purpose, the reason the corporation sells its products or services. Principles such as ethics, safety, self-determination, or innovation are often at the core of a company's culture. "While a vision articulates a company's purpose, values offer a set of guidelines on the behaviors and mindsets needed to achieve that vision."[7] Whether it is to inspire,[8] to nourish,[9] to help customers succeed financially,[10] or to fulfill dreams of personal freedom,[11] once the business archivist understands the organization's passion, the company culture, and how employees are motivated, the archivist will better understand how to promote heritage in order to contribute to the corporate goals. This is particularly important since the archives is not typically a revenue-generating department of the organization. Certainly there are numerous examples of companies using heritage to increase their bottom line by marketing and advertising products. Companies may have heritage brands or sell merchandise evolved from earlier eras in their history. For example, the Red Wing Shoe Company has heritage collections with modern designs that pay tribute to boots made when the company began, designs that were inspired by information found in the company archives.[12] Yet the contribution of the corporate archives is rarely monetary; it is an understanding of the corporate purpose and culture. The value of the archives comes from interpreting the corporation's heritage.

One way to demonstrate that the archivist understands the company's goals and vision is to align the archives mission statement with the overall organizational mission. This is particularly important in a business setting since the overall corporate mission is not about culture or heritage. "Work with, rather than against, the goals of the parent organization. Learn the values, language, and culture of the larger entity and describe your program accordingly. Frame your arguments, tailor your activities, and account for resources in ways that are understood by the larger entity. Pursue the archival mission faithfully, but always with the understanding that to flourish the archival program must be viewed as contributor to the larger enterprise."[13]

It helps to use the exact or similar words from the corporate mission statement. For example, in a previous iteration of the organizational strategy at Cargill, three key stakeholders—customers, communities, and employees—were identified as contributing to the corporation's success. The archives mission statement stated not only what the archivists do but how their work supports these stakeholders: "The Corporate Archives is responsible for identifying, organizing, preserving and making available non-current records of continuing value to Cargill. Items in the archives are used to provide information relating to the company's development, culture, programs, facilities, events and decisions. This heritage is used by Cargill business units and functions to manage Cargill's reputation, to connect with customers and communities, and to engage employees." As the corporate mission statement evolves and changes, the archives mission statement should be revised as well. It is the first step in demonstrating that the archivists understand the aspirations of the organization and know how to align their projects to help meet those goals.

Likewise, the archives' strategic plan should clearly link the work of the archivists to the organization's purpose. In this instance, it is not just the objectives of the corporation that are important but the goals of the division where the archives sits in the corporate hierarchy. The strategic plan should indicate how the archives contributes to activities at all levels of the company. Strategic plans should be flexible. Strategic directions change as the needs of the organization and archives change and as different opportunities arise. For this reason, it is helpful to review and revisit the strategic plan at regular three- to five-year intervals. For example, in a recent Cargill archives strategic plan, the archivists identified a number of Cargill businesses that were underrepresented in the collection. This meant it was more challenging to engage these colleagues with heritage when the archives had little information about the areas in which they worked. One of these was the Cargill Pork business. This business was sold in 2015, which was not something the archivists could have predicted when their documentation strategy was formulated in 2010. While the archives still has underdocumented Cargill businesses in the collection, collection development will be less business-specific going forward and will focus instead on acquiring materials from the corporation's intranet. The archivists have reasoned that they are poor predictors of Cargill's mergers, acquisitions, and divestitures. Instead, they will target specific areas of the intranet, which will yield information on corporate-wide decisions, strategies, and business plans, information that will be pertinent to all employees rather than particular business lines.

Business archives live in a constant state of change, often brought about by mergers, acquisitions, and divestitures. A number of well-established archives have lost their long-serving corporate archivists in recent years in this fluctuating environment. One would like to think this is a new development, but business archives have always been affected by mergers, restructuring, and consolidations.[14] This is part of the cyclical activity for business archives. As data from the Institute for Mergers, Acquisitions and Alliances (IMAA) indicates, the number of mergers and acquisitions has steadily increased since the mid-1980s, both in the United States (from 2,904 in 1985 to 16,849 in 2018)[15] and worldwide (from 3,287 in 1985 to 48,577 in 2018).[16] Change has been significant, ongoing, and should be expected; therefore the archivist has to be ready to demonstrate the value of heritage and the archives at a moment's notice. As David MacLennan, Cargill's CEO, is fond of saying, "The pace of change will never be slower than it is today."[17]

Managing through change requires flexibility and the willingness to work through the unknown. This can be particularly difficult during a reorganization and changes of leadership. Cargill experienced restructuring in 2016, which affected every employee. The archivists faced numerous unknowns for several months, including whether their reporting supervisor and hierarchy would change. It is always difficult to manage in an environment when the future is unclear. The uncertainty creates a stressful work environment, which can affect physical and mental health, perspective, focus, and family life. During this kind of time, healthful stress management techniques are extremely important. It is vital to continue confiding in family and friends, practicing relaxation techniques, eating a healthy diet, exercising routinely, and getting plenty of sleep[18] in order to maintain a rational perspective about what an archivist is able to control. While at work, it is equally important to continue routines, and part of the archivist's routine activities should be developing stories about how the archivists contribute to the company's success. At Cargill, the archivists needed to prepare for the possibility that they would move elsewhere in the corporate hierarchy, with supervisors who were less familiar with the archives and the value it provides the company. By demonstrating value, the archivists could also make a case for remaining in their current structure.

A good starting point for defining value is to maintain a kudos file, a record of those who have thanked the archivist for projects well done. These colleagues are likely allies who support the archives and find its services invaluable. At Cargill, the archivists are able to use these thanks as examples of how the corporate archives promotes the organization's mission by contributing to projects around the company. For example, the archivists support trademark challenges by establishing a legacy of owning and using a product name, contribute to corporate anniversaries, and confirm ownership of company property globally. These stories are more significant to the managers at Cargill than statistics; plus they provide a sampling of the breadth of the archivists' expertise and demonstrate the connections the archivist is able to make between the corporate heritage and everyday work of the organization. Every opportunity to demonstrate value is necessary for the continued support of the archives. These colleagues are important stakeholders, and their success is key to the success of the archives.

Storytelling techniques are also useful for relating Cargill's heritage to the present. As the interpreters of Cargill's history, it is the archivists' job to make the associations between Cargill's past and its future. These connections need to be not only relevant to work done in the company today but also thoughtful and concise. You should be able to understand their significance quickly. Stories are also convenient tools for demonstrating the archivist's knowledge. They establish the archivist's understanding of information important to the company and its employees, they link the company and its values, and they guide people to heritage. For example, when Cargill's second president wrote in 1923, "Our word is just as good as our bond,"[19] it is the archivist who explains that this statement is an early reflection of ethical integrity, which the company exhibits in its business practices today. It is up to the archivist to articulate the importance of this heritage as it pertains to company culture and daily practice.

In these instances, the archivist becomes the superhero, the defender, or as the Cargill corporate archives director likes to say, "The Guardians of Truthiness!" Facts are facts, but it is up to the archivist to present them as a compelling and understandable story. Archivists must make the history accessible and engaging.[20] For example, corporations often like to celebrate "firsts." What were they the first to do? Being the first in a field with a new idea, product, or innovation is a persuasive story. Sometimes advancements are confused with firsts, and it is up to the archivist to explain how this achievement moved the company forward and why it is significant, even if the company was not the first to do it. For example, Cargill started a grain laboratory in the early 1920s, and the techniques developed there helped Cargill mix and grade grains more effectively and accurately than its competitors. Was Cargill the first to have such a laboratory? There is no way to know for sure. The creation of the laboratory marks the beginning of Cargill's history of research and development, and its innovations and work with grain continue today as the company works with business partners to create healthier breads for consumers. Cargill was certainly early in the field trying to solve these problems. These investments are still significant, and they tell a compelling story about Cargill's business practices and history, even if the company was not the first to do it. Part of being a Guardian of Truthiness is managing perspectives of the archives' clients. This may mean that colleagues receive something different from what they thought they were looking for, but they will still have an engaging story to work with that is true, factual, and connects the company heritage to current endeavors.

Fostering Relationships

Building relationships is a crucial ongoing activity in a business environment. "Successful archival programs develop large and loyal constituencies, groups or people with vested interests in the archives."[21] There are typically few archivists in a corporation, and there are fewer natural allies than are found in an academic setting or historical society. Yet there are people who understand the purpose of the archives and the value of the corporation's heritage. Allies may include the corporate librarians, law librarians, and records managers. Those in public relations or marketing may have an interest in heritage, because it can assist with corporate storytelling, brand management, and advertising. These stakeholders form an important base for the work the archivists do, but it is equally important to find support throughout the company and to find new champions.

The archives exists to benefit the corporation, but a commonly heard sentiment is, "I didn't know we have an archives!" Since archivists never know where they will cultivate a new ally, it helps to be prepared with a short introduction to the work of the archives. Think of this as an elevator speech. It is helpful to briefly state what the archives is and to tell people what projects the archivist is working on, tailoring it to the individual if possible, based on their business or role. It can be useful to share something that will have broad appeal, such as a project for archiving email, placing a historical artifact on display in the area in which the person works, or discussing a recent donation. Ideally, one should be able to demonstrate in a short time the relevance of the archivist's work and heritage to current activities in the company. The goal is to engage someone's interest about the company's heritage, plant the seed that the archives exists, and suggest ways that the archivist's knowledge may be useful for future projects.

In addition to seeking support from natural allies and engaging those who are learning of the archives for the first time, it is equally important to target individuals within the organization whom it may be advantageous for the archivist to know better. A practice recommended by Jo Miller can be particularly helpful in building these relationships. Miller, CEO of Be Leaderly, focuses on helping women "advance into positions of leadership and influence."[22] Her advice is to work just 5 percent less and use this time to connect with fellow employees.[23] Consider approaching colleagues you work with, those you want to work with, and those you want to learn from. Ask these contacts for fifteen to thirty minutes of their time, and then engage with them wisely. Meetings may be used to learn about coworkers on a personal level, to discuss a project, and to discover how the archivist may assist them now or in the future. Meetings are also an opportunity to meet with specific people in other departments or leadership positions who are potential archives stakeholders. Whether you meet them for coffee or lunch, the time involved is minimal. Even if you have only one such meeting a month, by the end of the year, you know twelve people better than previously. In an organization where having a personal relationship is advantageous and where time is valuable, this strategy will help archivists build a network separate from their supervisor's and plant the seed of the archives as potential partner. Once a network exists, the archivists will be able to target their work to better incorporate heritage into their colleagues' projects.

Archivists in a corporation make up a small group of people who have very specific needs. These requirements are often different from those of their colleagues. For example, an archivist needs systems on which to store records and metadata for the long term, longer than most systems are designed to exist. The archivist needs a steady influx of records to continue responding to questions and providing informative answers into the future. Archivists' colleagues do not think about heritage on a daily basis, as their goals tend to be more immediate and directly related to the success of their own work. In order to greenlight projects and activities that the archivist is interested in, it is often better for others to want what the archivist wants, particularly those who have more leverage. An archivist must be opportunistic in seizing these moments when they arise in order to lead others to ideas and projects that will include heritage and benefit the archives. The involvement of another group outside the archives lends more awareness and significance to the project and the archives' work. Cargill's 150th anniversary was celebrated in 2015. The Cargill archivists knew that however the anniversary would be observed, they wanted to be included in planning the event. They also knew that they would need to be prepared for requests for their services, knowledge, images, and artifacts. They recognized that preparation for an anniversary celebration, in any of its forms, was not going to happen simply because the archivists were excited about it. The corporate archives director started planting the seed about planning for the anniversary with key stakeholders, supervisors, and colleagues in corporate affairs, marketing, and brand in 2010. This way, others knew the archivists were interested in the anniversary, and they understood what the archives had to offer. The archivists' interest was not enough for the company to scale up a potentially localized event, with anniversary activities led by individual countries and businesses, to a global celebration with a considerable investment of time and resources. This ultimately occurred when the company was able to tie the celebration to unveiling its new brand promise. The common look of the branding tied all of the global celebrations together, and ultimately more than 86 percent of employees interacted in some way with anniversary activities. One can assume that the employees learned positive things about the company that they could then share with potential customers and partners. The company's branding goals were met, and employees were engaged. The archivists provided information for the storytelling about the company heritage and were able to leverage the 150th to digitize significant images in the collection for use during the anniversary. The anniversary was successful and advantageous for the archives. The archivists were able to influence a project owned by another department to serve their own goals, and the celebration could not have happened the way it did without them.

A similar experience occurred with an opportunity to archive email. The Cargill archivists have long wished for a corporate-wide document management system and awareness of the necessity of managing electronic records. The archives has a system that stores images and documents, but to expand storage on a grand scale would require a significant financial investment and justification beyond the needs of two archivists. The corporation has invested in OpenText for storing structured data by some of Cargill's businesses, and the archivists recently began testing its use for keeping and storing email of long-term significance for the corporate affairs team. This is another example of a long-term goal that only came to fruition when someone else needed a solution to a problem. The issue was Cargill's plan to delete personal email files in personal storage table (.pst) formats because of their drain on the overall corporate storage system. The archivists and corporate affairs managers recognized that there is a need within the team to refer back to projects and information over a long period of time, and that significant documentation from the last fifteen years is largely electronic and in email format, which was stored in .pst files. The team's need to access this historical information gave the archivists an opportunity to experiment with a storage system and strategies needed for archiving and storing email. As knowledge managers in the company, liaisons to the records management team, and experts on storing information for long-term use, the archivists became the leads and owners of this project. Not only were the needs of the team met, the archivists' skills and knowledge were recognized, and long-term documentation goals were achieved. Additionally, the on-the-job learning the archivists experienced with archiving email and managing these electronic records contributed to their professional development.

The email project illustrates an important aspect of fostering relationships: learning to speak the language of the archives' audiences. Archiving terms such as *arrangement, description, processing,* and *reference* are not widely understood in the corporate world. When speaking to stakeholders, the archivists refer to the value added to the company, rather than the number of requests filled. The archivists learn and use the acronyms specific to their environment. They speak about managing and assessing risk. They learn to speak the language of information technology professionals. For the corporate affairs email project, not only did the Cargill archivists want to use a system built for storing structured data defined by short-term retention periods for long-term storage of unstructured data, but they also had to communicate their needs to multiple audiences. Corporate affairs colleagues needed to understand how and when to use the system. Information architecture groups needed to understand the archivists' use of the word "archives," the project design needs, and the archivists' knowledge of how users learn and engage with new technology. Records managers needed to understand the requirement for a permanent or long-term retention period, since the system is tied to managing retention. The Cargill archivists were able to use their knowledge of their various stakeholder groups, communicate with them using the terms they best understood, and act as a liaison so that everyone's needs were met.

The culmination of cultivating relationships should be that the archivist has a series of champions who will speak favorably about the archives and its services. "The key to building such support is knowledge of the work and the needs of other institutional programs. Talking with others [*sic*], learning their organizational goals and the audiences they serve—and wish to serve—will help identify those areas in which the archives can provide support."[24] These are defenders and clients who can speak about the value the archives has added to their work and about the knowledge they have acquired from interactions with the archivist. Ideally, these relationships will be built throughout the company in a variety of divisions, and throughout the corporate hierarchy. While it is challenging and time-consuming to create these connections and bolster these relationships on a regular basis, this is a critical part of helping the archives thrive in a business environment. Strong personal relationships are the undercurrent of successful transactions. Satisfied clients are key to the archivist's success, particularly when the clients are able to do their jobs better because of the contributions from the archives.

Leadership Skills in the Corporate World: A Personal Perspective

All of the skills required to aggressively promote the archives, such as marketing, communicating, and negotiating, can be learned, but they all require practice in order to use them effectively. "Developing leadership skills takes practice, patience, and perseverance. Individuals should consciously look for opportunities to lean into their discomfort."[25] In the business world, in small, lightly staffed archives, you must be creative in acquiring management capabilities, particularly when moving up often means moving out of the archives, or when moving into a management role means doing less of the work that originally attracted you to the profession.

It is important to draw a distinction between leadership in a corporation and corporate leaders. While the archivist may be recognized as an expert in his or her field, exemplify leadership qualities, and serve as a manager of the archives, the archivist may not be considered a corporate leader. In good corporations, leadership is recognized at all levels of the organization, and everyone's skills can shine outside of a management role, but the term *corporate leader* is often a separate distinction. High-potential employees and future leaders of departments and divisions, and possibly even future board members, are often identified and given specific leadership development opportunities within a company. This may include targeted management training and project management responsibilities unavailable to other employees. Corporate leaders often have a willingness to move, laterally or hierarchically, throughout the corporate structure. Archivists, while serving in a professional capacity, are often outside this group unless they express interest in upper management positions and are willing to leave the archives to serve the corporation in a different role.

It is possible to develop leadership skills and be known as a knowledgeable authority in a corporation, but archivists must apply their expertise toward the marketing of the archives. Where does an archivist find the opportunities to progress within the work environment, and when do they need to look elsewhere? Where do you gain the experience needed in order to be ready for available promotions? In a corporation, where strong leadership is considered an asset, how does the archivist demonstrate professional development when what archivists do is a specialized activity?

Self-awareness is the first step in identifying the skills the archivist will need in the corporation. What will help the archivist become the aggressive marketer they need to be for the archives? It can be difficult to identify and address weaknesses, and to identify projects and goals that will allow the archivist to acquire new abilities, but not all development can be toward one's strengths. Allow me to use myself as an example. Personally, I identified gaps in communicating effectively and strategic planning. My supervisor encouraged me to participate more in meetings, but first I needed to be able to speak with authority. Luckily, Cargill supports three Toastmasters clubs in the United States. Toastmasters International[26] is an organization that focuses on members learning communication and leadership skills by giving speeches in supportive environments and completing tasks that teach members to lead confidently. Cargill supports its employees by paying for memberships, but any situation in which you may speak in front of others and have your progress evaluated will provide similar support. Because of this preparation, I am better equipped when something inevitably goes wrong while speaking, and better able to formulate persuasive arguments and responses on the fly in both casual conversation and intense meetings. Public speaking is a skill that must be practiced in order to improve, and I try to find opportunities to talk about the corporate heritage and give tours regularly so that my abilities stay up to speed. Communicating well is a key attribute when cultivating relationships, articulating value, and persuading others of the usefulness of heritage.

In regard to strategic planning, prioritizing is not a problem for me, but long-range thinking about where the archives needs to be and how to get there is an area I needed to improve. After informing my supervisor that this was an area I wished to develop, I was encouraged to contribute to brainstorming the future of the archives, and to participate in strategic planning exercises within the division and in professional organizations. I took the lead on projects that challenged my project management skills, such as the work on archiving email. Learning on the job is the most beneficial option for the archivist and the corporation, but if those chances do not immediately exist, take advantage of educational opportunities provided by the organization. Human resources departments often provide affordable online courses or webinars on business-related topics for employees. Courses may cover aspects of strategic planning, but ultimately this skill needs to be put into action to be tested. Strategic thinking is critical in a corporation where it is important to align archival work with the forward direction of the company.

I have found another practice recommended by Jo Miller to be helpful when identifying necessary capabilities for advancing in the corporate world. Look at who you admire in the company, whether for their skills, leadership abilities, or level of achievement. Start by identifying what they did to achieve the level that they have, what projects they worked on, where they excel, where they have influence, for whom they work, and what their career path has been, for example. These things provide an idea of what the institution values in its high-performing employees. Then identify what you can do in your own role and work situation to address these values for your promotion. I identified a coworker for whom a new employment level had been created, between our mutual level and management, and took note of what he did well. He built a good relationship with his supervisor, he was respected by his stakeholders for his knowledge and completion of assignments, and he was a successful project leader. I set out to mimic his steps in my own space.

Lastly, remain up to speed on archival standards, tools, and practices. The Cargill Corporate Archives does not use Encoded Archival Description (EAD), our collections are not open to the public, and our finding aids are not shared online or with other institutions. Our collection management system shares some of the standard archival description fields, record group, abstract, box and folder list, but the archivists are the sole users of this system. We follow archival principles, but EAD is not applicable to our organization. However, when the latest EAD workshop was offered nearby, I asked for the opportunity to attend. While we may not use EAD at Cargill, numerous other archival institutions do, and I always want my skills to be current. This training may not be immediately relevant to my work at Cargill, but an understanding of markup languages and information organization is useful anywhere. We all must manage our development for the long-term, the role we have currently and the roles we will have in the future. Where one is today may not be where one will be working five years from now. The duties of the archivist within the organization may not be the same in five years. In a business environment it is important to remain knowledgeable and prepared, because forces of change are largely outside the archivist's control.

What Does Success Look Like?

Successful programs can be defined by many criteria, and it is important to identify how best to measure achievement within a corporation. For example, the Cargill archivists do not track reference requests, visits to the archives, or the hours spent responding to client questions. Stories are more meaningful than statistics for relating what the archivists do, how they do it, and whether or not they have satisfied customers. The number of requests responded to is not as significant as who the audience is and the information they seek. Acting as interpreters of corporate history, the archivists find "that business inquirers most often need the answer, they need it now, and want it in 'packaged' form. They are not, as a rule, much interested in where the answer came from or in the interesting twists in the process of finding it."[27] Clients are not typically interested in seeing the original documentation in which the archivists have found the answer to their question, with the notable exception being lawyers. In fact, the corporate archivists are the primary hands-on users of their collection. In this regard, the archivists act more like historians, doing the research and providing interpretation of past events. Discussing the end results or completed projects is more informative to their supervisors. When necessary, the archivists can call upon their champions to sing their praises. Corporate situations do exist where it makes sense to capture certain statistics. If public outreach is a key component of the archives, it can be helpful to track requests from people outside the company. If the company has a brand with a significant consumer following, then it is important to note engagement with these stakeholders. Meaningful measurement changes depending on the organization, its management, and the archives stakeholders.

If the number of requests fulfilled is not a meaningful measure of success, how else might the achievements and the quality of the program be evaluated? How do you assess if you have the appropriate amount of institutional support? How do you know if you have a solid program that may weather inevitable business fluctuations? Bruce Bruemmer, Cargill Corporate Archives director, developed a scale to determine the health of a corporate archives (see figure 1).[28] What does *healthy* mean? It does not mean a perfect score or representation in all categories. It is an indication of corporate-wide recognition, financial support, and stability. It is a sign of trust in the archives and archivists, and acknowledgement of their contribution to corporate goals. Gaps in too many areas could indicate where an archivist needs to spend more time building relationships and marketing heritage. The scale should be viewed as a work in progress as there may be areas that have been overlooked that are more applicable to different settings. That being said, the scale is a starting point for analyzing a successful business archives program.

Let us explore these measures by looking at the Cargill program:

1. The archives opened in 1988, and the first full-time professional archivist was hired in 2000. It had previously been staffed by volunteers and a librarian who worked in the archives part-time. Recognizing the need for professionally trained staff acknowledges that managing an archives requires specialized skills that are separate from the knowledge of librarians or records managers and should not be added on to others' responsibilities.

1. Every five years the archives has had a professional on staff.
2. Number of professionally trained archivists or records managers.
3. Has the archives reported to a new manager within the year?
4. Has the archives moved in the organization within the year?
5. Are there business archives peers within twenty miles?
6. Is a major company anniversary to be celebrated within the next two years?
7. Is there a separate line item or budget for the archives?
8. Does the CEO know who you are?
9. Do any board members (not including the CEO) know who you are?
10. Does your manager encourage professional activities?
11. Has your company increased its annual earnings over last year?
12. Has your company been acquired in the last three years?
13. Does your archives have any environmental controls not normally available elsewhere?
14. Does your archives hold the official minutes of the company?
15. Have you participated in company media training?
16. Does the archives have a presence outside the firewall?
17. Have you traveled by plane on business unrelated to professional meetings within the past year?

FIGURE 1. Corporate archives health scale, developed by Bruce Bruemmer.

2. A second archivist was hired in 2007. The company has a separate records management department with seven people. The archives also has a part-time employee who primarily processes records.

3. For the first time since an archivist was hired, the Cargill archivists have a new manager. It is unusual to have such stability in a corporation with sixteen years under the same supervisor. It is more common for business archives to move from department to department, or to report to new managers in their division on a regular basis. Each new supervisor needs to understand what the archives is, what it does, and how it contributes value to the company. Training a succession of new supervisors, who must be able to advocate on behalf of the archives, can be exhausting depending on the frequency of such training.

4. The corporate archives has always been within Corporate Affairs. Placement within the organization can affect the focus of the archives' work whether it is with the legal department, public relations, marketing, or elsewhere in the company.

5. There is a thriving archival community in the Minneapolis and St. Paul area and a local archives group, the Twin Cities Archives Round Table,[29] which includes other business archives members. Access to other professionals is important for networking, educational opportunities, and collaborating.

6. Cargill celebrated its 150th anniversary in 2015, and the archives was involved with supplying images, contributing to success stories, and supporting the headquarters celebration. Anniversaries often rely on the support of archivists and can generate goodwill for the archives. Now that this anniversary is past, the archivists need to focus their energies on remaining relevant to the organization, so that the archives will be able to assist with the next big anniversary in 2040. Goodwill only lasts for a short period before the archivists must reinvest their time in projects demonstrating their value.

7. The budget for the archives is incorporated into the budget for Corporate Affairs. While financial management is no longer their responsibility, the archivists have additional layers of approvals for travel and major purchases. Corporations often try to consolidate budgets so that employees are not managing small pockets of money, but this means less control and freedom to operate now that the budget is outside of the archives' administration.

8. Both archivists have met with and interviewed the CEO without the presence of intermediaries. Being on a first-name basis with the CEO can be unique to a corporation's culture. Awareness of the archives and positive personal encounters with the CEO and senior-level management increases the potential for high-level support of archival endeavors.

9. Both archivists have met with and provided information to family owners and board members. Again, good relationships provide the potential for high-level support.

10. Both archivists receive financial support and the time to partake in professional activities. This support indicates that the company values professional development outside of daily work and acknowledges the specialized nature of archival work and training.

11. Positive and negative company earnings affect funding for projects, staff, travel, and the general mood throughout the company. Earnings fluctuate constantly, affecting the business climate for public and private enterprises.

12. Cargill has not been acquired by another company. Mergers, divestitures, and acquisitions can significantly affect the stability of the archives, its staff, and its collections, either by

changing the workforce, forcing the archives to relocate, dividing its collections, or finding space to store new records and artifacts.

13. The archivists have some control over the temperature of the archival storage area and
    additional humidity from building improvements. This control was acquired after years
    of lobbying for help managing the fluctuating humidity in the geographical region.
    How well you are able to argue for specialized controls indicates an understanding of the
    unique needs of the archives, as well as the willingness to spend money on improvements
    that may affect a small number of employees and area of the building. Positive relation-
    ships with facility services are beneficial since that department is typically responsible for
    the building structure, lights, furniture, and public spaces, all of which affect the physical
    archives as well as activities the archives may participate in, such as public exhibits.

14. The board minutes are held with the corporate secretary's office and are not shared with
    the Corporate Archives. It has been difficult to persuade other departments that the
    archives is a trusted corporate asset that can provide a secure storage environment and
    limited access to records, if necessary. It can be particularly challenging to argue that the
    archives serves the company as a whole and to bridge silos of information at Cargill. The
    level of trust between departments and an understanding that the archives represents the
    best interests of the company are aspects of corporate culture unique to each organization.

15. The corporate archives director has been given formal media training, indicating that he
    has the trust and authority to speak with members of the media on behalf of the company.

16. The corporate website has a section for company heritage, but the archives is not repre-
    sented. This is not unusual when the archives stakeholders and clients are entirely inter-
    nal. Companies that have a broad public base and significant popular brands, such as
    the Coca-Cola Company or General Mills, are more likely to have public access to the
    archives via the Internet and social media.

17. The archivists rarely travel on business for the company. There is low awareness of the
    archives globally, and the archivists have been unable to capture records and artifacts from
    other locations, conduct oral histories, or share heritage more broadly.

Overall, the Cargill archives is healthy. There are some areas where the archivists have been successful, and other areas where they need improvement. These measures may not fit every situation
or institution, and they could be expanded to be more inclusive of different types of archives. One
measure that is missing relates to understanding the archives' internal business clients: what divisions or businesses do they represent, and does the archives have stakeholders that represent the
corporation as a whole? Has the archivist reached an audience beyond the archives' natural allies?
These measures may also change in companies with consumer brands where the archivists interact more with the public. In these cases, counting requests from external stakeholders and noting
which brands they reference would be reasonable measures. Other institutions may want to note
where their funding comes from—an archives-specific endowment or grant funding? The scale may
be adjusted by organization type depending on what is critical to the archives' success. At Cargill,
broad, high-level support is critical for the archives. The health scale provides a starting point by
which to evaluate whether or not the archivists' contributions are acknowledged and rewarded in
the organization. The quality of the program and the positive recognition it receives will hopefully
translate into professional and financial support for the archives and archivists. A healthy archives

will have trust from all levels of the corporate structure and a wide range of stakeholders. And archivists will have the ability to speak on behalf of the organization about the topic they know best, the corporate heritage.

Conclusion

The leader of a business archives must be part champion, part marketer, part storyteller, and part historian. The fluctuating and changing business world requires fluidity with prioritizing and promotion in order to lead a successful corporate archives program. In this environment, an archivist relies on partnerships to remain relevant. The time invested in forging relationships is well spent, particularly when the archives' stakeholders praise the work of the archivist and share these compliments with the archivist's managers. Sharing the value of the archives and corporate heritage is an ongoing activity that requires creativity and the willingness to try new things. Even if you are not naturally an aggressive marketer, with practice and personal development, you will be able to craft a persuasive story for an archives inquiry, speak at a moment's notice about how the archives can contribute to business goals, and demonstrate how heritage is relevant to the corporation. Ultimately, it is rewarding and fulfilling to encounter business colleagues who seek out the archivist well aware that the corporate archives exists, curious about the corporate heritage, and hopeful that the archivist will share expertise and help them succeed with their endeavors.

NOTES

[1]	Philip F. Mooney, "Archival Mythology and Corporate Reality: A Potential Powder Keg," in *The Records of American Business*, ed. James M. O'Toole (Chicago: Society of American Archivists, 1997), 62–63.

[2]	Dolores Hanna, "Kraft Foods, Inc.: An Interview with Dolores Hanna," in "View from the Inside: Corporate Executives and the Records of American Business," in O'Toole, *Records of American Business*, 69.

[3]	Harold P. Anderson, "Business Archives: A Corporate Asset," *American Archivist* 45, no. 3 (1982): 265.

[4]	Nutrena Animal Feeds, http://www.nutrenaworld.com/, captured at https://perma.cc/35CR-QKHK.

[5]	Truvia, https://www.truvia.com/, captured at https://perma.cc/7M2B-56GL.

[6]	Bruce H. Bruemmer, "Brown Shoes in a World of Tuxedos: Corporate Archives and the Archival Profession" (presented at the Annual Meeting of the Society of American Archivists, Washington, DC, July 31–August 5, 2006).

[7]	John Coleman, "Six Components of a Great Corporate Culture," *Harvard Business Review*, May 6, 2013, https://hbr.org/2013/05/six-components-of-culture, captured at https://perma.cc/938K-EX86.

[8]	NIKE, Inc., "About NIKE," http://about.nike.com/, captured at https://perma.cc/C4MG-HCLL.

[9]	Cargill, Incorporated, "About Cargill," https://www.cargill.com/about, captured at https://perma.cc/9PL9-3WX5.

[10]	Wells Fargo, "The Vision, Values & Goals of Wells Fargo," https://www.wellsfargo.com/about/corporate/vision-and-values/index, captured at https://perma.cc/B7MV-LEU8.

[11]	Harley-Davidson, Inc., "Our Company," https://www.harley-davidson.com/us/en/about-us/company.html, captured at https://perma.cc/S6YX-AUQ4.

[12]	Red Wing Shoes, "Redefining 'Lady-Like': Introducing the Women's Collection," September 3, 2016, http://www.redwingheritage.com/us/USD/journal/redwingwomens/, captured at https://perma.cc/D4ND-SY2T.

[13]	Edie Hedlin, "Meeting Leadership Challenges: Lessons from Experience," in *Leading and Managing Archives and Records Programs: Strategies for Success*, ed. Bruce W. Dearstyne (New York: Neal-Schuman, 2008), 164.

[14]   Elizabeth W. Adkins, "The Development of Business Archives in the United States: An Overview and a Personal Perspective," *American Archivist* 60, no. 1 (1997): 8–33; James E. Fogerty, "Archival Brinkmanship: Downsizing, Outsourcing, and the Records of Corporate America," *American Archivist* 60, no. 1 (1997): 44–55; Gregory Markley, "The Coca-Cola Company Archives: Thriving Where Dilbert, Not Schellenberg, Matters," *Provenance, Journal of the Society of Georgia Archivists* 26, no. 1 (2008): 7; Duncan McDowall, "'Wonderful Things': History, Business, and Archives Look to the Future," *American Archivist* 56, no. 2 (1993): 348–56; David R. Smith, "An Historical Look at Business Archives," *American Archivist* 45, no. 3 (1982): 277.

[15]   IMAA, "M&A Statistics," *Number & Value of M&A North America*, https://imaa-institute.org/mergers-and -acquisitions-statistics/.

[16]   IMAA, "M&A Statistics," *Number & Value of M&A Worldwide*, https://imaa-institute.org/mergers-and-acquisitions -statistics/.

[17]   "Pivoting to the Future: Six Mega-Trends That Will Change Our Industry and Challenge Our Regulators," interview with Christopher Giancarlo, *MarketVoice Magazine*, January 15, 2016, 27.

[18]   Mayo Clinic, "Stress Relief," http://www.mayoclinic.org/healthy-lifestyle/stress-management/basics/stress-relief/hlv -20049495, captured at https://perma.cc/868Z-GQZW.

[19]   Wayne G. Broehl Jr., *Cargill: Trading the World's Grain* (Hanover: University Press of New England, 1992), 285.

[20]   John T. Seaman Jr. and George David Smith, "Your Company's History as a Leadership Tool," *Harvard Business Review*, December 2012.

[21]   Michael J. Kurtz, *Managing Archival & Manuscript Repositories*, Archival Fundamentals Series II (Chicago: Society of American Archivists, 2004), 222.

[22]   Be Leaderly, "About Us," https://beleaderly.com/about/, captured at https://perma.cc/D4ND-SY2T.

[23]   Women's Leadership Coaching, *Poised for Leadership* workshop materials, copyright 2009, attended June 11, 2010, Symantec Corporation, Roseville, MN.

[24]   James E. Fogerty, "Competing for Relevance: Archives in a Multiprogram Organization," in Dearstyne, *Leading and Managing Archives and Records Programs*, 118.

[25]   Donna E. McCrea, "Learning to Lead: Cultivating Leadership Skills," in "Leadership Skills for Archivists," *American Archivist* 74, no. 1 (2011): 106.

[26]   Toastmasters, https://www.toastmasters.org/, captured at https://perma.cc/P4K3-KQJ8.

[27]   Ellen G. Gartell, "'Some Things We Have Learned . . . ': Managing Advertising Archives for Business and Non-Business Users," *American Archivist* 60, no. 1 (1997): 59.

[28]   Bruce Bruemmer, email message to author, May 20, 2015.

[29]   Twin Cities Archives Round Table, https://tcartmn.org/, captured at https://perma.cc/AF3B-4J73.

9

An Exercise in Versatility:
Managing Archives
at a Historical Society

Lynette Stoudt

Introduction

It is 8:30 a.m. on a Monday, and I am unlocking the door of Hodgson Hall, a national historic landmark building located in Savannah, Georgia, opened in 1876 as the headquarters of the Georgia Historical Society (GHS). The alarm hums as I make my way to the panel to disarm it. Before I sit down at my desk to start the workday as the director of the society's Research Center, I walk through the building and grounds unlocking gates and turning on lights, checking for burned-out light bulbs and proper environmental controls, and hopeful that all systems will remain online for another productive day of work. Managerial responsibilities at a historical society can be broad and open-ended, and they often require flexibility on a day-to-day basis to successfully navigate varied tasks.

The GHS was founded in 1839 with the mission to collect, examine, and teach Georgia and United States history through education and research. It is the oldest continuously operating historical society in the South and for more than 175 years has facilitated historical research by operating a research facility and by offering a wide range of educational programs and publications. GHS manages the state's historical marker program, hosts the annual Georgia History Festival, administers a statewide affiliate chapter program, engages in educational programing throughout the state, and publishes a scholarly journal, the *Georgia Historical Quarterly*. The institution fulfills its mission by distilling and repackaging contemporary academic scholarship into programs and publications for a wider public audience. GHS founders adopted the Latin motto from Georgia's founding trustees: "Non Sibi, Sed Aliis"—Not for Self, but for Others—which characterizes the institution's commitment to public service.

In its long history, GHS relied on several partnerships to ensure its existence, including serving as a local public library, an academic library, and, from 1966 to 1997, a state-funded and state-run branch depository of the Georgia Archives.[1] GHS privatized from the state of Georgia in 1997 and today is a statewide, private nonprofit institution. As a nonprofit, by definition, it is an institution that conducts business for the benefit of the general public without a profit motive. In general, salaries are lower than other archives employment sectors, and since the budget is easily affected by the larger economic climate, jobs can be less stable. Managers at historical societies are regularly faced with friendly advice about how to improve operations, services, and programs from every direction including the board, funders, members, patrons, visitors, staff, and the general public, and we are expected to implement changes with a minimal budget, fewer staff, and less training than many other types of archival repositories.

I worked at GHS for more than twelve years, including more than five years as director of the Research Center until April 2018. According to my job description, the overall responsibility of the director of the Research Center was to serve as team leader of the division and primary contact and expert for the institution on library and archives matters. My own definition of my responsibilities was to ensure that Research Center staff were able to carry out their important work; that researcher needs were met, so they could be successful in navigating and using our collections and resources; that board members, donors, members, and the public continued to believe in and support our mission; and, as a Research Center team, that we met or exceeded the requirements of our division set forth by the larger administration. Within each of these basic functions were numerous daily tasks. Although I kept a detailed account of my daily activity and prioritized my daily to-do list well into the following weeks, other pressing priorities often entered my schedule, and I never knew from which direction they might originate. It was rare that I was able to sit at my desk and work on a project from start to finish, with no interruptions. Flexibility and effectively balancing competing demands were two elements that played an important role in successfully meeting these responsibilities. Many of us expect that as we move into management positions, our time will be spent planning and coordinating work rather than actually carrying out the work, but this was not the case in my small institution.

After a general description of GHS's institutional management and leadership structure, I will discuss elements of my job description, including human resources and staffing; collection management; public services; fundraising and development; outreach and education; professional development; and, of course, other duties as assigned.

Institutional Leadership and Management Structure

As an institution, GHS has a legacy of recognizing that strong leadership is the key to advancing its mission and that each staff person plays an important role. There was a general understanding among most senior administrators that we could not afford to be risk averse in developing new projects, programs, and services as it would cause the institution to stagnate. I had the good fortune to work with administrators, colleagues, and staff who embraced new ideas and were continuously thinking about ways to improve operations and otherwise increase the reach of the institution. This working environment was not necessarily what I expected walking into my first job at a historical society.

Coming from a largely academic archives background in California, I did not expect a small southern historical society to share so many of the progressive and forward-looking qualities of higher education, but this approach is what drives the success of the institution. My own initial, misinformed impression underscores the daily struggle that many historical societies face in dispelling misconceptions about their unique role in educating the public. This was not a heritage society dedicated to preserving the viewpoint of a single subset of the population, as stereotypes often suggest, but an institution dedicated to collecting, preserving, and providing access to materials representing the diversity of the state and teaching Georgia history through a variety of educational programs, publications, and services. Most senior staff had worked at GHS for more than ten years and were evolving as leaders and, in turn, growing the institution.

The high-level governing body was a group of twenty-four board-elected, statewide leaders who made up the Board of Curators, which largely served in an advisory capacity.[2] GHS had a hierarchical organizational culture, with the president and chief executive officer serving in the top leadership position.[3] The executive vice president and chief operating officer (COO) established the division budgets and managed the daily operations of the organization. I reported directly to the COO and led the daily operations of the Research Center. The Research Center was located across the street from the administration building. The physical separation from administration resulted in a certain level of autonomy that was successfully maintained by clear lines of communication with the COO and by keeping other senior staff informed about projects or issues that pertained to their division. In terms of my own leadership and decision-making, I relied on strong communication with the president to understand the overall vision for the institution.

There was an institutional strategic plan in place that was revisited as needed, but not at regular intervals. This organization-wide plan was broad, and because it was not updated regularly, it did not include current archives priorities. Most of the organizational planning was relatively short-term, from six months to one year. In this planning environment, it was challenging to formalize long-term divisional priorities. Rather than losing sight of these priorities, I maintained an "opportunity agenda," an informal list of objectives that, when the opportunity arose, I could address with administrators or other stakeholders.[4] This informal list with talking points was committed to memory and included high-level objectives that were either absent from the archives division or required strengthening such as the implementation of large-scale digitization priorities, establishing a records management program, reaching new audiences, and development of an IT infrastructure. Although my approach was less formal than the strategic approaches that Peter Gottlieb discusses in chapter 2, we must sometimes conform to our institution's management culture to be effective leaders. This approach allowed me to be prepared at all times to clearly articulate strategic objectives when the opportunity arose—which could potentially occur at any time, from senior staff meetings to casual conversations. The more consistently the message was delivered and the more often it was heard by administrators in the context of the institution's larger vision, the better the chances of administrators' taking note. As David Carmicheal states in chapter 1, administrators "must share the vision of the archives if they are to support the repository adequately."

As the director of the Research Center, I was responsible for establishing the annual goals and objectives of the division and, working with other senior staff, ensuring that they were consistent with the larger institutional mission. I worked collaboratively with Research Center staff to develop goals that were based in standards and best practices and submitted them to the COO for review and approval. Generally, these included processing projects, cataloging, engaging users, increasing access to collections, and the like. As a small nonprofit, what we were able to accomplish was inextricably linked to our budget. Large projects were generally tabled until outside funding could be identified and secured. As an institution with limited resources, we were not generally on the cutting edge of archives advancements, but we could achieve the milestones of larger institutions in time by engaging in partnerships, training, securing outside funding, and shifting staffing resources as necessary. Whether funding was available or not, it was important to start advocating for priority projects as soon as I realized a need and to educate administrators about their significance.

Human Resources and Staffing

As the director of the Research Center, I administered personnel regulations, submitted perfor-mance reviews, and assisted administrators in personnel actions such as hiring and termination. In addition, I helped craft position descriptions, worked with staff to manage interns and volunteers, trained staff, established goals, developed work plans, and otherwise supervised five division staff members. The positions included two archivists, one librarian, and two reference assistants.

This was my first management position, and I found human resources to be one of the most challenging components of archives management. Without formal training in human resources, I relied mostly on the knowledge and experience that I gained on the job and a detailed understand-ing of GHS's in-house policies. Personnel management took a lot of time and included compo-nents that were sometimes less concrete than other managerial areas. There were the prescribed tasks like staff training and administering performance reviews, and there were the less tangible areas like building relationships and forming a cohesive team. As a leader, it was important to know the staff under my direction. As in any team environment, we are only as strong as our weakest link. In order to strengthen our team, I identified areas needing improvement and developed those areas in individual staff members. Sometimes it was as easy as forwarding a link to an online training resource or suggesting a more efficient way of performing a task. An employee's success is also the manager's success and benefits the entire institution.

I kept up to date with staff activity through regular check-in meetings and monthly staff meetings where each staff member (including me) provided a verbal report on their activities. In addition to discussing projects and upcoming events, Research Center staff meetings were also an excellent opportunity to discuss shared concerns. For example, in a recent meeting, someone noted a sudden rash of patrons not abiding by instructions to keep archival materials flat on the table. Since we all participated in providing reference services, we discussed the verbal instructions we gave to patrons and how best to visually show proper handling, and then brainstormed ways to update written instructions.

As Peter Gottlieb and David Carmicheal have suggested in earlier chapters, ongoing, clear communication with staff is critical in developing and sustaining relationships. In fact, a lack of communication or poor communication is the most frequently cited organizational problem.[5] We have probably all experienced a time in our professional career when we were excluded from an email or conversation where information that affected our work was exchanged, and we were the last to learn about it. I have both experienced and witnessed the frustration when communication breaks down, and I tried to avoid this whenever possible. Since the Research Center was physically separate from all other GHS operations, communication issues often arose. When I learned about an activity or event that impacted Research Center operations or staff, I communicated it to the staff immediately, so that we could be as prepared as possible.

Resources for positions at GHS were scarce, and some positions in the Research Center were hourly with no benefits. These circumstances, combined with lower wages than other archives sectors, meant that it could be difficult to recruit and retain staff. As a small nonprofit, the institution was also susceptible to layoffs in a slowing economy and the reduction or elimination of existing benefits if required to maintain certain levels of staffing. In my relatively short time as a manager, I learned that without staff in key positions, the division suffers and the fallout can affect many elements of operations for years to come. The Research Center underwent one round of layoffs during my employment, and while positions were vacant, backlogs grew, important management tasks remained undone, and the long-term impact was challenging to address for future staff. In this funding environment, it was important to advocate not only for new positions as appropriate, but also for existing positions when budgets were threatened. As often as possible, I underscored the value of positions and individual staff members to administrators, even in times of financial stability.

The importance of a collaborative team with the right skill set was also critical. Sometimes these elements can be difficult to discern during a short interview. I have learned that an applicant with a skill set that matches the job duties perfectly on paper might not be a good fit in terms of building a cohesive and diverse team. I wish I could say that all of my hiring decisions were successful, but I can say that I learned something new with each experience. Not all staff members come to us with the exact required skill set, but if they have relevant experience, are able to think critically, and are motivated to learn new skills, they will almost always contribute to the success of the institution.

Unlike the larger human resources departments of academic institutions and government agencies, small institutions like GHS have fewer resources to support even a single full-time human resources position, and there are generally fewer formal policies and regulations. In the absence of comprehensive formal policies, and without a dedicated department to administer personnel actions, problems sometimes arise. For example, issues may be handled inconsistently and on a case-by-case basis, staff may be called to complete duties that are far outside their job description, and discipline might be applied inconsistently. Inconsistency in implementing human resources actions often negatively affected staff morale and brought about a feeling of distrust toward administrators and the institution in general. As a middle manager, I was responsible for the two-way communication between administrators and the Research Center staff. I was both an advocate for staff and an enforcer of administrative policies and procedures. It was challenging to maintain a sense of teamwork when staff heard about or observed personnel actions that they did not perceive as fair or in keeping with written policies and procedures. Personnel matters are distracting and take time away from other duties, and they will only escalate if not addressed. Above all else, it was important to listen to staff and recognize their concerns. I was not always in a position to directly address those concerns, but I could communicate issues to administrators and advocate on behalf of staff, if appropriate. As Michael Kurtz notes, "How management treats people can define the whole character of an organization," and it is important to remember that staff members are our most important resource.[6]

The hierarchical management structure at GHS was not conducive to my own management style, though I was able to navigate it. The Research Center had a flatter management structure with greater collaboration across job functions. A less structured environment proved to be more efficient in an environment where our small team needed to remain flexible, be able to adapt to change, and effectively respond to challenges and new opportunities. As a manager and team leader, it was critical to maintain a collaborative, cooperative, trusting environment where staff at all levels felt comfortable expressing their ideas and opinions and were encouraged to think creatively. Whether in monthly meetings or informal conversations, when staff members commented about inefficiencies they observed, I solicited feedback about possible improvements. This could be anything from the best place to locate forms at the reference desk to desired search features of a new software platform. I wanted to know what was working for us, what did not work, and where we could improve. Managers must be open to comments and constructive criticism and not take it personally. In order to improve our operations, we must be willing to change the status quo. In my experience, there was almost always room for improvement, especially in an institution that was more than 175 years old. We must not dwell on problems, but must move forward to define solutions. We all bring different experiences to the table, and our diverse viewpoints can help make lasting, positive change. This was amplified in a smaller institution, where we saw the direct impact of our contributions to the institution and its users on a daily basis.

Collections Management

Collections management was a large undertaking at an institution that has been collecting for almost two centuries with limited collections management resources along the way. I was responsible for the management and maintenance of all collection materials including archival collections, books, maps, objects, serials, and other resources. This work included developing and implementing the institution's acquisition and deaccessioning policies and procedures, establishing best practices, and overseeing all technical services activities.

The key to implementing effective collections management at GHS was to collect data about the status of the collections, identify needs, and prioritize projects to address those needs. In identifying needs, my goal was to accomplish the collection management milestones of larger institutions, either using available resources or seeking outside funding assistance, depending on the project. Looking back, I see that our collections management projects had a substantial impact on the institution: processing a majority of the backlog archival collections, gaining physical and intellectual control of the objects collection, and documenting and improving cataloging processes for maps, journals, and books. Improved collections management benefited researchers and staff alike by providing improved access to collections.

When I first arrived at GHS as an archivist in 2005, staff was in the process of selecting a vendor for their first online public access catalog (OPAC). Although Machine Readable Cataloging (MARC) catalog records for archival collections and books were contributed to the Online Computer Library Center (OCLC), the institution had never implemented an OPAC. Outside funding for this important project was required, so a grant funder was identified and a successful proposal was submitted. This project became phase one of a much larger, multiyear initiative that involved several components including transcribing typewritten finding aids into electronic format and implementing *Describing Archives: A Content Standard* (DACS); conducting a backlog survey of archival collections and implementing collection-level processing; implementing

Encoded Archival Description (EAD); surveying, cataloging, photographing, and rehousing the objects collection; implementing a digital image catalog; cataloging the map collection; implementing Archivist's Toolkit; and finally, developing and implementing an online database of EAD finding aids. My role in retooling GHS's collections management activities was to identify areas needing improvement; to investigate standards, best practices, and resources for implementing change; to establish a phased, project approach; to create work plans; to help develop project budgets; to identify potential funding agencies; to assist in writing grants; and finally, to manage project work and staff throughout each phase. Even a small historical society with limited resources can accomplish the objectives of larger institutions over time. The entire plan was carried out over ten years, all with support from the Institute of Museum and Library Services, the National Historical Publications and Records Commission, and other funders and project partners. Most importantly, all activities mentioned above were sustainable by the institution.

Planning for the first project was underway when I arrived at GHS, and it was clear that improving access to collections was an institutional priority at that time. After submitting a successful grant and completing the OPAC implementation project, administrators saw the direct benefits to the institution, most notably heightened awareness about GHS and an increased use of collections by the public and GHS staff in other divisions. It was important to administrators to see increased use of the collections not only in local/regional projects, but also nationally and particularly in the academic sector. This first project laid the groundwork for each subsequent project and provided an opportunity to educate administrators about the processes, equipment, and standards required to implement a successful comprehensive collections management plan, with an emphasis on increased access to collections as the ultimate goal of each project. We also highlighted other positive impacts of each phase, such as potential cost savings, streamlining staff workflows, adopting national standards, freeing up valuable shelf space, reaching different users, and improving the overall user experience.

I should also mention that all of the above collections management activities were accomplished without an information technology (IT) department or even a full-time IT staff person. At an institution with limited capacity and technology resources, it was easy to get discouraged about taking on technology initiatives, but finding the right project partners and vendors made all the difference in implementing a successful plan. The increasing availability of open-source collection management software also enables small institutions like GHS to implement more effective collections management strategies.

Public Services

Delivering high-quality public services was critical to the success of GHS as the Research Center was the only division that interacted directly with the public on a daily basis. The Research Center served about four thousand on-site researchers each year and thousands more through online resources and research services delivered to off-site patrons. The collections were noncirculating, and we were actively engaged in digitizing and delivering collections online via our in-house digital image catalog, the Digital Library of Georgia, the Digital Public Library of America, and other online resources. About 75 percent of on-site researchers resided in the state of Georgia. On average, archival collections received the most use of all GHS resources. Unlike other archival institutions where I have worked, where on-site patron usage could often be predicted with some certainty, we found no indicators at GHS to help us predict on-site usage, and we never knew what volume of patrons or tourists to expect in the reading room on any given day.

GHS is open to the public and serves a variety of patrons including students, faculty, genealogists, independent researchers, authors, lawyers, journalists, realtors, tour guides, and others. GHS also receives tourists from the many tour buses traversing Savannah's historic district. As a team, we placed an emphasis on quality customer service. However, as an institution situated somewhere between an academic special collections library, a government archives, and a public library, our mission, policies, and procedures were often unfamiliar to patrons. This provided daily opportunities for our staff to educate visitors about who we are and what we do.

The Research Center occupies a beautiful historic building, but the public reading room was not ideal for providing access to archival materials. There were four large walnut tables standing on iron legs that were bolted to the floor. These original tables were not movable, so archival research was limited to four to six seats at the table adjacent to the reference desk, so that staff had adequate sight lines for collections security. All other areas in the reading room were open to using main collection books, vertical files, microfilm, and other resources housed throughout the large room. In addition to patrons, tourists also visited the reading room, where we presented small, rotating exhibits. Tourists were required to place their belongings in a locker and only allowed to use collection resources if they registered with staff at the reference desk. Staff vigilance was important, especially on busy days. Two staff members were always scheduled on the reference desk during public hours, so that one person remained in the reading room when the other was pulling archival collections from the adjacent secure, climate-controlled storage building.

In my position, I was responsible for managing all public services activity; recommending and drafting policies, procedures, and fees; administering requests for digital reproductions and use permissions; monitoring statistics; and determining needed services, including identifying the most effective way to provide them and the resources necessary to support them. As the staff person ultimately responsible for managing public services, it was important to remain engaged with the patrons we served. Although we generally had sufficient staff to cover reference shifts, I still worked a couple of shifts per month and filled in when needed. Working directly with patrons was the best way to assess current policies, procedures, and services and enabled me to better articulate concerns to staff and administrators.

Reading room policies and procedures closely resembled those at many academic library special collections. Policies and procedures were revisited regularly to ensure patron and institutional requirements were met and to better streamline workflows. Before implementation, many policies were vetted and approved by our attorney. Fee structures for reproductions and other services were similar to other statewide historical societies. The institution received limited annual state funding to help operate the Research Center. To help meet the costs associated with operating the Research Center, administrators required that we collect a $5 per day research fee from patrons who were not members of GHS; this fee was sometimes met with contention and discouraged on-site collections usage.[7]

I was responsible for handling patron complaints and difficult patrons. Thankfully, we did not receive too many of either. Complaints sometimes pertained to the research fee or our limited public hours, which were cut when we lost two positions during the last recession. Patrons often wrongly assumed that we are affiliated with and offer the same services as larger academic institutions and government agencies in Georgia. Most complaints were due to confusion about our policies and procedures, which could easily be cleared up in a cordial conversation. Each encounter reminded us that we must clearly describe who we are as an institution and be proactive in communicating our policies, procedures, and services to patrons to avoid misunderstanding.

To many of our constituents, public hours were commensurate with access to collections. This was largely true a decade ago before the implementation of online resources and digital projects. However, now patrons can navigate all of our cataloged collections online without thumbing through thousands of typewritten finding aids in the reading room and can view a growing number of collections in digital format from anywhere in the world. A decrease in public hours allowed staff more time for technical services activities such as creating access to unprocessed collections and digitizing collection materials, and more time to handle off-site reference requests and research appointments on days we were closed. Even though we gained back the positions lost during the last round of layoffs, we retained the same public hours, which resulted in increasing access to collections overall. Each staff person was assigned both public service and technical service tasks, and the hours allowed us to maintain a good balance in order to complete our work effectively.

Fund-Raising and Development

As a nonprofit, by definition, we are an institution that conducts business for the benefit of the general public, without a profit motive. We largely relied on membership, endowments, grants, and outright monetary gifts to fund all aspects of what we do (staff, overhead, facilities, collection development, collections care, etc.). We had limited financial capacity for implementing new programs and projects unless new funding sources could be secured. As part of my job, I drafted and reviewed proposals, solicitations, fund-raising and promotional materials, grant reports, and other documents related to funding for the Research Center. I also supported donor cultivation events and worked directly with monetary donors. We received a relatively small amount of state funding to help support Research Center operations, and each year, senior staff met with our elected officials to urge continuing support. The major annual fund-raising event was the Trustees Gala, which was part of the larger Georgia History Festival.[8] Research Center staff mostly served in a supporting role for this event, identifying collection items to be reproduced and used in promotional materials or for event décor and assisting with event setup and teardown.

In a development-driven funding environment, administrators largely recognized the importance of leveraging our unique collections and the meaningful role they played in educating the public. During special tours of our facilities, Research Center staff created temporary exhibits of treasures from the collection, in addition to highlighting items of interest to potential donors. Collections were incorporated into promotional materials for fund-raising, and our distinguished legacy of collecting, caretaking, and creating access to collections was underscored. Projects and programs involving the collections were also highlighted to demonstrate our commitment to education and delivering history to the public.

At GHS, division budgets were established and managed by the COO with little input from senior staff. Without control of the division budget, I continually advocated for the Research Center division to ensure that administrators recognized the value and importance of what we did.

Whenever possible, I urged that our collections be utilized as part of programs, publications, and educational offerings. If staff in other divisions could not easily locate GHS resources on a desired topic, Research Center staff was available to assist. I emphasized that we were there to serve other divisions and administrators in the same manner we serve the public. The collection forms the foundation of GHS's very existence, and the collection and its caretakers are integral to the institution's continuing success.

Administrators generally identified and communicated first with potential, high-profile donors, but I learned that excellent customer service is also important in fund-raising. We never know when a new donor might walk through our door to begin a research project. On more than one occasion, patrons became monetary supporters because they recognized a need while conducting research. The greatest example of a patron turned Research Center donor began with a simple visit to our reading room to conduct research on a historic neighborhood. During his first visit, the patron requested a color photocopy, but our facility was not equipped with a color photocopier. He was otherwise impressed with his visit, and soon after, we received a check in the mail to purchase a color photocopy machine. After further engagement with this patron and discussion about a mutual concern for painting conservation, he funded two major conservation projects and established an endowment fund that today ensures an annual collections conservation budget. This experience underscored for Research Center staff and administrators the importance of excellent customer service and the potential for developing relationships with Research Center supporters. These relationships can be more challenging to cultivate, but the outcome can be remarkably impactful for the division.

Outreach and Education

The words *outreach* and *education* were not listed in my job description. However, there were a few elements included, such as presenting special programs and instructional activities to extend our services and facilities across the state, managing in-house exhibits, and administering incoming and outgoing loans of collection materials. With a small staff committed to many other priority activities related mostly to collections care and public service, it was challenging to ensure adequate time for additional outreach and educational activities. At a minimum, we offered on-site orientations for a variety of classes and groups, administered exhibition loans, and developed and prepared three or four small, in-house exhibitions per year.

Outreach and education were areas where I hoped to increase Research Center staff involvement. However, with limited capacity and competing demands, it was challenging to carve out the necessary time. Ultimately, the question became, What activity could we give up or reduce in order to create more time for this increasingly important enterprise? Or how could we incorporate outreach into existing activities? We were expected to carry out the tasks outlined in our job descriptions, and anything outside those tasks required prior planning and approval from administration. Prioritizing managerial tasks was not always easy and often required a strategy for triaging incoming requests that were usually deadline driven. In a hierarchical management structure, requests from the top generally took priority, and others were prioritized based on time sensitivity and could sometimes be delegated to other staff when appropriate.

Our programs, education, and communications staff worked closely with the Research Center staff to develop project and program opportunities to engage new users and create awareness about our collections. With the help of other divisions, we were more proactive in our efforts. Other divisions largely took the lead on projects, and we supported these activities as the collection specialists. Our support included identifying and digitizing collection materials for regular articles and social media, and pulling collection materials and assisting with in-person and virtual student and teacher-training visits. Because Research Center staff were less involved in planning these activities, we sometimes had less input and ownership of the final product. However, these cooperative efforts helped support important institutional objectives while expending less Research Center staff time.

GHS's programs division also administered a statewide Affiliate Chapter Program. This program offered resources to nearly two hundred local historical organizations around the state of Georgia.[9] As part of this network, affiliate members may engage GHS archivists to visit their organization to survey collections, provide needs assessments, or present educational sessions on various topics related to collections care and access. These visits extended GHS's reach, assisted smaller organizations in securing support from their leadership, and helped improve collections care and access statewide.

Professional Development

I was promoted to the Research Center director position in 2012 after serving several years as the senior archivist at GHS. Before joining GHS, I worked at academic institutions and at a for-profit company as an archivist/records manager consultant. This was my first management position, and I was unsure what the transition to management would entail. I understood the assigned duties of the director position and was confident in my ability to perform the tasks required of the position. Also, I had previous experience in several areas of the job description and had worked with strong archival leaders in past positions. However, there was no in-house management training offered to help in the transition. Essentially, I served as the senior archivist one day and the director of the Research Center the next. It was clear that simply holding the director position did not somehow endow me with the leadership skills I needed to be successful. To be effective in this new position, I needed to seek training and educational opportunities outside my institution to help bolster the knowledge and experience I had already gained.

While historical societies do not always have the necessary resources to fully support professional development activities, professional development was a component of my job description and was expected by administration on some level. As in many positions, professional development is not well-defined and is largely left up to the individual. I was not given a professional development budget, so requests were funded on a case-by-case basis by administration as funding allowed. Professional development leave was always granted for approved requests, but the level of financial support varied from no support to partial and occasionally full financial support. Professional development is important in any position, but for someone like me, in a small institution without immediate access to a larger network of colleagues, it was vital. In my experience, the best way to ensure at least partial funding of requests was to demonstrate a strong institutional need for the training or workshop, or, if requesting support to attend a conference, to highlight your participation on a panel or on a committee.

My involvement in local and regional groups, particularly the Society of Georgia Archivists (SGA), provided unending opportunities for the growth and development of my own abilities and skills, which affected positive change in my institution. I served on the board of SGA for six consecutive years as mentoring program co-chair, director, vice president, president, and past president. Regional organizations like SGA provide a nurturing and collaborative environment to practice skills like administering budgets, committee and project management, setting agendas, managing meetings, and public speaking. In addition, it allowed for networking with professionals in geographically diverse areas. In fact, more than one collaborative grant project idea was born when casual conversation commenced after the adjournment of a meeting.

Another important professional development opportunity was the Archives Leadership Institute (ALI).[10] I was fortunate to participate in this valuable program as a member of the 2014 cohort. ALI is a grant-funded, weeklong leadership intensive. The program provides advanced training to archives leaders with a goal to positively effect change in the archival profession. The program helps leaders identify personal strengths and weaknesses and to identify institutional assets and determine how to best utilize them. ALI helped me develop a greater understanding about the importance of advocacy—not just outside my institution, but also internally. I also developed skills in "asset thinking," or looking at assets instead of needs, and understanding and leveraging affinities.[11] Most importantly, we identified our leadership strengths and areas for future growth.

I recognized that I would never have all of the answers, and I did not want to limit the capacity of my institution to better care for collections, provide enhanced access, or otherwise improve operations due to my lack of knowledge. It was critical to keep up-to-date on archival standards and advancements as much as possible in order to move the institution forward and ensure my own success as a leader, even if it meant that I must fund certain professional development opportunities out of my own pocket. I occasionally sought training in areas even if the institution was not yet positioned to implement a desired project. This allowed time for advanced planning, so that I could be prepared to implement when funding was available.

I also advocated for professional development requests submitted by other Research Center staff. It was important to facilitate the growth and skill building of staff members to strengthen individual team members and the Research Center division as a whole. Also, to encourage staff to remain up-to-date on professional literature, we maintained recent journals from professional organizations like SAA and the American Library Association in a readily accessible location and allowed time during the workday for all staff to review.

Other Duties As Assigned

We've all got them. No one mentions these tasks in library school, and they do not necessarily appear on our job description. They are more varied and likely more frequent in small institutions with fewer resources. For example, without regular, on-site cleaning staff, tasks sometimes included replenishing paper products in restrooms or the break room, carpet sweeping the reading room, sweeping and dusting collection storage areas, and other tasks associated with keeping a well-maintained facility.

The Research Center facility includes Hodgson Hall, opened in 1876, and the Abrahams Annex, built in 1970. Facilities management was not listed as a major component of my position, but I spent time almost daily on facility-related concerns including climate control monitoring, landscaping, electrical, furniture, equipment, and other related tasks. This activity was fundamental to the preservation of our collections and the health and safety of our staff, and it was vital to make time for facilities-related work even on busy days with competing priorities. Facilities tasks included working directly with vendors such as security and fire alarm services, electricians, plumbers, roofers, restoration specialists, HVAC companies, and pest control services. With the exception of our public reading room, all areas in the facility were secure, staff-only areas, which meant that staff had to accompany all vendors when they were on-site. Some vendors required a monthly time commitment, and others conducted quarterly maintenance and inspections. This position demanded a hands-on approach to ensure that facilities tasks were completed in a timely manner. In addition to identifying issues, I was also prepared to assess and fix some issues, from changing light bulbs to resetting HVAC components, the elevator, burglar alarms, and fire alarms, and accessing all areas in the buildings on any given day, including the attic and rooftop.

Emergency preparedness, response, and recovery were other functions of my position that were not included in my job description. These duties should be included in all archival management position descriptions as they are critical to the preservation and security of the collections and the overall success of the institution. We had a comprehensive disaster and recovery plan that covered many types of disasters, both major and minor. The plan was updated annually by me and a designee from our administrative division, and we reviewed the plan each year with the entire staff. Twice in recent years, we implemented our disaster plan in preparation for hurricanes threatening our coast; in times of impending disaster, preparation was the priority and took precedence over all other job functions. We also participated in a local group, Savannah Heritage Emergency Response, which is one of twenty-six cooperative disaster networks around the nation launched after Alliance for Response forums.[12] These groups provide a venue to get to know your local first responders, and, more importantly, they ensure that first responders know you, your collections, and your facilities. These important partnerships, coupled with a detailed disaster plan and staff who were trained in implementing the plan, helped ensure the long-term preservation of our collections.

Conclusion

The endemic challenge of working in a smaller, nonprofit institution was that we simply did not have the resources for a state-of-the-art facility or the ability to fund all positions necessary to keep up with growing demands. In an environment where staff members work to carry out daily assigned tasks, address legacy issues, and take on new projects and programs to remain relevant, time is at a premium. It can be frustrating to work in a chaotic atmosphere where we must sometimes be reactive rather than proactive on important matters. Flexibility and the ability to effectively balance competing demands were two qualities that played an important role in successfully managing an archives in this environment. A willingness to take on new and unfamiliar responsibilities was also required to be successful.

I recognized that my leadership ability was the key to moving the Research Center forward. I am a proponent of leading by example, and as the individual ultimately responsible for the staff, collections, and facility, it was vital to stay fully engaged in the activities of the division. Ongoing engagement included rolling up my sleeves and pitching in where needed, holding regular meetings with staff, and otherwise keeping up-to-date on all activities related to the work of the Research Center. In good times and bad, leaders take responsibility for the actions of their team and must be prepared to answer to administrators when issues arise.

I learned that leadership goes beyond accountability. We set the tone for our team and stakeholders both inside and outside our institution. We must not only remain motivated, but also motivate our team. Individuals are motivated in different ways, so situational thinking is important in determining the best way to navigate each unique situation. If we simply treat staff as we wish to be treated, there will be fewer motivation and morale problems. Also, staff who are motivated will excel in performing their duties. An administrator once asked a Research Center supporter what they liked most about me, and the supporter replied that they could tell that I cared. When we are enthusiastic about what we do and advocate for the work of our institution (and our profession), people notice. Stakeholders will support an institution with passionate staff and leaders who believe in and care about what they do.[13]

Like archives leaders in other types of archival repositories, I had many responsibilities and had to manage a demanding workload while working effectively with administrators, senior managers, staff, and other partners. Our decisions impact a diverse assortment of stakeholders, all with different relationships and connections to the institution, including researchers, funders, collection donors, members, board members, and the larger community. In an environment with minimal resources, it was essential to identify assets and determine how they could best be utilized to strengthen the institution. We must seek opportunities for collaboration and partnership in an effort to add value to our collections and services and better connect users with our resources.

Managing a historical society archives is not the right fit for everyone, but for the right person, there is a tremendous opportunity for professional growth and development. We are not paid at the same level as our counterparts in other archives sectors, and there can be less job stability. However, successfully navigating the challenges that a historical society presents can be very rewarding. We may not be experts in every area of responsibility, so we must be willing to learn and grow. Given administrative support, and with a collaborative approach, motivated leaders can make a great impact on their institutions.

NOTES

1.   Albert S. Britt, *Overture to the Future at the Georgia Historical Society* (Savannah: Georgia Historical Society, 1974), 10, 12–13.

2.   "Board of Curators," Georgia Historical Society, http://georgiahistory.com/about-ghs/board-of-curators/, captured at https://perma.cc/P3QF-3SHA.

3.   Michael J. Kurtz, *Managing Archival and Manuscript Repositories*, Archival Fundamentals Series II (Chicago: Society of American Archivists, 2004), 38.

4.   Larry J. Hackman, *Many Happy Returns: Advocacy and the Development of Archives* (Chicago: Society of American Archivists, 2011), 12.

5.   G. Edward Evans, Patricia Layzell Ward, and Bendik Rugaas, *Management Basics for Information Professionals* (New York: Neal-Schuman, 2000), 57.

6.   Kurtz, *Managing Archival and Manuscript Repositories*, 116.

7.   "Location, Hours, and What to Bring," Georgia Historical Society, https://georgiahistory.com/research-the-collection/visiting-the-library-archives-hodgson-hall/, captured at https://perma.cc/3UB6-GU2P.

8.   "Georgia History Festival," Georgia Historical Society, https://georgiahistoryfestival.org/, captured at https://perma.cc/EG7J-5J8A.

9.   "Affiliate Chapter Program," Georgia Historical Society, http://georgiahistory.com/education-outreach/affiliate-chapter-program/, captured at https://perma.cc/SX5S-W26S.

10.   "Archives Leadership Institute," ALI: Archives Leadership Institute, https://www.archivesleadershipinstitute.org/, captured at https://perma.cc/VEQ6-N8FZ.

11.   "Luther K. Snow: Asset Mapping," Luther Snow: Assets for the Good in Groups, http://www.luthersnow.com/uploads/PDF_File_73102809.pdf, captured at https://perma.cc/6DM3-YNXG.

12.   "Alliance for Response Networks," Foundation of the American Institute for Conservation of Historic and Artistic Works, http://www.heritageemergency.org/initiatives/alliance-for-response/networks/, captured at https://perma.cc/2NQ7-8CMM.

13.   Evans, Ward, and Rugaas, *Management Basics for Information Professionals*, 355–56.

Management and Leadership in a Nonprofit Archives: A Lone Arranger, New Professional Perspective

Samantha Norling

Introduction

In the early years of a professional archivist's career, the foundation is laid that determines what type of manager and leader the archivist will be within that institution, in the broader archival profession, and as a representative of the profession to nonarchives audiences. This is particularly true for those archivists who find themselves recently out of graduate school and in their first professional position with management responsibilities in a young institutional archives program. While there is clear value to the lessons that can be learned from archivists with decades in the field, the experiences of early career archivists as they establish themselves and grow archival programs within their institutions can also provide valuable insights and unique perspectives into archival leadership and management. In this chapter, I will identify six elements for successful management and leadership of a nonprofit archives program and then reflect on my past three years as a new professional archivist managing an institutional archives program in a large art museum, using those six elements as a framework.

In just over three years in my first professional position as the primary manager of the Indianapolis Museum of Art (IMA) Archives, much of my experience in and still-developing philosophies about archival management and leadership have been shaped by the art museum environment in which I work. Though this chapter will be full of examples gleaned from my time as the IMA archivist, many of the situations I will describe are not unique to the museum environment or even to the nonprofit world; they can have applications for archivists with management responsibilities in a variety of settings. As well as representing the experience of museum and nonprofit archivists, my management and leadership approaches are often influenced by my placement as a lone arranger archivist in a small institutional archives program, which will give this chapter particular significance for other lone arranger archivists responsible for their program's success.

Management versus Leadership

In preparation for writing this chapter, I took the opportunity to revisit archival literature and introduce myself to literature from other fields on the topics of leadership and management. While I will not be providing a detailed literature review, there were a few takeaways that shaped my thinking around management and leadership in relation to my experience at the IMA and my understanding of nonprofit archives in general.

The distinction between managing and leading was particularly important to me as I organized my thoughts. What struck me about the authors writing about management was their tendency to define *management* in terms of functions and the elements necessary for a complete archival program. In *Managing Institutional Archives*, Richard Cox provides a list of the "essential elements for managing institutional archives":

- mission statement;
- adequate financial resources;
- written procedures for caring for the archival records;
- professional archivists;
- in-service and continuing education commitment;
- adequate facility for storage and use of archival records;
- and cooperative programs with other archival operations.[1]

Cox was not alone in associating management primarily with the basic needs and functions of archival programs, as this was a common theme when authors discussed management in an archival context.[2] Extrapolating from this association, the definition of a successfully managed archives program would be a program that has all of the above elements in place. While this statement is not untrue, adding characteristics of good leadership into the equation provides a more complete picture of what it takes to establish an archival program that not only exists but also thrives.

In contrast to the association of archival management with an archives programs' basic needs and functions, archival leadership was often defined in terms of actions, with an emphasis on vision, change, and relationship building. This distinction introduces a more human element into considerations of what makes a successful archives program. Often, leadership was positioned as a necessary complement to good management practices.[3] Bruce W. Dearstyne succinctly expressed this relationship between management and leadership in *Leading and Managing Archives and Records Programs* when he stated, "Management—getting the job done effectively and the service or product delivered reliably—is difficult enough, but leadership is of a different magnitude because it involves moving the program from its present status toward a new (hopefully better) state of affairs."[4]

When considering these writings, it became clear to me that both management and leadership skills are essential when creating and expanding successful archives programs. With both, an archivist would have the ability to not only craft policies and procedures and secure adequate funding, facilities, and staffing necessary for a functioning archival program but also increase the relevance and the perceived and actual importance of the archives program within the home institution, adding to the capacities of the program in the process. Good archival leadership can also transcend the institutional context. Archives program managers with the ability to lead have the potential to establish their programs as models for the field. Archival leaders also play a significant role in furthering the profession and, by taking their message outside our professional circles, can even improve understanding and the perceived importance of archives and archival work among nonarchives audiences.

My approach to the rest of this chapter will be to explore the relationship between management and leadership as described above in the context of a nonprofit institution's archives program. First, I will outline those elements that make up a successfully managed archives program in a nonprofit setting and include suggestions for leadership approaches to fortifying those elements in a new program. To place those elements in context, the founding and six-year history of the IMA Archives program will serve as my primary case study of a nonprofit archives program. In the case study, I will explore both the management decisions that went into the program's creation, as well as the ways that relationship building and strategic visioning have contributed to the growth of the IMA Archives—both in terms of resource allocation and the perceived importance of the program within the institution. While most of the examples in this chapter will be derived from my experience as the lone archivist at the IMA, it is my hope that this chapter will have broad application in a variety of archival contexts.

Elements of Nonprofit Archives Management and Leadership

Institutional archives programs have been established in a wide variety of nonprofit organizations. Churches, charities, public hospitals, schools, professional associations, labor unions, and both private and public museums are just some that come to mind. It is unlikely that any two nonprofit archives programs will look exactly alike, as there are many variable factors and institutional circumstances that impact the founding of an archives program. In the spirit of Richard Cox, I have identified what I consider to be the essential elements for managing and leading nonprofit archives, which together provide a solid foundation and identity for a new nonprofit archives program:

- institutional mandates and reason for founding
- placement within the organizational structure
- professional staffing
- funding and facilities
- institutional alignment
- audience identification and inreach/outreach

While each of these elements will look different within the context of an individual archives program, some generalizations can be made to gain a better understanding of what each element could look like in the creation and ongoing management of a fully functioning nonprofit archives. Each element builds on the previous, and the successful archives manager and leader will be able to evaluate and define each in turn through policies, procedures, and initiatives while advocating for and securing needed resources from the home institution. When considered together, the six elements can aid in evaluating the strength of the archives program in terms of its alignment with both institutional priorities and professional standards. A new nonprofit archives program can be considered fully functioning once all six elements are completely defined and supported by the archives' organization.

Institutional mandates and reason for founding

What sets nonprofit archives apart from most other types of archives is that they are often established within organizations that do not set the preservation of historical records as a priority, unlike in a library or historical society setting. For most nonprofits, there is also no clear legal mandate for preserving historical records in a formal archives program with professional staff, as is the case for government archives guided by records laws. Faced with this reality, it falls to the nonprofit archives program manager—ideally a professional archivist—to be creative in management and leadership of the archives. In this environment, it is crucial for the archivist to establish standard archival policies and procedures that will become the needed institution-wide mandate for depositing records created by staff, executives, and others as determined by the collecting scope.

Lacking the institutional priority or legal mandate to preserve institutional records, there are a variety of reasons that nonprofits establish formal archives programs. The most common reason is an upcoming anniversary or commemoration for which the institution hopes to leverage its historical documents and artifacts. In other cases, a nonprofit archives program may be established in conjunction with a significant change in the organization, such as a move to a new building or the establishment of a new division within the organization. These are events that have the potential to bring to light or trigger the production of a significant amount of documentation that requires a level of management and care that exceeds the capacities of existing record-keeping practices or facilities.

These initial reasons for founding an archives can influence the perceived "purpose" of the program among executives and other staff at the institution. Because the initial push for founding an archives program in a nonprofit rarely encompasses the full scope of the program's activities and needs once it is up and running, it is important for an archives manager to be able to evaluate the perceived purpose of the archives among stakeholders and users, which often varies from person to person and tends to change over time. In so doing, the archives' manager can take action to change any misperceptions that may linger as the program becomes more established.

Placement within the organizational structure

The location of an archives program within a nonprofit can vary wildly from organization to organization, depending on a variety of factors. One of the greatest determinants of placement is whether or not the organization already has an existing unit whose purpose has some alignment or convergence with archival activities. For example, a nonprofit with an active research branch or learning center may situate the institutional archives within that unit. In that arrangement, the archives would serve as an additional resource to support the research activities of its staff and other users.[5] In a museum setting, there are often multiple potential units in which an archives could find a home. The most common are within a research library or as part of the registration department, which is staffed by information professionals who manage the museum collections. If a nonprofit already has a records management program or a department that has significant records management responsibilities, an archives could be founded as an extension of those existing activities.

Another significant factor in determining the placement of an archives program within a nonprofit is the primary purpose of the archives at the time of its founding. As discussed above, nonprofit archives are often founded in anticipation of significant anniversaries or commemorations. If this is the case, the primary purpose of the archives for the organization at that time is to utilize archival holdings for both public and internal celebrations of a specific person, event, or the broad history of the organization. This initial purpose aligns the archives with marketing activities and may result in the placement of the archives within the marketing department.[6] Similarly, an archives program could be founded within a development department if founded as part of a major capital campaign.

Though it may seem that the placement of an archives would not need to be revisited by managers once the program is founded, it is not uncommon in a nonprofit setting to see significant restructuring of individual divisions or the entire organization on occasion.[7] This reality may be more common for nonprofit and corporate archives than for those in an institution where the archives serves a core function, such as in a library or historical society setting. A successful archives manager and leader should be able to anticipate or even initiate these potential shifts and leverage a reorganization to improve the placement of the archives program within the institution. The manager should also be mindful of how a shift in placement within the organizational structure could potentially impact staffing levels if full- and part-time employees may also find themselves relocated.

Professional staffing

As in any archival setting, the ideal staff of an institutional archives would include at least one full-time professional archivist. Unfortunately, this is not always the case for new archives programs in nonprofits, which can sometimes be managed by volunteers, part-time employees, or employees with no background in archives who have had archival duties added to their existing responsibilities. An archivist joining an existing nonprofit archives as the first manager with professional training in the field should consider the evaluation and revision of existing policies and procedures as a top priority. This review will provide an opportunity to align the archives program with professional standards that may not have been followed previously. For lone arranger archivists, ensuring institutional support for continuing education is crucial both for the professional development of the archivist and for keeping the program compliant with professional standards.

New nonprofit archivists may find that their direct supervisor does not have a solid understanding of the purpose and needs of an archives program, let alone the benefits that it could provide to the organization. For this reason, it is important to communicate basic archival principles and practices to the supervisor early on to establish a common vocabulary and lay a solid foundation for discussions of the archives program. Similarly, it is important in this situation to meet with colleagues representing a variety of departments. This may very well be the first time that some staff members have ever met an archivist or been asked to deposit their records in an archives. The reality is that staff impressions of their institution's archivist can affect their likelihood to comply with records policies and collaborate with or rely on the archives for their project needs. In a nonarchival institution, the archivist ends up representing the archives program in the minds of staff, executives, and other users within the organization, which makes relationship building essential. This may seem like a significant challenge in the beginning, but a successful archives manager and leader will recognize that most meetings or one-on-one interactions with other staff members and executives could be an opportunity to raise awareness of the archives. It is not uncommon for everyday interactions to reveal new ways in which the archivist or the archival collections can support ongoing activities of the institution.

Many archivists working in a nonprofit setting are lone arrangers, working as the only archivist in a nonarchival institution.[8] This poses an added challenge for archives managers in gaining recognition and securing resources for the archives. Effective communication skills are crucial for small department managers, as is the ability to form a vision for the archives that aligns with institutional priorities. Until the archives manager demonstrates the relevance of the archives by contributing to high-priority projects and/or helping to meet institution-wide goals, it is unlikely that the manager will be given the opportunity to increase the permanent staffing levels. Even temporary, grant-funded positions may not be an option if the archives is not considered a priority, as grant writers and development departments within nonprofits often have to prioritize the number and types of grants that they apply for each year. As the archives competes with other departments for the opportunity to pursue grants, the perceived relevance of the program and proposed projects becomes even more important, as it can affect both staffing and funding opportunities.

Funding and facilities

Along with adequate human resources in the form of at least one professional archivist, an archives manager should work to secure enough financial and physical resources from the institution to support basic archival functions. Budgets in nonprofits are generally set on an annual basis, which means that an archives manager will need to anticipate the needs of the archives at least one year out, and even further in advance if a larger funding request will need to be made. Regardless of the particulars involved in the budgeting process, it is important for an archives manager to be able to "speak the language of funding managers" and understand what Paul C. Lasewicz has referred to as the "strategic motivations of senior executives"—something that institutional archivists of all kinds may struggle with.[9] As with many of the other elements discussed here, this requires that the archivist maintain a solid understanding of current institutional priorities, with particular emphasis on those that raise revenue. While archives are not traditionally big revenue earners when compared to other departments, their ability to support the activities of revenue-generating departments and projects could provide the leverage needed to successfully advocate for additional funding for the archives program. This would also aid the archivist in avoiding painful budget cuts. Archival managers should maintain detailed information about how previous years' funding was utilized, coupled with usage statistics and examples of fiscal impact that the program has made. Both can serve as leverage when the annual budget cycle begins.[10]

Closely related to the topic of funding is the provision of adequate facilities for the archives, including enough office space to accommodate staff and any interns or volunteers. This space should be outfitted with any necessary furniture and equipment and include dedicated spaces for working, such as a processing area. Typically, a greater investment on the part of the home institution must be made in regards to adequate facilities for the storage of archival material. This requires not only enough space for the current holdings but also room for growth, and in an environment that supports the long-term preservation of those records (i.e., space that is secure as well as temperature- and humidity-controlled).

In a nonprofit setting, it is not uncommon for archival storage conditions to fall short of professional standards. When this is the case, an archives manager should be able to evaluate whether the existing facilities can be made to work and what the best way to do so is, in order to build up to professional standards. A strategic archivist will be able to identify or create opportunities to expand the space dedicated to the archives or to improve on the conditions. This opportunity may come up when a building renovation or office rearrangement is being planned. In order to take advantage of those opportunities, archivists need to be proactive and not reactive; direct supervisors and relevant executives should be aware of the archives' needs *before* the opportunity arises, to allow them to factor the archives into special budget and facility considerations.

Institutional alignment

Of the six elements for managing and leading a nonprofit archives program, perhaps none is more important than institutional alignment. It is this element that makes it possible for an archives manager to more successfully advocate for the other elements discussed above. Institutional alignment is the degree to which the archives program reflects and supports the current and long-term strategic priorities, goals, and activities of the institution. The greater the alignment, the more success an archives manager will have in making the case that the archives program not only requires but deserves a continuing investment from the institution.

To bring the archives program into alignment requires a deep understanding of the institution's mission and current priorities and a knowledge of the ways in which each department is working to accomplish both. The ability of the archives manager to develop a vision for the archives that supports that mission and the activities of other departments, and then to articulate that vision in such a way that earns the support of others, requires interpersonal and communication skills that exceed basic management responsibilities and extend into the realm of leadership. A deep understanding of an institution's mission and activities grows over time, but this growth can be furthered by embedding the archivist where appropriate, such as through participating on task forces, attending interdepartmental meetings, and developing an active records management program that requires regular contact with departments and discussions of their documentary output.

Institutional archivists are in a unique position within their parent organization in that their work not only brings them into contact with all departments and staff from those units but also makes them experts with regard to the functions—and by extension the needs—of those units and their staff. This is necessary in order to set short- and long-term goals for the archives that align with the institutional priorities, but it also puts the archivist in an important position to serve as a change agent in the institution. By recommending cross-departmental or even organization-wide changes or new initiatives, the archivist can become a more vital member in the workings of the institution, improving on both the perceived and actual importance of the archives program in institutional operations.

Audience identification and inreach/outreach

For archivists working within a nonprofit institution and charged with preserving the organization's records, the primary users of the archival collections are almost always the staff, executives, and stakeholders within the institution itself. Depending on the nature of the archival records transferred to the archives, an archivist may find that the majority of the holdings must remain closed to outside researchers. This may be necessary in order to protect proprietary information and institutional assets as well as the privacy of the institution's donors and staff. While this may challenge an archivist's inclination toward open access to information, there are often sound fiscal and legal reasons to keep those materials restricted to general staff or specific departments, and the institutional archives manager should work to understand and follow those precedents.

As a result of the generally closed nature of records held in institutional archives, outreach in this context tends to look more like "inreach," with a focus on internal audiences. Inreach can take many forms, and it is up to archives managers to be strategic in utilizing their knowledge of the priorities and activities of various departments to communicate the ways in which archives can provide support to specific initiatives. This approach allows a nonprofit archivist to increase the internal user base and, by extension, the relevance and recognition of the program within the organization. Complementary to this approach, a nonprofit archivist must consider regular education of staff and executives as the greatest form of inreach, whether it be through scheduled trainings or chance conversations in the hallway, where appropriate. Elizabeth Yakel put it best when she said, "Education is a continuous, cumulative, exhausting, and rewarding process . . . All other achievements, indeed the strength of the entire program, hinge on instructing the institution's employees and managers about the potential role and benefits of an archives."[11]

While institutional records make up the majority, if not all, of the holdings of nonprofit archives, some programs collect related manuscript and other special collections, as determined by the collecting policy. These may be the papers of former board members or donors, or archival collections on subjects relating to the work of the home institution. For nonprofit archives that accept collections from external sources, a fully formed marketing strategy must include both inreach and outreach components to speak to all potential audiences. Outreach to external users will resemble traditional archival outreach common in other settings. The challenge to nonprofit archives managers in this regard is not the consideration of how to reach external audiences, but rather how to balance those outreach activities and the needs of external users with organizational inreach and the needs of internal users. Prioritizing external users and raising the public profile of the archives by ignoring internal audiences may endanger the status of the archives as an institutional priority,[12] compromising the ability of the archives manager to build a strong program with all of the elements described above.

Archival Management and Leadership in the Art Museum

As I begin my fourth year as archivist at the IMA, writing this chapter has given me the opportunity to look back and reflect on the ongoing evolution of my management and leadership styles as an early career, lone arranger archivist in a nonprofit setting. My predecessor, the IMA's first archivist, laid a solid foundation for the new program by writing and implementing a variety of policies and procedures, creating collection-, box-, and/or folder-level inventories for most of the archival hold-ings, and managing the first year of a two-year-long NEH grant to digitize our most significant col-lection. As my knowledge of the IMA grew, I found myself more purposefully setting priorities and pursuing new initiatives to increase the capacities, visibility, and relevance of the archives program. These new priorities and initiatives gave me the opportunity to both advance and strategically divert from the path set by my predecessor for the benefit of the archives program.

The Indianapolis Museum of Art is an encyclopedic art museum located near downtown Indianapolis, Indiana. The museum's 152-acre campus includes the Virginia B. Fairbanks Art and Nature Park and the historic Oldfields estate of the Lilly House and Gardens. Since 2009 the IMA has also stewarded the Miller House and Garden property in Columbus, Indiana. The main museum building includes two theaters, event spaces, staff offices, and a library, along with the storage and gallery spaces where the permanent collection of artwork resides. While the IMA was founded more than 130 years ago as the Art Association of Indianapolis, the IMA Archives was not formally established until 2010, when the museum hired its first archivist.[13]

The archives is the primary repository for institutional records of all types, in both physical and digital formats. The IMA Archives is also home to archival collections documenting notable indi-viduals, art communities, collectors, and artists in Indiana—many with direct ties to the history of the museum and its collections. The primary users of the archives are IMA staff members, though many of the records and manuscript collections are open to external researchers. For the past three years, I have served as the institution's second lone arranger archivist—my first professional posi-tion after graduate school. To place the six elements for managing and leading nonprofit archives in context, the founding and six-year history of the IMA Archives will serve as a case study. As I share some of the most notable experiences from my time with the IMA Archives that relate to the six elements, I will discuss both the management decisions that went into the program's foundation, as well as the ways that relationship building and strategic visioning have contributed to the growth of the IMA Archives.

Institutional mandates and reasons for founding

The establishment of an IMA archives program had been advocated by librarians and registrars for years, gaining momentum in the lead-up to the institution's 125th anniversary in 2008. In anticipation of that yearlong celebration, and as archival holdings grew to a capacity that could no longer be managed by the registrars on top of their regular duties, an IMA Archives Start-Up Committee was formed. The committee sought advice and consultations from local archivists and paper conservators. With their guidance, the committee pursued two grants in 2007 that would support initial start-up costs for the IMA Archives, including the hiring of a professional archivist for two years. Unfortunately, neither application was successful.

Two years later, the IMA staff who had been championing the archives cause had the final push needed to secure institutional support from executives. When the Miller family gifted their iconic midcentury modern property to the museum in 2009, a considerably large archival collection doc-umenting the design, construction, decoration, and maintenance of the home and landscape was also transferred to the museum. The historical significance of the archival collection was undeni-able, but within the context of institutional priorities and resource allocation, the initial return on the IMA's investment in hiring its first professional archivist, budgeting for supplies, and allocating space to the archives came when the archival collection was inventoried and made available to aid in the historic preservation, interpretation, and marketing of the midcentury property.

The nature of museums as cultural heritage organizations makes this type of nonprofit one of the more likely to establish and maintain institutional archives programs. Within the context of a museum, the institutional archives can serve the mission of responsible stewardship of the museum collection, as well as the advancement of scholarship through publication and educational programming. However, the professional museum community has no external standards mandating that a museum establish a formal archives program. The proper care and management of records has always been part of the American Alliance of Museums (AAM) accreditation process,[14] but the requirement is not that the museum have an established program with a professional records manager or archivist. What the accreditation review process is primarily concerned with are the procedures set and carried out by museum registrars in caring for the permanent collection, not all institutional records broadly.[15]

Placement within the organizational structure

For the IMA Archives, the placement within the museum's organizational chart could have gone one of two ways: under the Registration Department, which had been responsible for the management of historical institutional records up to that point, or the Stout Reference Library, which was one of the smallest but oldest departments in the institution, serving a curatorial research function.[16] Either possibility would have had a major impact on the culture and priorities of the archives program. Ultimately, the IMA Archives and the archivist position were combined with the library to form the Library & Archives Department. This placed scholarship and research at the center of the archival mission, prioritizing access to the records for "the administrative support of current museum activities, the successful stewardship of the IMA collections, and for historical research conducted by staff and the public."[17]

The IMA Archives has already experienced a major shift in organizational placement in the six years since its founding. When the program was established, the Library & Archives Department was situated under the management of a chief information officer (CIO) at a time when technology-based projects and innovation were a priority for the institution. With this priority, my predecessor was encouraged to apply for a National Endowment for the Humanities (NEH) digitization grant. Though the grant application was successful, the CIO who encouraged the application left soon after the award was announced, leading to an organizational restructuring that set the stage for my first major challenge as an archives manager.

By the time I began working at the IMA, the archives had a new placement within the institution as part of the new Audience Engagement division. This division is primarily responsible for public programming and the museum's interpretative functions. Institutional priorities had also shifted from technological innovation to attracting and creating "exceptional experiences"[18] for new audiences, with an emphasis on in-person programming.[19] Within this context, I was still responsible for managing the completion of the two-year-long digitization grant. It became clear to me early on that the original plan from the grant application to deliver the collection online through our Archon portal was no longer a viable option, as the addition of thousands of digital objects was causing the system to freeze with increasing frequency. Though I was a new addition to the project team and only a few months into my first professional position, I understood that if

I didn't advocate for the success of this project on behalf of the archives, there was nobody else in the institution with a reason to do so.

This realization was a major turning point for me as a new professional in my first management position, as it solidified my sense of responsibility for the archives program and reputation and pushed me to assert that responsibility. I immediately brought my concerns to my supervisor, making the case that the user experience would be significantly compromised in the Archon environment and emphasizing our responsibility to NEH to deliver a quality online collection. The high visibility and publicity surrounding the receipt of the grant in 2012 gave us the leverage needed to garner support from our department head and museum director. As a solution, the archives was able to collaborate with the IMA Lab to migrate the digital images and metadata to the museum-wide digital asset management system (DAMS) and to create what became the Digital Archives Portal.[20]

The result of my first foray into asserting myself as manager of and advocate for the archives program was more than I could have anticipated. First, the migration to the new DAMS opened up new avenues of convergence between the archival collections and the museum's permanent collection of artwork. Second, the Digital Archives Portal was very well received across the design, museum, and archives communities and will continue to support the online delivery of digitized IMA Archives content online into the foreseeable future. As an archives manager and leader, this experience has given me the confidence to take on challenges as they come up, with the knowledge that there is always the possibility to turn a challenge into an opportunity.

Professional staffing

When I joined the IMA as its archivist, the Library & Archives Department had only two full-time staff members, me and the head of Libraries & Archives.[21] The low staffing level for the department was the result of a period of layoffs that the IMA had gone through about a year before I joined the staff, and many departments were still feeling the effects of that downsizing. With no opportunities to expand staffing levels on the horizon, but with a significant amount of work that still needed to be accomplished, I felt some pressure to utilize volunteers or interns to complete projects. As a recent graduate who had been in school and then entered the job market in a depressed economy, I had witnessed and heard about many troubling employment, volunteer, and internship practices in the archives field.[22] As a result, the idea of relying on unpaid labor for certain projects, even those that did not require professional skills, did not sit well with me. In addition, my perception was that, within a nonprofit organization where resources are scarce and the archives is one small program among many, avoiding the use of volunteer and unpaid internship labor would help to prevent resource allocators from conflating the value of those positions with the value of professional archives staff and the archives program in general. For these reasons, I did not pursue the creation of an intern position until the opportunity presented itself to make it a paid position.

Soon after I started working at the IMA, the Library & Archives Department received a generous directed donation to support the ongoing work of our staff and care of our collections, to be used at the discretion of the Head of Libraries & Archives. Since we were a two-person department, my opinion was sought as to potential uses of the money. The possibility of finding the resources to support a paid internship position had been on my mind, so I shared my thoughts with my supervisor. The graduate public history program that I had come out of at

Indiana University—Indianapolis is widely recognized for its progressive internship program that places students in Indianapolis-area historical and cultural heritage organizations for yearlong, part-time internships funded through a cost share with host institutions. The cost to hosts goes directly to providing interns with monthly stipends, a set number of paid course credits per year, and health insurance—all managed by the university's human resources department. Luckily, this use fell within the scope of the donated funds, and my supervisor agreed to host an intern who would work primarily on archives projects while providing general help in the library. Three years later, we are currently hosting our third public history graduate intern, and we have seen the mutual benefits to both our department and the interns every year.[23]

By sharing this experience, I hope that other archives managers will recognize that advocating for students and new professionals within our repositories by creating paid internship opportunities, part-time positions tailored for students, or truly entry-level jobs for recent graduates of archival programs has implications that extend beyond our repositories. Where compensation is not possible, there are ways to construct and design meaningful internship opportunities that do not devalue our work but instead raise it up as a combination of both skills and knowledge that can only be learned at the highest level through purposeful mentorship. We will all benefit when this becomes the dominant perception, and lone arranger and small-shop archival programs stand to gain the most.

Funding and facilities

For the last couple of years, reducing the draw on the museum's endowment to improve financial stability has been a major priority for the IMA. This has been accomplished incrementally and in a variety of ways, the most obvious of which has been a general decrease in departmental and project budgets. Both fortunately and unfortunately, the annual budget for the IMA Archives is so small relative to the overall institutional budget that we have not been targeted for cuts that would impact our operations. However, this has left virtually no room to request funding for special projects, and as head of a non-revenue-generating department, I have little leverage to bargain for increased financial support as a stand-alone unit. That being said, there are many opportunities for collaboration within the museum environment, particularly for an archivist who regularly works with other departments and has a unique understanding of the work being completed throughout the institution.

Having formed positive work relationships with colleagues from departments around the museum, I have been able to identify common needs of the archives and other units. By working jointly, we can present a stronger case to executives for increased financial support of projects that benefit the archives program and its collections. This cause is often furthered by my proven willingness to assist with other department's needs when they overlap, even peripherally, with the work of the archives. Recently, the IMA was going through the process of reaccreditation with AAM. As previously discussed, formal archives programs are not factored into the AAM accreditation process, but it turned out that I was still able to play a role in the IMA's preparations. As our architect and facilities staff prepared the museum building for a visit from the accreditation committee, it came to light that active architectural records were in a very disorganized state and in a location that needed to be cleared before the walk-through. I was called in to assist with the cleanup and reorganization of the records, and in the process, it became clear that there was need of more archival intervention before the end of the records life cycle to ensure proper preservation of architectural records while still active.

To make a long story short, we were able to temporarily relocate the records, and the archives and facilities departments have joined with the horticulture department to reconfigure a former supply room to serve as a satellite architectural archives room. This space will house both archival and active architectural drawings, specifications binders, and facilities- and landscape-related special project documentation. By collaborating with facilities and horticulture—two of the largest departments in the museum, one of which is a major institutional priority at the moment—I will be able to significantly expand the square footage of archives storage and double the amount of flat files available for proper storage of architectural drawings. Facilities and horticulture both benefit in that their active and inactive records will be properly stored and fully inventoried for the first time, and I will be able to ensure the preservation of those active records until they are ready to be officially transferred to the archives. The creation of this satellite archives would not have been possible if I had been alone in making the case for the additional storage space and funds for additional equipment, and if I had not stepped in to assist with the accreditation process, even though that process did not specifically focus on the archives program.

Institutional alignment

As strategic plans often come from the top, with priorities trickling down to each department within the institution, it has been necessary for me to get creative with aligning archival projects with overall strategic priorities of the museum. In my time at the IMA, I have tried a variety of approaches to incorporating archival collections and projects into the ongoing museum activities that have the full support of executives and stakeholders. Sometimes this means dropping other projects to prioritize the processing or digitization of specific collections with tie-ins to upcoming exhibitions or new public programs. More often, I have been able to provide reference services (sometimes unsolicited), pulling information from the archives that has contributed to new internal policies, branding initiatives, and strategic plans, as well as external press releases, website and newsletter content, and even promotional videos. Though these contributions from the archives often play a relatively small role in the full scope of these activities and initiatives, together they have made a big impact in the perceived relevance of the archives program in the eyes of executives and colleagues from other departments. Over the past three years, this has led to a marked increase in the number of internal requests for archival material to provide background information or featured content for a wide variety of projects.

The biggest challenge for me as a manager, in this regard, is to recognize when playing a supportive role for other departments' initiatives compromises my ability to fulfill the archives' primary mandate to collect and preserve those records within the institution that have enduring value. This is a realization that I have learned the hard way and that I continue to work on as I set priorities for the archives program and for myself. Prior to each fiscal year, all museum employees set goals for themselves and their departments that are measurable and can be achieved within that year. I have learned to use that process as an opportunity to set concrete and measurable goals for myself that strike a balance between traditional archival projects (such as processing) and those museum-wide projects to which I can contribute archival content or lend my skills and knowledge as an archivist. While unexpected opportunities to utilize the archives collections will always come up, I have learned to regularly revisit my annual goals and department priorities to avoid taking on unexpected projects that may divert too much from the archives' needs.

Audience identification and inreach/outreach

As the case study up to this point has shown, the primary audiences for IMA Archives collections and projects are internal staff, executives, and stakeholders. Meeting the needs of these internal audiences has always been the priority for me when planning outreach activities. Most of my promotion to internal audiences is passive: each time I work with members of the IMA community, regardless of how big or small the project, I approach it as an opportunity for them to take away information about the archives that they didn't previously have, and hopefully to realize that the archives can be a useful resource for their department's activities. I have also relied on more purposeful forms of inreach to educate IMA staff and executives about the archives collections, procedures, and archival work in general. Pop-up exhibitions of recently processed collections and presentations to staff regarding ongoing projects have been some of the well-received forms of inreach.

Raising the profile of the IMA Archives outside the museum has been prioritized as secondary to inreach, though it is important to attract external audiences that may be interested in our related special collections or our open institutional records groups.[24] Outreach to non-IMA audiences has taken many forms: contributing physical materials or digitized content to art exhibitions; including or featuring archival content in marketing communications and public relations messaging (primarily museum publications); and creating an online presence on Tumblr.[25]

The Tumblr blog *Documenting Modern Living* (http://digitizingmillerhouseandgarden.tumblr .com/) was established in 2012 at the beginning of the Miller House and Garden digitization project. I inherited the Tumblr from my predecessor and shared posting duties with a grant-funded archives assistant. An initial review of the blog's content revealed an opportunity to expand the scope to include "behind-the-scenes"-type posts that would introduce the archivists and professional archives work that had previously been invisible on the blog, which had up to then focused on the collection. Though the collections continued to make up the primary blog content, adding posts that highlighted archival work not only expanded the audience for the blog to library, archives, and museum professionals but was also a way to introduce a more general audience (in this case, primarily design and architecture enthusiasts) to professional archivists and the work that we do. By undertaking similar initiatives, archival managers in repositories of all types could contribute to an increase in public awareness of archives while promoting their collections.[26]

Conclusion

By identifying the essential elements for the successful management and leadership of an archives program in a nonprofit setting, and by sharing my experiences managing the IMA Archives as a case study of those elements, I hope that, above all, I have conveyed that the decisions we make as archivists have implications beyond our individual repositories. This is true especially for those of us in management and leadership positions within our home institutions and in the broader archives profession—regardless of how many years we have been in the field professionally. The decisions we make on a daily basis as managers, the long-term goals and priorities that we set for our programs, and the relationships built with colleagues not only shape our collections and their use but also have the potential to impact the profession and the public perception of archives and archivists. By setting high standards for acceptable labor practices through ethical volunteer and internship programs and the creation of truly entry-level positions, we pay it forward to each new cohort of archives professionals. Every time we introduce new audiences to archives and archival work, whether they are colleagues in other departments or individuals exploring our archives' online presence, we have the potential to improve public understanding of archives and their value in any number of settings and situations. Most importantly, by establishing and expanding solid archives programs, we end up not only preserving our home institution's records in perpetuity and making them available for use but also strengthening those very institutions through support of their fundamental work, regardless of what type of work that may be and regardless of institutional context, nonprofit or otherwise.

NOTES

[1] Richard J. Cox, *Managing Institutional Archives: Foundational Principles and Practices* (New York: Greenwood Press, 1992), 25–26.

[2] Additionally, the role delineation statement of the Academy of Certified Archivists (http://www.certifiedarchivists.org /get-certified/role-delineation-statement/, captured at https://perma.cc/J5F2-AA46) includes "Managing Archival Programs" as one of the primary domains and details tasks associated with successful management. Those tasks closely mirror Cox's list of elements.

[3] For additional readings on management and leadership in an archival context, see George Mariz et al., "Leadership Skills for Archivists," *American Archivist* 74, no. 1 (2011): 102–22; Michael J. Kurtz, *Managing Archival and Manuscript Repositories* (Chicago: Society of American Archivists, 2004); Bruce W. Dearstyne, ed., *Leadership and Administration of Successful Archival Programs* (Westport, CT: Greenwood Press, 2001); and Terrence F. Mech, "Leadership and the Evolution of Academic Librarianship," *Journal of Academic Librarianship* 22 (September 1996): 345–64.

[4] Bruce W. Dearstyne, "Leading Archives and Records Programs: Perspectives and Insights," in *Leading and Managing Archives and Records Programs: Strategies for Success*, ed. Bruce W. Dearstyne (New York: Neal-Schuman, 2008), 293.

[5] An example of this setup is the Mary H. Littlemeyer Archives of the Association of American Medical Colleges (AAMC), which forms a single department with the AAMC Reference Center, a special library that serves the business and medical research needs of AAMC staff.

[6] The placement of archives within marketing or communications departments is fairly common with corporate archives, where company history can be leveraged for advertising campaigns.

[7] In only three years at the IMA, I have seen two departments merge, as well as individual units shift to be placed under new divisions and multiple staff positions transferred to different units. None of those changes affected the placement of the IMA Archives within the museum's organizational structure, but such a change is not out of the realm of possibility.

[8] For a detailed review of archival work as a lone arranger, see Christina Zamon, *The Lone Arranger: Succeeding in a Small Repository* (Chicago: Society of American Archivists, 2012).

[9] Paul C. Lasewicz, "Forget the Past? Or History Matters? Selected Academic Perspectives on the Strategic Value of Organizational Pasts," *American Archivist* 78, no. 1 (2015): 62.

[10] For a more complete discussion of the utility of reference and other statistics in the budgeting process, see Cox, *Managing Institutional Archives*, 32.

[11] Elizabeth Yakel, "Institutionalizing an Archives: Developing Historical Records Programs in Organizations," *American Archivist* 52, no. 2 (1989): 204.

[12] Deborah Wythe, ed., *Museum Archives: An Introduction*, 2nd ed. (Chicago: Society of American Archivists, 2004), 49.

[13] For an overview of the rise of museum archives programs in the United States, see Ann Marie Przybyla's chapter, "The Museum Archives Movement," in Wythe, *Museum Archives*.

[14] The single mention of "records" in AAM's Standards and Best Practices documentation states as a requirement that "A system of documentation, records management and inventory is in effect to describe each object and its acquisition (permanent or temporary), current condition and location and movement into, out of and within the museum." Alliance of American Museums, "Standards on Collections Stewardship," *Standards and Best Practices*, http://www.aam-us.org /resources/ethics-standards-and-best-practices/collections-stewardship, captured at https://perma.cc/NDD3-2TKK.

[15] This is an important distinction for institutional archivists working in a museum environment. While museums *are* cultural heritage institutions, the primary scholarly and interpretative collection within the museum will always be its permanent collection. Institutional records may support the interpretation and research about the permanent collection, but they will rarely be the focus of exhibitions, public programming, or other public-facing collections pages. If the museum archives also collects related special collections, those may be treated in a similar fashion as the permanent collection, and archivists may serve curatorial functions regarding those collections.

[16] Art research libraries are very common in major art museums and have historically formed a central function of art museums since their founding. In the case of the Indianapolis Museum of Art, the library had been in existence since 1906, when the Art Association of Indianapolis became the John Herron Art Institute. The important role that research libraries have played in art museums reflects the scholarly roots of museums, which makes them a natural home for museum archives programs.

[17] Indianapolis Museum of Art Archives, "Mission," revised 2014, http://www.imamuseum.org/research/archives, captured at https://perma.cc/YSX4-QDN2.

[18] At the time of this writing, the mission of the IMA is "to enrich lives through exceptional experiences with art and nature," with the core values of "stewardship, service, and excellence." Indianapolis Museum of Art, May 20, 2015.

[19] It is important to note that the emphasis on public programming is not explicitly written into the museum's mission statement. My understanding that programming targeting new audiences is one of the largest institutional priorities has been gleaned during my time at the museum by paying attention to those activities that get the most support—in this case, both fiscal and marketing. The ability to evaluate institutional priorities through the actions of executives and other stakeholders in relation to certain activities of the institution is an important skill for an archives manager to have. With an understanding of institutional priorities, the archives manager can then strategize to bring the archives program and activities into alignment with those priorities.

[20] The IMA Lab is an in-house group of digital designers and developers. They complete digital projects for the museum, as well as for outside clients (lab.imamuseum.org). The Digital Archives Portal (archive.imamuseum.org) was their first archival product.

[21] This position was and is currently filled by a career librarian with limited archival experience.

[22] During my time in graduate school, the archives job market was a consistent worry, not only for me but for my peers, both in my program and in others throughout the country. Prior to the creation of the Students and New Archives Professionals (SNAP) Roundtable in the Society of American Archivists in 2012 (http://www2.archivists.org/groups/students-and-new -archives-professionals-snap-section, captured at https://perma.cc/AL9P-DPEF), there was not much of an outlet for archives students and recent graduates to voice their concerns. Individual blog posts and entire online communities sprang up to give voice to this group. One such example is You Ought to Be Ashamed (https://eatingouryoung.wordpress.com /about/, captured at https://perma.cc/LUU5-E3HP), a blog active from 2010 to 2014, which was dedicated to pointing out troubling employment and internship practices in position descriptions and providing a space for students and new archivists to voice their concerns and share grievances. In response to this blog and the more general feeling of concern among students and recent graduates, SAA president Jackie Dooley's presidential address in 2013 was titled "Feeding Our Young" and focused on how SAA and professional archivists and archives programs in general were meeting—or not meeting—the needs of students and recent graduates (Jackie Dooley, "Feeding Our Young," *American Archivist* 77, no. 1 (2014): 10–22).

[23] At the time of this writing, we are now hosting our third public history intern. Our two past interns were dual-degree students also pursuing master's degrees in library science. More information about the program can be found at http:// liberalarts.iupui.edu/history/index.php/public/internships, captured at https://perma.cc/WLC4-H4ZN.

[24] There was initial hesitancy from some archives program stakeholders (primarily the registrars who originally collected and preserved the archival records and then advocated for the official creation of the archives) to the idea of making some of the institutional records available to outside researchers. Through collaborative projects of various kinds, I have had the opportunity to both implicitly and explicitly display my professionalism and sensitivity to issues of privacy and confidentiality regarding the archives, helping to put the registrars at ease about the reality of our institutional records as public resources, whenever possible. While their inclination is still to err on the side of caution and restriction, I am now trusted to make decisions about which record groups, individual items, or pieces of information should be closed and which can be opened. This allows me to follow my inclination as an archivist to prioritize open access to our records.

[25] Due to the primarily supportive role of the IMA Archives within the museum, the creation of archival-specific programs open to the general public has not been a priority for the institution. Instead, the archives has contributed to programming for key audiences, such as the Second Century Society and IMA Alliance—two groups of longtime members and donors to the museum.

[26] I have previously written about this Tumblr experiment, the results, and my suggestions for other archivists considering a similar move on the SAA's *ArchivesAWARE!* blog, "Asserting the Archivist in Archival Outreach: A Case Study and Appeal," January 28, 2016, https://archivesaware.archivists.org/2016/01/28/asserting-the-archivist-in-archival-outreach-a-case-study -and-appeal/, captured at https://perma.cc/JT9H-MNL3. We have continued to feature archives staff and work on our general IMA Library & Archives Tumblr, http://libraryarchives-imamuseum.tumblr.com/, captured at https://perma .cc/9R7W-694H.

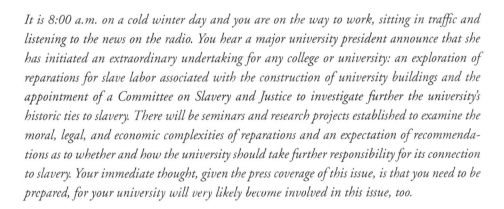

11

Leadership and the Management of College and University Archives

Megan Sniffin-Marinoff

It is 8:00 a.m. on a cold winter day and you are on the way to work, sitting in traffic and listening to the news on the radio. You hear a major university president announce that she has initiated an extraordinary undertaking for any college or university: an exploration of reparations for slave labor associated with the construction of university buildings and the appointment of a Committee on Slavery and Justice to investigate further the university's historic ties to slavery. There will be seminars and research projects established to examine the moral, legal, and economic complexities of reparations and an expectation of recommendations as to whether and how the university should take further responsibility for its connection to slavery. Your immediate thought, given the press coverage of this issue, is that you need to be prepared, for your university will very likely become involved in this issue, too.

College and university archives can be a source for significant research and teaching, will support crucial administrative functions, and should add rich texture to the life of an academic institution. Such archives and their staffs have the potential to provide a foundation for advancing scholarship in a wide variety of disciplines, to collaborate with faculty in teaching, to work with a wide range of administrators to ensure effective recordkeeping, and to support the management of the life cycle of college and university records in all formats. University archives, then, can play an important role in advancing the mission of higher education.

In many colleges and universities, there is a long history of success in some or all of these areas.[1] In many institutions, however, there is not full or continuous appreciation of what services an institutional archives is able to or should provide. How can academic archivists (this term will be used for college and university archivists) position their archives to live up to their potential and to thrive? What are academic archivists required to know, other than the core knowledge of the field, for their archives to succeed and for their own personal success? Academic archivists should expect that the requirements to lead start with vision, assertiveness, persistence, flexibility, a collaborative nature, and excellent communication skills and also should include ambition, passion, fearlessness, optimism, the ability to recognize opportunity, a willingness to change, and a good sense of humor.

Most academic archivists would react to the situation of a college's or university's historic ties to slavery, noted in the scenario above, by assuming they should contribute to any efforts to identify research sources of historical significance. But do the staff and administrators at academic institutions working on such projects automatically think to use the resources of the institutional archives to help address questions being raised? Do they know archival research resources even exist, or where they are? Do they understand how the practices and even the ethical standards of archivists can be helpful to an institution struggling with a difficult issue? No, not always, even at institutions with well-established archives. But mindful leadership, coupled with thoughtful management, together can conspire to ensure that an institution in a situation such as the one described, or others, are well served by archives and archivists and that archives and archivists are valued and well supported.

What follows is not a description of how generally to manage college and university archives or their related areas, common for academic archives, of manuscript or special collections. In addition to basic works about managing archives useful to academic archivists, there are numerous writings addressing specific issues in managing the functional areas of college and university archives.[2] Instead, the focus here will be on identifying and describing those circumstances of an institutional archives in a college and university environment where leadership matters most: gaining authorization and authority; addressing administrative placement; connecting with the larger organization; working with colleagues across other academic institutions; and encouraging staff development.

What Is Leadership?

Defining *leadership* is challenging. There is, of course, an entire publishing industry devoted to defining and outlining ways to become a great leader. In my current institution, a whole school is devoted to this and to the publication of texts, case studies, and articles on the subject.[3] Many academic institutions offer numerous workshops on improving leadership skills. These workshops lead to self-assessment, using a combination of individual and group instruction supported by texts such as the well-known Gallup Press book, *Strengths Based Leadership*.[4]

In a related field and particularly illuminating is the Council on Library and Information Resources' *Reflecting on Leadership*.[5] In this small compilation of essays, three library leaders—Karin Wittenborg (University of Virginia), Chris Ferguson (Pacific Lutheran University), and Michael A. Keller (Stanford University)—reflect on long careers leading libraries in academic institutions. In each case, there are examples of paths taken (or not taken) and decisions made (or made for them) along the way. What stands out in their reflections are discussions of how they survived and thrived within the structure of an academic institution and also their thoughts on the personal qualities of leadership. For while some leadership skills can be learned, archivists need to realize that, to become a leader, he or she needs to focus on leadership qualities that will make the biggest difference in the ability to set or keep the archives on course. These qualities will be called upon to advance both basic and complex archival agendas. This focus will also lead to generally improving your leadership abilities.

Leadership and Gaining Authorization and Authority

College and university archives get established for different reasons, such as the need to address a significant upcoming institutional anniversary; the result of cleaning up anything from a closet to an office to a warehouse of records; or, for institutions coming of age more recently, specifically to address digital or digital forensics challenges in institutional record keeping. Not all academic archives start out with the founders anticipating or even knowing what switch they turned on and what direction the work of an archives might take.

To lead successfully, every academic archivist must have clear authorization and guidance to conduct the business of a college or university archives. Without it, an academic archivist cannot lead, for there will be confusion about your role and authority, and your attempts at creative leadership to address your challenges will not be able to sustain the archives in the short term or over time. This can be hard to accomplish and will require you to step forward to explain the purpose of an institutional archives to administrators who do not understand the concerns or have no interest. You will need to be prepared to explain your point of view, be convincing, and, simply, be a true professional, articulating your knowledge and expertise. This will toughen you as a leader and is an important opportunity to position yourself as the person who will lead from the front for the institution on archival matters.

If you find yourself in the fortunate position of having an approved and written authorization for your archives—for example, a document defining what college and university records are and that the archives exerts authority over areas such as appraisal, acquisition, access, and preservation—then you will be seeking ways to update or improve upon that authorization as needed, to solicit support for your work and your mission. You need to expect your work to take you immediately away from your desk and out of the archives and to become an advocate for the services your archives will provide in support of the institution. In cases where the authorization for the institutional archives is not yet fully in place, other leadership qualities are necessary. You will need to seek out meetings to discuss this with the appropriate administrators or situations where you can prove the need for clarification.

Early in my career, I worked in a building with two very large walk-in attics where a century's worth of financial records was stored. The authorization for the archives was not solid. The archives was viewed more as a museum of interesting historical objects than as a true institutional archives. In the midst of a major storm, a massive amount of water began to pour onto the records stored in the two attics. News spread and chaos ensued. Despite the treasurer's aloofness to the archives and previous attempts to discuss financial records, I offered my department's assistance to help with cleanup and also to guide them in thinking through what was worth salvaging and why. In action, then, they were able to see the logic of having procedures in place to deal with risk and the cost-effectiveness of maintaining or destroying records. Initially thinking they needed to restore all that was damaged, they realized they did not, and they also began to understand our appreciation for the historical work of their department. We gained friends but, most importantly, we gained advocates and stakeholders in our operation. We called on them with ease as conversations began about improving the authority for the archives to manage part of the life cycle of the institution's records. Not every opportunity needs to be as dramatic as this, but as you get to know an institution and where the records challenges reside and are consequential, you should speak up and offer assistance.

The work of the archivist here will require planning and a thoughtful synopsis of the resources and support needed and why. The process will likely begin with conversations with the archivist's supervisor, who will take the request to the administration. Conversations will also often help to determine if the work of the unit is to extend beyond purely institutional records and include materials also important to documenting the history of a college or university, such as the personal archives of faculty. While faculty archives, for example, often fall into the category of "personal archives" and are sometimes serviced by "special collections," faculty are also employees with institutional records the archives should address. In my current institution, for example, more than 50 percent of our permanent holdings are faculty archives that also represent 50 percent of our use statistics. This issue can become complex for academic archives, so understanding the nuances in this area is an opportunity not only to educate the institution on the gray areas of records and personal archives typical in an academic institution but also to establish yourself as an authority and problem solver who will get called upon to lead discussions on these issues.

I have worked at and consulted for college and university archives new and small, middle-aged and medium-sized, and old and large over the course of my career. In each case, the issue of authorization has been a key to success. At my current institution, Harvard University, I have witnessed how the issue of rejuvenating the purpose and authority of the archives has enabled the archives to remain relevant and vital over time. The Harvard University Archives draws its authority from the Harvard Corporation, similar to governing boards or boards of trustees in many academic institutions. The members of the Corporation voted officially in 1851 to establish an embryonic archives, the result of a concern over the loss of historic documents, brought to the attention of the Corporation by Harvard president Josiah Quincy, who was preparing to write a history of Harvard as part of its 1836 bicentennial celebrations. Between 1851 and 1995, the authorization and authority of the Harvard University Archives has been amended by the Corporation a minimum of seven times. Most importantly, archivists in 1939, shortly after the establishment of the US National Archives, used those developments to guide the Corporation in defining institutional ownership of its records and outlining the responsibility of the Harvard University Archives for them. In that era of modernization of archives in the United States, there are hints in Harvard's authorization at what would later become known as records management.

By 1995, after many years of adjustments to its authorization, the Harvard archivists lobbied for the official recognition of a records management program run by the University Archives, and most importantly, the acknowledgement that Harvard's records were not just paper-based but were in all formats, including electronic records.[6] So, as our archivists today are actively involved in conversations on managing email, websites, and research data, we have profited from the foresight of our predecessors who knew that the work of the Harvard University Archives extended beyond others' assumptions of our written authorization and that changes needed to be made in anticipation. Our archival predecessors thought broadly, spoke up, and pushed to refine our authorizations and authority long before anyone really knew what they were talking about. We are benefiting enormously today from their leadership. As a leader and a professional in the field, you, too, need to keep a similar eye both on the present and the future, not saddling those who follow you with problems you can avoid and thinking ahead to help them.

Leadership and Addressing Administrative Placement

A thorough understanding of the parent unit to which a college or university archives reports is critical in considering strategies for leading and managing. Academic archivists always report up in the organization to those whose responsibility is not solely "archives." So understanding where you sit in the organization and the goals of the parent unit overall are critical to understanding how to lead within the limits you may discover.

A majority of academic archives are part of a library system. Other reporting structures vary and could include reporting to an officer such as a provost or a president, to a records or information management department, or to a communications unit. Within libraries, a common home base, college and university archives could be freestanding, perhaps incorporating aspects of records or information management, and report to a library director, an associate director, or a chief of staff; be part of a special collections/archives department led principally by a head of special collections reporting to a library director; or be part of an archives/special collections department led by an institutional archivist reporting to a library director. Much of this is determined by age, size, and budget and can change over time as an archives develops. In cases of large research institutions, there might also be multiple departments for university records, as with institutions with medical schools managing voluminous and specialized records involving university-based hospitals. In public colleges and universities, some reporting may also be directly to a state unit or even the state archives.

Building a good relationship with the parent unit to which an academic archives reports is imperative if the archives is going to receive the support and nurturing it needs for success. If reporting to a library, as an example, one of the major challenges is the most obvious. The mission of a library is broad, but that mission is often focused solely on serving the information needs of faculty and students and not necessarily those of the college or university's administration and staff or researchers from outside the institution. So basic constituents of the academic archives are not noted as a high priority, or a priority at all, to the overarching supervisory library. This issue of the difference of mission is also true for academic archives reporting through other administrative departments on or off campus.

In a library setting, academic archives can thrive in some areas. Particularly with the increased interest of faculty in introducing students to the use of primary sources, academic archivists can either take the lead or collaborate with colleagues working in manuscript and special collections to meet faculty and student needs. This is a key and visible leadership opportunity addressing an aspect of what is often a critical mission in advancing teaching at academic institutions. Especially with undergraduates, who are fascinated by the students who came before them as well as notable faculty, the materials of a college and university archives collection can resonate quickly. The primary sources in archival collections can be the basis for significant digitization projects too, along with those of special collections, and add to the goals of many academic libraries to place increasingly more of their holdings online. Academic archives can also support the library mission by serving as a source for faculty and student research. Even nonfaculty research leading to publication of articles and monographs, dissertations, or documentaries will echo the scholarly goals of libraries.

But archivists working in these settings must also step forward and speak to the importance and differing needs of their other core constituents. It is easy to get lured completely into the goals of an academic library, whose core audiences are students and faculty, and begin to ignore the needs of the staff and administration increasingly dependent on the archives' services as you lead your program forward. Providing conscious leadership to address the needs of multiple constituents and to explain why you are doing so takes time and effort, but it is critical. Much archives' staff time is required to provide university staff with resources to be used in writing public relations press releases, answering policy questions for university committees, gathering documents for architects and contractors, supporting the questions of registrars, or seeking background information on former staff for a human resources department, but little of this is relevant to the goals of the parent unit, in many cases a library.

Leadership and Connecting with the Parent Organization

Even though academic archives are usually placed in units with different priorities, academic archivists must make clear to those who supervise them that the archivist's work requires close working relationships with a variety of departments outside the parent unit and often higher up in the administration. With authorization for the archives in hand, it is imperative that you lead this charge and reach out to a wide range of departments where records are created. Leading here means stepping out from under the shelter of the parent unit and into the broader administrative world of the college or university. No one will take your hand; this is where you will need to lead the archival charge.

The image of academic archivists unfortunately can still be of those who work quietly in a library-like space, making old materials available to the few people who stumble upon them. It is less understood or appreciated by many, for example, that the role of the academic archivist is to lead in building and sustaining a collection of institutional resources, to help address institutional records issues in all formats, or to support an institution engaged in legal challenges. If an academic archivist does not execute a plan to identify and reach out actively to college and university offices and academic departments, then individuals and offices at the institution will control the fate of the archives simply by benign neglect or in determining *for* the archives what is important.

Identifying offices to benefit most from the services of the archives is a critical first step. There are a wide range of offices that work almost organically with an academic archives: those engaged with outreach such as communications, alumni, development, and athletics; those working with student and personnel records, such as registrars and human resource officers and well as student organizations; those with legal responsibilities such as legal counsel and privacy officers; those with financial responsibility such as treasurers and auditors; and those responsible for working with high-profile people or issues such as presidents, provosts, and marshals. Increasingly, those working in information technology have become working allies. Depending on whether or not the academic archives also collects the personal archives of faculty or works with faculty in support of instruction or personal research, these departments, too, can become regular constituents of the archives' services and resources.

All academic archivists need to understand the larger world of higher education, how it is structured, and how it works. One way to do this is to become familiar with the literature of this industry, such as the *Chronicle of Higher Education*.[7] It is equally important to understand the priorities of the parent academic institution. From multiyear capital campaigns, to major building projects, to diversity efforts, to transitions in information technology and research data management, to changes in the direction of academic departments and scholarly communication, there is work underway that archivists need to identify and to determine how to assist with associated records needs. Archivists who lead need to be a visible presence on campus and build a community of stakeholders.

In my work, I have found that an active community of stakeholders can come to your rescue. Having been asked to outsource a function that staff knew would have a negative impact on campus offices and the archives, an active group of stakeholders agreed, quite willingly, to speak to those we reported to about the suggested change. They made a strong case for themselves, and the idea was abandoned. It might have taken us months to get across the same points, but the statement came directly from high-profile campus offices that matter. The relationship building paid off for them and for us and also helped to illustrate the value placed on the archives by a wide range of individuals on campus.

Leadership and Working with Colleagues across Other Academic Institutions

Whether leading an archives or contributing in a functional area such as public services, technical services, or appraisal and acquisitions, archivists must continue to learn and improve. If they do not, opportunities will be missed, and the archives will become increasingly irrelevant to the institution over time. Evaluation and assessment of individual and group activity are essential. Leading involves not just planning but also examination and critique. It is easy to become so focused on the local and on immediate needs or pressure that the value of assessment and looking outward can be overlooked.

The changes taking place in higher education across the nation in research, teaching, and administration affect all academic archives. In addition to building relationships with local colleagues, academic archivists should set aside time to learn from others and develop working relationships with archivists at similar institutions. To lead your archives or your functional unit, consider organizing collaborative efforts to address issues of common concern with others in the academic archives community or with those whose challenges resonate with you. Recently, for instance, the academic archivists among the Ivy Plus Libraries started to meet annually.

This type of effort may mean that you need to step out into new areas uncomfortable at first or with those you do not know in order to solve problems. For example, many academic institutions have been working independently to establish secure and reasonable ways to collect, process, store, and make accessible records in the form of email. Archivists and colleagues at a number of institutions, in addition to speaking about individual projects at professional meetings and publishing work on individual projects, eventually began to meet to share ideas. The importance of the work was noticed by the Andrew W. Mellon Foundation and the Digital Preservation Coalition, which announced the formation of a Task Force on Technical Approaches for Email Archives. The task force is now "charged with assessing current frameworks, tools, and approaches being taken toward these critical historical sources." As was noted in the announcement of the Task Force, "*The community needs to articulate a conceptual and technical framework in which these efforts can operate not as competing solutions, but as elements of an interoperable toolkit.*"[8] The group is a mix of academic archivists along with those from other types of archives, libraries, government agencies, and for-profit companies. Particularly in addressing new and complex issues well beyond the resources of even well-endowed institutions, collaboration is now imperative and provides a stream of new opportunities for honing or using your leadership skills and abilities.

Academic archivists, especially those whose institutions set up campuses or programs outside the United States, will also find that their work increasingly requires them to collaborate with archivists from other institutions across the world. If you have spent the time building relationships within your institution, this is a moment when the benefits of relationship building can reap rewards. For example, having developed a good relationship with university legal counsel who understand your issues of concern, you will be more likely to obtain assistance with efforts in interpreting local laws outside the United States or understanding the data restrictions in some countries affecting the handling of financial, human resource, and student records. With faculty increasingly collaborating across nations on major research projects, particularly in the sciences, disentangling rights issues related to research data and the records created in support of research projects may mean negotiating university rights across countries and within a variety of archival traditions. As the work of those in colleges and universities is increasingly global, so, too, is the work of college and university archivists.

What's an Academic Archivist to Do?

Over the course of a career in colleges and universities, I have come to understand how important it is to be able to articulate clearly the mission and benefits of the archives to the parent institution and also as a direct report to a library or other administrative unit. In a few cases, this relationship started with indifference or even confusion about the role of the supervisory department in the institution's archival endeavors.[9]

With a greater interest in information security on campuses, changing approaches to teaching and learning with an emphasis on hands-on experiences, and academic institutions seeking to distinguish themselves and their legacies from others as they seek new resources, today is the best time I have experienced to make the case for a more central role, or a more appreciated role, of the academic archives. With librarians also understanding a little more about the role of institutional archives and possibilities for collaboration, it is also a time for academic archivists to step out from the sidelines of libraries to lead and garner support. This may even be the moment where the two missions—those of academic libraries and academic archives—can be mutually supportive or even integrated in ways where each party profits. There is opportunity in areas such as the collection and management of born-digital materials. For example, with increasingly more academic archives engaged in developing web archives, there is mounting archival expertise resonating with new collecting priorities in libraries. Academic libraries are struggling to redefine themselves. They are seeking new ways to play a role in support of the changing information needs of faculty, such as taking on responsibilities in research data management. In some institutions, where academic archives have collected the personal papers of faculty for generations, they have often, as a result, collected and managed research data in all formats. An institutional archives can contribute to the work of libraries here, too, bringing much-needed expertise in areas such as appraisal, ownership, privacy and rights management, and records management. Such an insertion can at times be risky business with a library profession that is reinventing itself and seeming to encroach on areas that archives have seen traditionally as "theirs"—or vice versa—as in the area of student instruction. But academic archivists are well placed to gain attention and support for their needs in this administrative structure if they are willing to be risk-takers and to educate and collaborate.

Leadership and Encouraging Staff Development

Leadership is not just a top-down responsibility. The head of an academic archives staff is not the only staff member required to exercise leadership. Each staff member responsible for operational tasks bears some responsibility too. In addition to implementing tasks to meet goals, as a leader, you should encourage staff to keep up with the latest developments in the field and contribute to planning. Working with staff to assume some leadership responsibility can create an esprit de corps. This becomes important during demanding times.

Effective leadership in academic archives begins with establishing, along with staff, a vision of what the archives is to achieve, a mission stating how to achieve the vision, goals to be accomplished, strategies to achieve those goals, and objectives with action plans—or, in the case of those working alone in an academic archives, formulating this path with yourself and your supervisor. It is common for staff working in higher education, including archivists, to participate in these goal-setting activities. As a leader, see that these performance plans provide the opportunity for staff members to take on leadership responsibilities. Take the opportunity to mentor either formally or through casual conversation as opportunities arise. As a leader, you should encourage staff at all levels to articulate how changes to their work or improvements in a functional area can add to the vision and the future of the archives.

What are some examples of ways staff can be encouraged to contribute? If, for example, an academic archives has adopted ArchivesSpace, staff can not only learn how to use the tool and input data but can also be encouraged, as part of their personal goals, to assess what parts of the tool need development or refinement for the archives work to become more efficient. They can work with archivists at other organizations to lobby for software development to increase the value of the tool to your organization. Staff who harvest academic websites can reach out to others working in this evolving sphere and report back on progress not just from other academic archives but also archives in other sectors of the archival profession. The list is endless as to the ways staff can contribute to the larger enterprise and to realize that they, too, are leading the archives.

Regular staff assessment is one way to encourage this kind of leadership and responsibility. Goal-setting meetings are often an opportunity to provide staff with the larger context for archival work in higher education and specifically about the work of an institutional archives. Many new archivists set out on careers without understanding the characteristics of working in one sector of the profession or another. But, once working in the field, whether at a private institution or in the public sector, it is important for all staff to understand where they work and what kind of organization they are supporting. I have found that a major reason for job dissatisfaction is that a person would rather be working in another sector of the profession or one with different expectations and goals. For example, while most college and university archives are open to the general public, the primary audiences served are faculty, students, university administrators, and other scholars. If an archivist is more interested in serving the general public or working with materials that do not consist of institutional records but rather manuscripts or community archives, it is important to use these opportunities to mentor a staff member, especially in the early stages of a career.

Those who work as lone archivists trying to manage an academic archives—especially a new archives or one located at a small institution—or doing so in combination with other responsibilities have different factors to consider in leading the charge for the archives. In these cases, it is especially important to confirm with a supervisor the mission and goals of the unit or department with an understanding that you might not be able to accomplish simultaneously all that is needed to address institutional need. These are the conversations to seek out to raise awareness and educate those above you not only about the limits of what one person can accomplish but also the possibilities to accrue from additional resources. Leadership in this case is likely more cautious, but it should be no less ambitious in the long term.

Anticipating Change

Even with the best of preparation, unforeseen and even sudden, large changes will occur periodically and dramatically affect the plans of an archives. Adjusting goals in archives is generally expected. The need to change processing priorities to make a collection accessible to a researcher, the rearrangement of schedules to accommodate a faculty member who wants to bring a class to the archives, or the sudden closing of a campus office whose records need to come to the archives immediately are all common, local occurrences. But the academic archives exists within the world of higher education, which has been volatile for almost a decade. This volatility will likely continue as colleges and universities examine their missions; as the audiences for higher education change, diversify, and expand; and as new and evolving technologies shape alternative forms of course delivery. Changes in the economy and in outside support for college- and university-based research can have profound effects on the priorities, workforce, development of facilities, and activities undertaken at all academic institutions. This change has and will continue to affect academic archives.

I have been affected by this kind of change numerous times. In one instance, the organization I worked for announced with almost no warning a decision to reorient its priorities and to reduce by one-third the organization's overall staff. This staff reduction occurred in a single day—the next day. As leader of a unit to be affected, my first instincts were to worry about those who would lose their jobs and how to ease their pain, as well as how to address the anxiety of the remaining staff. The second concern was to determine how to keep the operation functioning until goals and action plans could be amended. Even with planning and mentoring, situations like this will require rethinking priorities, and not everyone will agree with those priorities. Reorganization may be required. Some staff members may need to place coveted projects on hold or begin to work outside their comfort zones—for example, processors taking on public service work or public service staff taking on records management assignments. If you have a sound basis of mentoring staff and preparing them for change over time, this situation may be less troublesome, and staff will be somewhat better prepared for a shock or able to pivot. In cases such as these, you must lead from the front, speaking for the archives and the staff. You must remain visible and make the opportunity to speak regularly with staff, both collectively and individually. You must help people move forward for it will not happen naturally.

Another instance was of a happier sort but nonetheless caused stress among some staff. As part of normal goal-setting discussions, short-term goals for individuals had been set related to processing, cataloging, outreach, and access activities. Broader staff discussions about the future included anticipated work on digitization and preservation. Both were currently out of reach due to funding, but there were also a few raised eyebrows during planning discussions about the long-term value of spending time and funds on digitization at all when so many other issues—such as processing backlogs—needed attention first. Unexpectedly, a gift was offered to the archives to process, preserve, and digitize a select, large group of university records. Looking at the big picture and realizing that this gift might lead to additional funding to expand this work and also create an opportunity to engage in work in an area of emerging importance not only to the archives but to the parent unit (a library), I agreed to readjust our plans and to make this work. And it has, to great fanfare, but not without some initial, internal staff strife leading to questions about why we were resetting priorities in an area whose long-term values were still seen by some as experimental when we had more immediate needs. As a leader, you need to make choices to move your archives forward, and not everyone will be happy with you or your choices. You must recognize the stress points and address them. For example, many staff in this situation see the opportunity just as extra work. A discussion with staff about how to adjust performance goals and deadlines will help to reduce the stress of these situations. When given the opportunity, you must be visionary, take risks to allow for substantive change, and figure out how to make it work. An important quality of leadership is not to regret your choices. Leading an academic archives means taking risks without the assurance of positive outcomes.

Final Thoughts on the Importance of Leadership and Thoughtful Management in College and University Archives

The brief account about slavery and universities at the opening of this chapter is true. Brown University president Ruth Simmons, a descendant of those who were enslaved, not only began the process to address the university's historic ties to slavery but also threw down the gauntlet. Her decision challenged administrators at other colleges and universities to follow Brown's lead. It was inevitable that my own institution, Harvard University, would eventually accept the challenge to examine and evaluate similar historic connections to slavery. It was inevitable, too, that the Harvard University Archives would become involved in the matter. What was gratifying was the extent of support requested of the archives when work began.

With excellent staff forethought on the specific issue of slavery, coupled with a track record of various archives staff reaching out to establish working relationships with university administrators and faculty when the slavery issue arrived at our doorstep, we were ready. What we were stunned by, however, was the degree of participation the university requested of the archives: there was to be a project researcher, reporting to the president, embedded in the archives staff; work with a faculty team to provide leadership on research; and the creation of an exhibition to support a conference initiated by the university president, *Universities and Slavery: Bound by History*, exploring the relationship between slavery and universities, across the country and around the world.[10]

How did this project fall into place? Why now? Our involvement with an important university project was not due to an overnight archives success story, and it did not happen by luck. Much can be attributed to developing a culture of leadership across the staff. A consciousness of the critical role of leadership through goal setting, seizing opportunities, building relationships, and aligning the work of the archives with the administration got the archives to this point.

A few years after the relationship between universities and slavery first emerged in the news, the archives staff was in the midst of processing some of the earliest university records from the seventeenth and eighteenth centuries in preparation for a massive digitization project. They noticed much information from the period—including information about race, gender, and slavery—had been either unavailable or overlooked in the writing of well-established nineteenth- and twentieth-century university histories. Knowing the information was going to be useful to the study of the university and slavery, they suggested putting other work on hold and hiring several graduate students to take a deeper look at the collections to document the location of the pertinent materials. Processing staff—who normally cannot take the time for this level of detailed analysis—took the students' data and incorporated it into cataloging records, making the information available as quickly as possible.

In the meantime, when public services staff identified courses the archives should support, they reached out to a professor who was organizing a seminar on the topic of Harvard and slavery and offered assistance in locating source material. They were pivotal in the success of the course and the student research, leading to publication of some of the earliest findings. Public service staff members also became involved in the public recognition of the depth of the slavery issue: the placement of a plaque on a building acknowledging the lives of formerly unknown slaves living in a campus building known for its association with George Washington and former Harvard presidents but not for the existence of these unknown and enslaved residents.

Archives staff also were simultaneously discussing ways to improve the design of its exhibitions to make them more appealing and bring in more viewers. Two successful exhibitions gained unexpectedly good press through the tireless and organized efforts of staff. The archives was being noticed and was approached by the president's office about the possibility, related to another sensitive initiative, to provide historic context on the relationship between the military and Harvard. This would be a challenging exhibition to mount if a rocky history was to be acknowledged and to reflect archival sources, but it afforded the opportunity for the archives staff to work closely with the president's staff in dealing ethically and honestly with a difficult subject. The exhibition was a success. And it had the effect of opening the eyes of some top administrators to the power of their university's archives. While this work was underway, the archives was brought fully into discussions of the slavery issue and asked to take on a leadership role on the project. As the university has come to value the work and collections of its archives over time and also to trust the staff, the University Archives has become a true working partner in a high-profile, highly sensitive project.

Regardless of the outcome, from our perspective, the archives has already had a success. We cannot stop our efforts to step forward and continue to find ways to contribute, for there will always be new administrators and those who know nothing about what we can offer. But this current involvement is exactly the outcome to strive for as a way to illustrate to staff the need to take leadership seriously: in doing so, a college or university archives will appear to *naturally* play a meaningful role in the functioning of an academic institution—and to history.

NOTES

1   See, for example, some of the descriptions in Christopher J. Prom and Ellen D. Swain, eds., *College and University Archives: Readings in Theory and Practice* (Chicago: Society of American Archivists, 2008) and in a special issue devoted to college and university archives issues worldwide, *Comma: International Journal on Archives*, no. 1–2 (2007), available through Liverpool University Press Online.

2   Such general readings on developing and managing archives include Bruce W. Dearstyne, ed., *Leading and Managing Archives and Records Programs* (New York: Neal-Schuman, 2008); Bruce W. Dearstyne, *Leading the Historical Enterprise: Strategic Creativity, Planning and Advocacy for the Digital Age* (Blue Ridge Summit: Rowman and Littlefield, 2015); Gregory S. Hunter, *Developing and Maintaining Practical Archives: A How-To-Do-It Manual*, 2nd ed. (New York: Neal-Schuman, 2003); and Michael J. Kurtz, *Managing Archival and Manuscript Repositories* (Chicago: Society of American Archivists, 2004). Works on changing and managing college and university archives include, for example, William E. Brown Jr. and Elizabeth Yakel, "Redefining the Role of College and University Archives in the Information Age," *American Archivist* 59, no. 3 (1996): 272–87; Christopher J. Prom and Ellen D. Swain, eds., *College and University Archives: Readings in Theory and Practice* (Chicago: Society of American Archivists, 2008); and William J. Maher, *The Management of College and University Archives* (Metuchen, NJ: Society of American Archivists, 1992).

3   See, for example, Harvard Business Publishing, https://cb.hbsp.harvard.edu/cbmp/pages/home, captured at https://perma.cc/5PY3-JAKS. See also, for example, Linda A. Hill and Kent Lineback, *Being the Boss: The Three Imperatives for Becoming a Great Leader* (Boston: Harvard Business Review Press, 2011).

4   Tom Rath, *Strengths Based Leadership: Great Leaders, Teams, and Why People Follow* (New York: Gallup Press, 2008).

5   Karin Wittenborg, Chris Ferguson, and Michael A. Keller, *Reflecting on Leadership* (Washington, DC: Council on Library and Information Resources, December 2003).

6   Transcriptions of most of the votes of the Harvard Corporation related to the Harvard University Archives are found on the Harvard University Archives website, http://library.harvard.edu/university-archives/mission, captured at https://perma.cc/VR2J-JHGF. Josiah Quincy, *The History of Harvard University* (Cambridge, MA: John Owen, 1840).

7   The *Chronicle of Higher Education* is an example of a weekly journal providing up-to-date coverage of events and news affecting colleges and universities principally in the United States but with some international coverage. There are numerous other publications focusing on specific sectors of higher education that vary in importance to specific types of institutions.

8   The Andrew W. Mellon Foundation and the Digital Preservation Coalition, November 1, 2016, "Mellon Foundation and Digital Preservation Coalition Sponsor Formation of Task Force for Email Archives," https://mellon.org/resources/news/articles/mellon-foundation-and-digital-preservation-coalition-sponsor-formation-task-force-email-archives/, captured at https://perma.cc/FW59-E86L. See the final report of the Task Force at https://clir.wordpress.clir.org/wp-content/uploads/sites/6/2018/08/CLIR-pub175.pdf, captured at https://perma.cc/FTY8-2SV4 .

9   See additional strategies for tackling this issue in a volume written for library directors and archivists, Jeannette A. Bastian, Megan Sniffin-Marinoff, and Donna Webber, *Archives in Libraries: What Librarians and Archivists Need to Know to Work Together* (Chicago: Society of American Archivists, 2015).

10 See a conference description at "Understanding Harvard's Ties to Slavery," *Harvard Gazette*, February 28, 2017, http://news.harvard.edu/gazette/story/2017/02/understanding-harvards-ties-to-slavery/, captured at https://perma.cc/4QR8-4G9T.

12

Blooming Where We Are Planted: The Future of Archival Leadership

Rachel Vagts

On the final morning of the 2018 Archives Leadership Institute, a panel of seven veteran archivists sat in front of that year's cohort. The facilitator for the week, Mark Nigro, opened the session by inviting the new leaders to ask questions of their mentors. It was a session that balanced the experiences of the seven, who had approximately two hundred years of experience among them. As I sat there, my body and brain exhausted from the intensity of the week of the institute, I wondered, "What can I share about my experience that might help these leaders learn from my experiences, my successes and my mistakes?" Then I wondered, "Will they even care what I think?" But as I listened to the rest of the panel, I was again reminded that one of the great strengths of our profession is our commitment to mentoring, teaching, training, and supporting one another, generation after generation. As David Carmicheal and Peter Gottlieb reflect in the introduction, there is no shortage of books on institutional leadership and, in fact, no shortage of theories of leadership, either. From the noise of competing voices, some more legitimate than others, a more focused thought emerges: archivists have the potential to be leaders in the work we do each and every day. We have much to learn from the leadership experts, but we have much more to learn from one another.

It was in that vein that my experience as director of ALI began. I had attended the third year of the institute in 2010, at the University of Wisconsin, and was led by a number of archivists I considered mentors. The experience was life changing in that it affected the very arc of my career. When the call from the National Historical Publications and Records Commission came out for the next round of funding in 2011, I held close but in-depth conversations with other archivists about what might be next for ALI. Those of us who had attended the early years of the institute at Wisconsin deeply appreciated the relationship between a reputable library school, continuing education resources, and the group of well-respected archival leaders who had created the institute. And so it was not that we thought the institute could be better but rather that it could be different.

As Gloria Steinem once noted, imagining is another form of planning, and so we imagined: what would, could, we do? Eight archivists, six of whom had attended the institute, worked to create this new version. For six years, we have done just that, first at Luther College and then at Berea College. As archival leaders, we patterned leadership for our peers, providing a setting where the challenging topics of our work could be discussed.

Who Are the Archival Leaders?

The most frequent question that I was asked during my years as the director of ALI was "Who is the right person to attend ALI?" This query was frequently followed by "Should they already be leaders? Or perhaps want to be a leader? Are they managers already? Is it for people who have been recently thrust into a leadership role?" Even in conversations with close colleagues and archival friends, the subject of who the institute is looking for arose. When I asked one particular person if he was going to apply to ALI, he responded, "No, I'm happy where I am. I don't want to move to a new job." For many of us, that is a consideration: archivists find themselves in many different places in their institutions, taking on leadership and management positions. And as we have seen, the experience may challenge many who attend ALI to take on a new opportunity. Truly, a new generation of leaders in our field has attended the institute.

As the institute moved into a third iteration at Berea College in 2016, one addition to the program was its first real assessment. In earlier years, assessment had been done of each cohort's experience, but there had not been a comprehensive review of the program. That assessment took place in 2016 and 2017 with the Archives Leadership Institute Steering Committee and director working with Dr. Rob Smith, Berea College's director of assessment. The report surveyed 134 past participants (a 62 percent response rate) using a survey tool with twenty-six items including both open-ended and forced-choice responses.

The assessment found that the goal of growing tomorrow's leaders in the archives profession was largely being met. When asked if they had used the skills they developed at ALI, the respondents generally responded positively, with 86 percent saying that they had achieved this goal at least to a moderate level. Participants reported that they felt energized by the institute, that it led to their being seen as leaders at their institutions, that it gave them new skills or the confidence to lead in new ways they had not learned in a textbook. In his report, Dr. Smith wrote, "While there is always room for improvement, it is clear that ALI has carried out a high quality leadership development program that has positively impacted many future leaders in the professional archives field."[1]

Of the ALI participants surveyed, 88 percent reported that they had at least moderately increased their leadership roles. Among the types of leadership roles the institute participants reported they had achieved were the following:

- elected or appointed positions
- new leadership positions
- increased responsibilities
- increased mentoring activities
- leading new initiatives
- professional presentations and publications

The ALI participants were also surveyed about the impact attending ALI had on the development of their professional network. More than 86 percent of the respondents felt that attending the institute had enhanced their ability to make use of their professional network, and more than 83 percent reported that their professional networks had been enhanced. While the assessment report states that it isn't possible to know for sure why these enhancements occurred, the outcomes may demonstrate the importance of having an archives-specific leadership development program. In fact, over the years, as the institute has evolved, changed, and relocated, the one constant has been the cohort of approximately twenty-five archivists, and it is this cohort model that appears to impact the participants' enhanced professional network and the benefit that enhancement brings.

In its summary, the report recommends five strategic areas for improvement:

1. ***Outcomes.*** The Steering Committee is encouraged to continue its consideration of the desired outcomes for the institute before deciding on and designing the programming for the next institute. Once the outcomes are set, they should be explicitly aligned with specific elements of future ALI programming.

2. ***Extended support for practicum projects.*** While there are many reasons that practicum projects might not reach completion, they are nonetheless a signature assignment that will undoubtedly provide some excellent assessment material down the road. Moreover, they represent the most direct impact that ALI has on the field, in general. As such, the Steering Committee should consider ways that it might offer continued support well after the institute ends, perhaps in a more structured way, to ensure that more of these projects are completed.

3. ***Leadership roles and responsibilities.*** Comments from participants revealed six clear ways in which they felt their leadership roles and responsibilities were increasing following their participation in ALI. Emergent themes such as these represent opportunities to increase the relevance of ALI programming, which will likely be reflected in stronger achievement of outcome 2. As such, future institutes would do well to consider these themes and match institute programming to those common themes.

4. ***Professional networks.*** The Steering Committee might also consider what it could offer by way of "post-institute" interventions/events that facilitate and support participants' use of their professional network. While a combined 60 percent of respondents reported achieving this outcome to at least a moderate extent, the modal response suggested that this outcome was achieved only to a slight extent by a sizeable minority of participants. Thus, it represents one area that, depending on the intervention, could carry with it a sizeable return on investment.

5. ***Professional networks.*** Also noteworthy was the relatively low use of professional networks for collaborations. Thus, another low-cost improvement could be to design future ALI programming with the explicit purpose of increasing collaborative uses of professional networks.[2]

These recommendations create a starting point for a continued conversation about the ongoing needs for leadership development in the archival field and about how we can continue to develop our existing programs and create new ones to support the profession.

What Will Our Archival Leaders Need?

In his chapter on using strategic approaches, Peter Gottlieb addresses the question of what archival leaders will need by talking about how we can shed the traditional and outdated versions of what an archives is. This requires us, as leaders of organizations and our profession, to find new ways to share our vision, through our communication plans, as David Carmicheal writes, or through our actions as we work with our stakeholders as well as our staff and colleagues. Taken as a whole, leading is a state of being for archivists, with the added pressure to be conversant, if not fluent, in our vision of archives, in and outside our organizations.

We continue to see pressure on our organizations to be distinctive, especially in ways that can be leveraged for fund-raising purposes. But there is also an ever-increasing expectation to be more efficient, more transparent, more accessible, more flexible, and more creative, often with fewer resources than before. This was a common refrain among the ALI participants during the years it was held at Luther College. The facilitator for that program, Luther Snow, worked with each cohort on the first day to challenge them to look at their assets and to think in a positive, generative way about challenge, rather than playing a zero-sum game, as it is often tempting to do. This exercise invoked new styles of leadership for the archivists who were in attendance. Too often, we spend the majority of our time examining the weakness, the challenges, rather than putting time into developing the possibilities.

In his chapter on communication, David Carmicheal raises the issue of values and the tendency that the archivist's individual values may be projected onto the institution. In this discussion, he suggests conducting a personal values inventory. As leaders, it is crucial that we spend some time on self-assessment, whether it is of our values, our unconscious biases, or our personality types. We must look at these self-assessments and use them to inform our leadership development.

Carmicheal's point is a significant one and is reflected in my own work life. Several years before I left Luther College, the merged library/information technology department participated in a StrengthsFinder workshop. I found the experience to be very helpful, not only for assessing my own strengths and style but also for learning more about my colleagues and how their personal strengths and styles worked with my own. After the first year of ALI@Luther, one comment we received in our evaluation addressed the need for self-assessment during the week—it was an area absent from the curriculum. We began to include the StrengthsFinder survey tool and for five years collected the top five strengths of all the participating archivists. Notably, some strengths, like Input and Context, show up again and again. Based on the descriptions of those strengths, this result makes sense—they sound like the description of an archivist! Consider the description of Context: "People who are especially talented in the Context theme enjoy thinking about the past. They understand the present by researching its history."[3] The other common Strength, Input, is even more on point: "People who are especially talented in the Input theme have a craving to know more. Often they like to collect and archive all kinds of information."

But whatever the personality assessment test or tool, I agree with Carmicheal's conclusion that self-awareness will help develop a vision that is clear to the staff, supporters, and administration of your organization. I am someone who loves to brainstorm and is happiest coming up with new, often big ideas. Having this trait affirmed has helped me to communicate more effectively and has encouraged me to keep some of the more harebrained ideas to myself. Especially when working with new people, I can clarify that I am an expansive thinker who likes to throw many ideas into the mix before settling on one approach; the ability to describe myself enables me to be a better colleague and leader. The point is not to scare others with the size of my ideas but to prepare them for spitballing as a necessary part of my own process. My favorite line from the definition of the Activator Strength (my number two Strength) is "the process isn't pretty."

Managing individual communication styles and having self-awareness are also crucial as we work in a multigenerational workplace. Even in a small institution like my own, our staff spans six decades. As both a leader and a manager, I have learned that this range can create a wide variety of styles and approaches to our work. Rather than struggle with that wide breadth of inputs, it is important to work to appreciate the gifts that each person brings forward from their perspective. And while it may feel like we are in a special moment, I believe that multigenerational workplaces will likely continue to exist for the foreseeable future.

The ability to appreciate individual differences is particularly true when working as a supervisor. David Carmicheal lays out a clear and thoughtful approach to this in his chapter on communication. For leaders and managers, the supervision and evaluation of others' work can be the hardest part of the job, and his crucial advice to set goals and schedule regular check-ins and assessment is a good one. The hardest guidelines to follow are the ones that are unspoken (as a friend once joked, the "Great Hidden Expectations"). We are more effective as leaders when we maintain a level of transparency and use established, mutually agreed-upon methods of communication. This is true in a workplace supervisory setting or in any of the many special projects or professional tasks we take on. We need to be open and clear with expectations and respect those expectations. The same is true with how we develop our policies, work with our donors, and the like. When you move on to the next role in your life, whether a new job or retirement, someone will replace you; how we lead now will make an impact on how the work will continue after we are gone.

The need for leaders to be self-aware is reinforced in Peter Gottlieb's chapter on building relationships. I particularly related to his emphasis on staff relationships characterized by reciprocal understanding and support as well as a willingness to hold themselves individually and collectively accountable for achieving agreed-on goals.[4] At a recent staff meeting, one archivist asked me what my theory of leadership was. I have to admit that even though I have directed a leadership program for six years and would consider myself a leader, I found myself at a loss for words to define what my overall philosophy of leadership is. Even the process of thinking about an answer takes some unpacking of my own experiences and those of close colleagues.

As the head of an archival program, I have aspired to the goals of trust, mutuality, and cooperation. This development of trust and cooperative relationships is crucial to providing true leadership in an archival organization. Having strong internal relationships will definitely impact the ability to improve external ones as well. As a leader, I want the rest of my team to forge relationships that further the mission and reflect the values of the archives, and I need to trust that they will do so ethically and professionally. I will not be in every conversation, and perhaps, as a result, decisions or outcomes will veer from my goals as a director. Enabling others to act independently on behalf of the archives also means that credit for successes will land widely. This can all be challenging. Archival teams need to pull together to achieve unit-level goals, even if we might take different paths to get there. Additionally, we all want to be recognized for our work and our role in accomplishing a goal. As leaders, we must learn how to balance taking credit for the work that has been done with also giving credit where it is due—and sometimes being okay with not being acknowledged individually at all.

This is particularly true in situations where a leader or manager's style comes into conflict with other members of the department. In some instances, it is a personal style difference, and in others, it creates a toxic environment that can be difficult, if not impossible, to recover from and change. As a leader, it is crucial to once again be self-aware and assess the situation. Reaching out for support from institutional resources should not be seen as a shortcoming. In some cases, peer support will be useful, and in others, the leader may want to seek additional support and training, utilizing professional development or working with a job or life coach. Additionally, if external forces are creating a hostile environment for you as a leader, be prudent. Document the situation and create a paper trail that will assist you if a more formal response becomes necessary. Finally, having experienced a number of these situations, I have decided to take an optimistic approach to them. I do my best to believe that all are acting with the best of intentions, even if it does not seem that way, and to work to understand what their intent was and how to turn that intent into something positive for all.

Developing New Leaders

Quite possibly, the most significant thing we must do as archival leaders is develop new leaders. This has been an underlying mission of programs like ALI, but how do we identify these potential leaders? Do leaders know they are leaders? Do they require someone else to identify that capacity within them first?

Each year, I reached out to former institute participants and asked them to nominate others in the field who they felt would benefit from an experience like ALI. On more than one occasion, I would receive a response from a nominee who was surprised that they had been recommended because they had not considered themselves a leader. Some of our best applicants and cohort members came from those nominations.

Having peers in your corner, giving you feedback or a nudge on your leadership path, can be crucial. Anne Ackerson, former executive director of the Council of State Archivists, suggested in a blog post titled "Why You Need a Personal Board of Directors" that you should develop a group of peers that can be counted on "to help you make strategic decisions about your career needs[,] to be a mix of people who can see the landscape from a 30,000-foot level as well as offer on-the-ground advice for navigating it."[5] Development of this type of strategic network is crucial to your personal leadership development. My own board has evolved over the years, but it is a group that I count on for good counsel when I need an external view of just what I am doing with my life. Carmicheal echoes this recommendation in chapter 6, "Developing Leaders." As he says, it is very important to make sure that you are including people who will be honest about the good and the bad and can work with you in a way that helps you continue to develop your skills and career, rather than just affirming you.

Another challenge that Carmicheal identifies as crucial in leadership development is professional expertise and development. As an organizational leader, it will be important to be conversant in all areas of the field. This can require one to show some humility. It may require you to admit that you do not know something that you probably should. This is a personal and long-term challenge for me and is why I must trust my advisors. There is nothing wrong with asking a question on a listserv, but sometimes it is better to have a kitchen cabinet of colleagues that you can consult first.

Whether you aspire to leadership or you find yourself in a leadership position without warning, ongoing success will require you to develop many of the skills that Carmicheal outlines in his chapter on leadership development. In fact, communication, teamwork, and self-awareness are many of the skills that were included in the curriculum of the most recent ALI at Berea College. These skills are all crucial to achieving real success as a leader. And it does not come easily to everyone—our styles vary without the pitfalls of qualitative judgment, which is why it is critical as leaders to offer to begin to identify and mentor these skills in other archivists who have leadership potential.

In my career, I have been very fortunate to have several people in our field who did that for me. My graduate archival studies professor and a supervisor at my first job told me early on how crucial it was to attend professional conferences and be engaged in professional organizations. Later, an archival colleague in Iowa offered me an appointment to an SAA subcommittee, and I began my tenure of service to the society. It will be particularly important for us to identify a diverse group of new leaders as the faces in our profession continue to represent a growing number of diverse communities. We need to think about what challenges might be faced by our new leaders when they come from underrepresented groups and how we can support their leadership development—even if it requires us to change our long-held conventions and models of leadership. We must operate holistically by addressing a life cycle of recruitment that brings in promising new archivists; reaches further back into undergraduate programs and high schools; and rethinks nondegree on-ramps to the profession. We must build the deep bench now for the leaders of the future.

As we continue to move forward in the twenty-first century, we must pay special note to the challenges for women in leadership. In the 2004 A*Census survey of the profession, it was reported that one of the most surprising findings was the gender shift that had occurred in the field since Ernst Posner's 1956 study. In 2004, 65 percent of archivists were women, a near reversal from the earlier study, which found that 67 percent of archivists were men.[6] In addition, that percentage increased in the younger demographic groups, with nearly 80 percent of all archivists under the age of thirty being women. In the fifteen years since A*Census was conducted, that gender imbalance has continued, with a higher percentage of women coming into the field and more and more moving into management roles.[7]

While the percentage of women in the field has continue to rapidly increase, racial diversity has increased much more slowly. Posner's 1956 study did not include data about the racial identity of archivists, leading one to believe that there may have been only white archivists. Brenda Banks presented a diversity report on A*Census at the SAA 2005 Annual Meeting sharing data comparing the 2004 study and David Bearman's study of the profession in 1982. The A*Census data reported that 7.6 percent of the profession self-reported as being nonwhite and non-Latino, compared to 2.8 percent in the Bearman study.[8] The most recent survey of SAA members that asked for demographic information was the Women Archivists/SAA Salary Survey, conducted in 2017. The survey had 2,100 responses, with 87.7 percent of the respondents self-identifying as white.

In the six years that I was director of ALI, I am grateful that we increased our racial diversity among the cohorts. Partial responsibility goes to our directed recruiting efforts with the Mosaic program participants, the Archives and Archivists of Color Section, and the Latin American and Caribbean Heritage Archives Section, but the most effective tool was recruitment by past ALI cohort members, especially the efforts by participants of color who reached out to their friends and colleagues to vouch for the program. One of my great concerns about the institute during the years that I was the director was the lack of racial diversity among the steering committee, faculty, and staff, but when we were putting our plans together for the institute, we had trouble recruiting archivists of color to work on the project. Our work now to diversify the cohorts and to develop more leaders from racially diverse backgrounds will help ensure that this is not the case in the future.

Leaning In, Falling Back

While women and men face many of the same challenges and opportunities in leadership and management roles, there are also quite a few that are unique for the woman leader. Sheryl Sandberg's 2013 book, *Lean In: Women, Work, and the Will to Lead*, began a conversation not only in the archives profession but also across much of the popular press. At the 2014 Society of American Archivists Annual Meeting, there was a session titled "Lean In: Archival Management and the Gender Dynamics of Leadership." Six women managers spoke on a panel about the status of women in the profession, with a specific focus on how gender affects management. I was at that session, and it was a very good, frank conversation. But not surprisingly, because of the topic and perhaps its frankness, it was not recorded; far too often, the potential negative of speaking openly about gender inequity outweighs the positives of preserving these conversations. Recently, Sandberg has followed up her book with a further discussion about the *Lean In* phenomenon and the resulting workplace pushback.[9] The annual Women in the Workplace study conducted by LeanIn.org and McKinsey & Company affirms those findings. The most recent 2017 study reported several key findings, including that progress for women appears to be stalling and that most people often overlook the unique challenges faced by women of color. Indeed, however thoughtful the 2014 SAA panel, it was composed solely of white women. What we do know is that women are falling behind early and more and more with each step.[10] In a female-majority profession, it would be nice to think that we would not face the same kinds of challenges, but even if our archives organizations are led by women, we are often part of a larger parent organization that is not. The challenges increase for people of color in the field, where their representation in leadership is even lower. Unfortunately, those challenges don't disappear when we do make it into leadership roles. Issues of gender pay equity create challenges for leaders as we work to be fair but also desire to have our own value fairly compensated.

Women in leadership and management also face additional challenges in communication and management style. In October 2015 Alexandra Petri published an opinion piece in the *Washington Post* titled "Famous Quotes, the way a woman would have to say them during a meeting."[11] The piece was in response to an article written by Jennifer Lawrence after the Sony hack revealed that she had been paid less than her male costars in the movie *American Hustle*. The opinion piece by Petri received a great deal of notice, in part because it was funny:

> To illustrate this difficulty, I have taken the liberty of translating some famous sentences into the phrases a woman would have to use to say them during a meeting not to be perceived as angry, threatening or (gasp!) bitchy.
>
> *"Give me liberty, or give me death."*
>
> **Woman in a Meeting: "Dave, if I could, I could just—I just really feel like if we had liberty it would be terrific, and the alternative would just be awful, you know? That's just how it strikes me. I don't know."**

"I have a dream today!"

Woman in a Meeting: "I'm sorry, I just had this idea—it's probably crazy, but—look, just as long as we're throwing things out here—I had sort of an idea or vision about maybe the future?"

"Mr. Gorbachev, tear down this wall!"

Woman in a Meeting: "I'm sorry, Mikhail, if I could? Didn't mean to cut you off there. Can we agree that this wall maybe isn't quite doing what it should be doing? Just looking at every-thing everyone's been saying, it seems like we could consider removing it. Possibly. I don't know, what does the room feel?"

But Petri's satire also received notice because, by and large, it is true. Studies have shown that in positive performance evaluations, women are more likely to receive critical feedback.[12] Similar find-ings reflect the impact of women's negotiating for salary.[13] As leaders, both male and female, it is crucial that our profession take action and begin to address this inequality. Anne Ackerson, former executive director of CoSA, has been an outspoken proponent of gender equality in the museum field. In 2017, she cowrote with Joan Baldwin the book *Women in the Museum: Lessons from the Workplace*, a thorough look at the role of women in museums. Although museums and archives are not exactly the same, they have many similarities, including resource issues and, as phrased in the book, roles as "Guardians of America's Patrimony."[14] In the book, they address many issues affect-ing women in the museum world, most of which resonated with my own experience in the archival profession. It is time a similar book was written by and for archivists.

Some of the universal challenges women face in leadership is the gender bias that takes place in everyday communications. Women are more likely to be called "bossy" or other similar but even less flattering words, often for behaving in a way that will bring praise for a man. In my own experience, I have been told to "put some sugar on it" when writing emails detailing the neces-sary next steps in a project and that my attempts at mentorship with a young male colleague were "condescending." One senior administrator told me I was "wound a bit too tight." A survey by the Center for Creative Leadership found that women were twice as likely to be described as bossy, even though "bossy" behavior was observed in men and women in equal numbers.[15] Even more concerning is the perception that bossiness makes it less likely for women to be promoted into additional leadership roles. In the white paper produced from their survey, the authors point out the additional challenge for women in leadership:

> While these results seem unfair, they would not surprise women's leadership scholars. Decades of research shows that there are gender biases in leadership, and women often face a "double-bind" in the workplace (Eagly & Karau, 2002; Jamieson, 1995). When people think of leaders, they tend to think of men and stereotypically masculine traits (e.g., independence, aggression, competitive-ness). Yet women are generally still expected to conform to stereotypically feminine traits (e.g., nurturing, nice, altruistic) in the workplace. This leads to a "double-bind" in which women who exhibit feminine traits are seen as lacking strong leadership qualities, while women who exhibit masculine traits are seen as unfeminine, mean, and unlikable.[16]

Faced with these leadership challenges, what are we, as a profession, to do? First, we must begin to take a good look at the challenges and develop an intersectional strategic plan for building our lead-ership skills, pathways, and respect within the profession. Ackerson and Baldwin are doing great work in this area for the museum profession. Their most recent book, *Women in the Museum*, is a must-read for archival leaders, and the important conversations that are taking place in the museum world should be happening in the archival world as well. Equally useful for archival leaders is their blog and related book, *Leadership Matters*.[17] In a recent blog post, Ackerson and Baldwin shared the results of a gender equity study they conducted with museum workers.[18] With 709 responses, they found that 62 percent of all respondents had been affected by gender discrimination, with the most frequent forms related to lack of respect, pay inequity, and verbal or sexual harassment. In their commentary about the posting of the results of the survey, Ackerson and Baldwin note that at the time of the blog post (July 23, 2018), there had been no response from any of the museum professional organizations, including the American Association for State and Local History, which they had earlier praised for requiring salary information in all job postings on its website. This leads one to consider what the role of our professional organizations is in both leadership development and issues like racial and gender equity in our field—issues that I would argue are intertwined and must be addressed together. One of those pathways has been the development of an archives-focused leadership program.

In addition to what the profession must do, what can we as leaders and managers do to diversify the archives and to support the work of women in our field? At the end of *Women in the Museum*, the authors share their "Gender Equity Agenda." The agenda is divided into six sections, including boards of trustees, individuals, institutions, professional associations, graduate programs, and funders. Each section includes important suggestions, but there are a number that are key for us as leaders and managers to consider if we want to diversify our profession and work to improve the environment for the many women in it who are or wish to be leaders.[19]

As leaders, we need to work at all times on two fronts: both advocating for ourselves, those who are currently in leadership, and looking toward the future, making sure that the new leaders who follow us will continue to work for diversity and equality. We need to share our stories and create transparency, both in terms of salary inequality and the challenges that many of us are facing as we work within traditional, often patriarchal institutions that often are not willing or able to listen to the concerns we are bringing forward.

While Ackerson and Baldwin's recommendations for individuals are useful for self-leadership, the recommendations they make for institutions highlight where archival leaders and managers can have the most impact. These recommendations cover many issues, including the following:

- Make a commitment to gender diversity and equity, coming from the top.
- Build diverse leadership from the ground up; make the leaders rather than searching for them.
- Insist on equal pay for equal work, and require transparency for understanding the criteria for salary levels.
- Develop flexible, family-friendly policies including flexible scheduling, telecommuting, compressed workweeks, and/or on-site childcare. Make sure that staff with children are able to advance equitably.
- Make mentoring and coaching a priority.
- Look outside the field for ideas, information, and solutions and share them with your colleagues.

And perhaps, most importantly, withhold judgment. As leaders, we must give one another the benefit of the doubt—and if we're lucky, others will do the same for us.

The issues that we face are not only in the archival field, but I hope that with our skills at both preserving and telling the stories of those who have come before us and creating the context of history to understand our present, we can work together to reduce these inequalities for our fellow archivists. And that is true leadership.

A Leadership Program of Our Own

The need for a leadership training program for archivists was identified in February 2003 when Kathleen Williams, then at the Smithsonian Institution Archives, sent a letter to the SAA Council expressing her concern that available continuing education offerings were focused primarily on technical topics and did not provide the leadership training necessary for midcareer archivists.[20] Peter Hirtle, the SAA president at the time, responded to her letter in August 2003, including the comment that Max Evans, then executive director of the National Historical Publications and Records Commission, shared a similar concern. Additionally, the issue had been discussed in other venues within SAA, including the Archives Management Roundtable, the Continuing Education Committee, and the SAA Fellows email discussion list.

One year later, Kathleen Williams joined the NHPRC as a deputy director; at this point, she and Max Evans first discussed an NHPRC-sponsored program that would eventually become the Archives Leadership Institute. In 2006 the proposal to support an institute was approved, with NHPRC staff member Lucy Barber shepherding its development. The University of Wisconsin-Madison was awarded the initial two-year grant to host the 2008 and 2009 sessions and then a three-year award to continue ALI until the summer of 2012. In those five years, 132 people attended the institute.

In 2013 the Institute of Museum and Library Services funded the Nexus Project: Spanning Boundaries to Transform Library Leadership (2013–14) to continue to study the development of leadership programs in libraries, museums, and archives. In each of these cases, both funders (the NHPRC and IMLS) identified that the rapidly changing operation of archives and other information organizations requires that members of our profession have access to high-quality, high-impact training that will expand their ability to exercise leadership within their institutions and the profession as a whole.

ALI@Luther (2013–15) was developed by Sasha Griffin (project coordinator) and me (project director) together with the Steering Committee (Terry Baxter, Brenda Gunn, Geof Huth, Beth Myers, Dan Noonan, and Tanya Zanish-Belcher). We worked to develop a program that would provide cutting-edge training each year for twenty-five midcareer archivists who had either recently moved into a leadership opportunity or were actively interested in seeking such an opportunity.[21] The institute utilized a weeklong intensive leadership training, a follow-up workshop, and a practicum project to help participants develop the ability and tools to transform the archival profession in practice, in theory, and in attitude.

What makes ALI unique and a program we can emulate as well as scale is that it took the essential building blocks of leadership development and put them in an archival context. The institute is led by archivists, with the support of professionals from other fields who could share their leadership development expertise; essentially, it was and is ours. But the institute also has limitations. The model it has used since its inception has been a weeklong residential experience with approximately twenty-five participants. It is possible that our field has more than twenty-five people who have leadership potential at any given moment or people who may not be able to spend a full week in a setting like ALI. It is also true that there are archivists who felt that they were beyond the time in their career when they should attend the institute or those who have attended and would like to develop additional leadership skills. We must continue to develop settings where archivists are able to meet those needs.

One aspect of ALI that supports the "archivists teaching archivists" model is the peer mentor program. From 2013 to 2018, the institute was supported by a steering committee made up of archival leaders. Each cohort of twenty-five participants was assigned a steering committee member as a peer mentor. This is not the only mentor program in the archives profession; both SAA and the Business Archives Section of SAA run mentoring programs, as do some regional archival associations. What makes the ALI program unique is the small group cohort and the intensive time that the peer mentor and mentees spend together during the institute. In addition, participants are required to develop a leadership project that they will complete after ALI. The concept of the practicum project was designed to require participants to quickly put into action the leadership skills they learned at the institute.

In their book *Women in the Museum*, Ackerson and Baldwin discuss the importance of not only having role models in the field but also going beyond to developing mentors and sponsors.[22] The mentor, as a sounding board, can be a crucial development tool for all leaders, but particularly for women (and other diverse leaders) in the archives profession who are seeking to navigate the sometimes difficult waters of leadership development. Even more crucial to that development is the role of the sponsor. As defined by the authors, a sponsor is "an out and out advocate for you in your institution. This is the person who raises your name for new assignments or promotions, works to get you training you need (and deserve), advocates on your behalf for a salary increase, and helps with social networking appropriate for the office. If the mentor is the Sherpa, carefully guiding and counseling you along your career journey, the sponsor is the special ops force with one highly targeted mission: *you*."[23]

So what will archival leadership look like ten years from now? Or twenty? The good news is that archivists care about leadership, and many have taken advantage of the opportunities the profession has to further develop those skills, through training like the Archives Leadership Institute; through service to the profession as members of the Society of American Archivists, the Council of State Archivists, the National Association of Government and Records Archivists, and the many regional archival organizations; and through existing mentorship programs. But we need to do more. One great challenge to our leadership is the burden of debt that so many of our newest members of the profession carry as they enter the field. The cost of a graduate education has gone up as traditional programs with hands-on training and funding to support the cost of education have become more scarce. It may soon be time to look at new models for the training and education of archivists that will alleviate that challenge. As archival leaders, we need to examine the impact that the decisions made by higher education and graduate programs are having on the training and development of new archivists and on our profession. The decisions that are being made by those outside our profession are beginning to limit the options that archival leaders and managers are able to make. We must begin to develop new avenues for training and education that support our field, not the financial needs of large educational institutions that may not be invested in the development of archivists.

Finally, the challenges and opportunities of leadership that archivists face are not unique to our profession. While there are many benefits to having an archives-specific setting in which to discuss leadership and to develop our leaders, we also need to work with our library and museum colleagues to develop strong leadership development opportunities and practices. We must learn and build on the body of work that has been developed in these related fields. If there is one thing that I have learned in my years of working with our emerging archival leaders, it is that our colleagues have an abundance of talent and gifts. Now we need to continue to do what is necessary to support and develop those talents to continue the rich history of ethical service that archivists have given to preserving the historical record.

In her 2018 SAA presidential address, Tanya Zanish-Belcher laid out her recommendations for what those next steps might be. She provided a hopeful and optimistic vision for our profession and left us with these important thoughts:

> **Be strategic and mindful about your archives career and service.** Dedicate yourself to what you truly care about and are willing to spend the time on.
>
> **Leaders are made, not born.** Consider every experience you have as an important step on your path and as a part of your individual story.
>
> **Believe in yourself and share yourself with others.** Smile and say hello to someone at this meeting you don't know. Share a story from your archives. Find a mentor. Be a mentor. When a colleague calls on you for advice, answer.[24]

I am biased, of course, because Tanya is my mentor and has helped me become the leader I am today, but her words give us all inspiration for the next chapter of archival leadership. We will need to build on our experience to lead into the next phase of our career and work. Each challenge that we've faced should teach us something for the next time, because there will always be challenges—internal or external, physical, emotional, of our own making, or completely out of our control.

How will you, as an archival leader, make that difference? How will you handle that challenge, that disaster, that miracle? I hope this book has inspired you to think about your own leadership practice. Perhaps it's caused you to reflect on leaders from your past, good and bad. Sometimes your leadership development will lead you to pursue new challenges. Other times, you will find opportunity to grow where you are. One of my former colleagues and current mentors affirmed for me the strength of "blooming where I was planted." Leadership growth occurs in many ways. It will take practice and experimentation, and some wrong steps, but with careful mentoring and your own growth, it will happen. You will be the person that someone else calls a leader.

NOTES

1. Archives Leadership Institute Outcomes Assessment Report, September 1, 2017, https://drive.google.com/file/d/0ByGqHZFjjlM3Y3lHM0V6bWt1TXFTcWgyYlI4N24yNm1PYmtF/view, captured at https://perma.cc/WP8W-UABD.

2. Archives Leadership Institute Outcomes Assessment Report, 11–12.

3. CliftonStrengths, https://www.gallupstrengthscenter.com/home/en-us/cliftonstrengths-themes-domains, captured at https://perma.cc/3W7H-A2WA.

4. Chapter 5.

5. "Why You Need a Personal Board of Directors," *Leading by Design*, August 20, 2017, http://leadingbydesign.blogspot.com/2017/08/why-you-need-personal-board-of-directors.html, captured at https://perma.cc/TL9P-MQBJ.

6. Ernst Posner, "What, Then, Is the American Archivist, This New Man?," *American Archivist* 20, no. 1 (1957): 3–11, http://www.jstor.org/stable/40289554, captured at https://perma.cc/Q43Z-3ZLA.

7. A*Census, p. 333, https://www2.archivists.org/sites/all/files/ACENSUS-Final.pdf, captured at https://perma.cc/N6DR-3ARU.

8. A*Census, https://www2.archivists.org/sites/all/files/Banks-ACENSUS.pdf, captured at https://perma.cc/6QFP-B33S.

9. Kristen Bellstrom, "Sheryl Sandberg: These Are the Biggest Obstacles for Women Trying to 'Lean In'" *Fortune*, September 27, 2016, http://fortune.com/2016/09/27/sheryl-sandberg-women-in-the-workplace/, captured at https://perma.cc/3X47-YYVY.

10. "Women in the Workplace," https://womenintheworkplace.com/, captured at https://perma.cc/68HT-CS6Z.

11. Alexandra Petri, "Famous Quotes, the Way a Woman Would Have to Say Them during a Meeting," *Washington Post*, October 13, 2015, https://www.washingtonpost.com/blogs/compost/wp/2015/10/13/jennifer-lawrence-has-a-point-famous-quotes-the-way-a-woman-would-have-to-say-them-during-a-meeting/?utm_term=.67aff78da925, captured at https://perma.cc/5Z2G-FA72.

12. Kieran Snyder, "The Abrasiveness Trap," *Fortune*, August 26, 2014, http://fortune.com/2014/08/26/performance-review-gender-bias/, captured at https://perma.cc/LA75-NK37.

13. "Social Incentives for Gender Differences in the Propensity to Initiate Negotiations: Sometimes It Does Hurt to Ask," abstract, https://www.sciencedirect.com/science/article/pii/S0749597806000884, captured at https://perma.cc/MQ9D-LXJ6.

14. Anne Ackerson and Joan Baldwin, *Women in the Museum: Lessons from the Workplace* (Routledge, London: 2017), 14.

15. "Bossy: What's Gender Got to Do with It?," https://www.ccl.org/articles/white-papers/bossy-whats-gender-got-to-do-with-it/, captured at https://perma.cc/3ZJ8-ZLPW.

16. Cathleen Clerkin et al., "Bossy: What's Gender Got to Do with It?," p. 10, https://www.ccl.org/wp-content/uploads/2015/04/Bossy2.pdf, captured at https://perma.cc/K8FJ-ESXM.

17. *Leadership Matters*, https://leadershipmatters1213.wordpress.com/, captured at https://perma.cc/R6NG-B48C.

18. "Some Thoughts About Museum Women—ALL Women," *Leadership Matters*, July 23, 2018, https://leadershipmatters1213.wordpress.com/2018/07/23/some-thoughts-about-museum-women-all-women/, captured at https://perma.cc/ML3Y-7SF8.

19. Ackerson and Baldwin, *Women in the Museum*, 198–202.

20. Brenda Gunn, "The Zeitgeist of Leadership, the Madison Chronicles: Lessons Learned from the Archives Leadership Institute" (presented at Society of Georgia Archivists-South Carolina Archival Association Joint Annual Meeting, Augusta, October 29, 2010).

21. Although the initial development of ALI@Luther was targeted at midcareer archivists, in practice the participants have been from all phases of their careers.

22. Ackerson and Baldwin, *Women in the Museum*, 188.

23. Ackerson and Baldwin, 189.

24. Tanya Zanish-Belcher, "Keeping Evidence & Memory: Archives Storytelling in the 21st Century (Presidential Address, SAA Annual Meeting)," August 17, 2018, *Off the Record*, https://offtherecord.archivists.org/2018/08/17/keeping-evidence-memory-archives-storytelling-in-the-21st-century-presidential-address-saa-annual-meeting-august-17-2018/, captured at https://perma.cc/NC4T-P576.

Annotated Bibliography

The purpose of this section is to provide readers with an annotated list of sources about leadership and management of archival programs that were significant for our discussions in the first six chapters. It includes sources far beyond the scope of archival repositories themselves, reflecting our conviction that leadership and management have many of the same essential attributes and characteristics regardless of where they emerge and where they are practiced. While it has attracted growing attention in the last ten years, leadership and management of archives per se remain topics seldom written about in the professional literature. Consequently, sources included here extend from the world of for-profit businesses, to archives' sister professions of librarianship and museums, to archives themselves. Bruce Dearstyne's *Leading and Managing Archives and Records Programs* (2008) includes an excellent bibliography of works on leadership across a range of fields, up to roughly 2007. Because there is no need to list all of those publications again, this bibliography concentrates mostly on publications that have appeared in the last ten years. It also includes all the monographs that we found most useful in writing the chapters in Part I of this book.

Articles and Chapters

Anderson, Christopher J. "Special Collections, Archives, and Insider Theft: A Thief in our Midst." In *Management: Innovative Practices for Archives and Special Collections*, edited by Kate Theimer, 45–60. Lanham, MD: Rowman and Littlefield, 2014. Anderson narrates a case study of insider theft of manuscripts from a university collection and the investigation of the crime that ensued. He explains the steps that were taken to improve security in the wake of the theft and concludes with the lessons he felt were learned from the incident.

Davis, Susan E. "A*Census: Report on Archival Leadership." *American Archivist* 69, no. 2 (2006): 407–18. Davis analyzes data relating to leadership from the Society of American Archivists' 2004 census of US archivists. She finds differences among archivists in their identification with and participation in archival professional organizations and argues that these differences can reflect variations in readiness to assume leadership in such organizations. She also looks at census data on archivists holding management positions and calls attention to an impending turnover in their ranks due to retirement.

Eaton, Fynette. "Managing Organizational Change in Archives: Taking Control." In *Management: Innovative Practices for Archives and Special Collections*, edited by Kate Theimer, 105–19. Lanham, MD: Rowman and Littlefield, 2014. In this case study of organizational change at a large archival repository, Eaton describes phases of work including planning, background research, and implementation of a change management plan. She ends by emphasizing the need for continual communication and for understanding the culture of the organization undergoing change.

Greene, Mark A. "Useful and Painless Strategic Planning: 'Make a New Plan, Stan.'" In *Management: Innovative Practices for Archives and Special Collections*, edited by Kate Theimer, 183–97. Lanham, MD: Rowman and Littlefield, 2014. Greene recounts a strategic planning process at a university archives and manuscripts collection. He explains in detail the planning process and the process of gaining employees' confidence and cooperation. The lessons he emphasizes from this planning include maintaining a flexible approach, open-mindedness, positive attitude, and a sense of humor.

Grimm, Tracy, and Chon Noriega. "Documenting Regional Latino Arts and Culture: Case Studies for a Collaborative, Community-Oriented Approach." *American Archivist* 76, no. 1 (2013): 95–112. Stressing that the recent growth and development of Latino population in the US raises important issues about how to build the documentary record of their communities, this article examines the Latino collections development practices at two institutions: the Chicano Studies Research Center (University of California, Los Angeles) and the Institute for Latino Studies (Notre Dame University). The analysis of these institutions' methods leads the authors to call on archivists not only to follow currently recommended collection development methods but also to support Latino communities themselves and, in particular, their archives.

Hackman, Larry. "Leadership and Infrastructure in Archival Programs." In "Perspective: Leadership Skills for Archivists." *American Archivist* 74, no. 1 (2011): 107–9. In this section, Hackman proposes two "infrastructures" that archival leaders should construct and maintain: one involving professional standards, program status within a larger organization, and sufficient resources; the other involving management and operational approaches like planning and evaluation that help an archives continually consolidate achievements and build on them.

Jimerson, Randall. "Teaching Leadership." In "Perspective: Leadership Skills for Archivists." *American Archivist* 74, no. 1 (2011): 115–22. Jimerson argues that the way archivists interact with the public is another arena where they can exert leadership. Using leadership knowledge and skills that Jimerson recommends all professional archivists learn through formal training, they should advocate to the public the fundamental purpose, goals, and values of archives. Among these are social values such as diversity, social justice, and equality.

Joffrion, Elizabeth, and Natalia Fernandez. "Collaborations between Tribal and Nontribal Organizations: Suggested Best Practices for Sharing Expertise, Cultural Resources, and Knowledge." *American Archivist* 78, no. 1 (2015): 192–237. To investigate the administration and outcomes of collaborative cultural heritage projects between tribal and nontribal participants, the authors used a combination of quantitative and qualitative data from responses to a survey sent to participants. They organize their findings under six headings, each of which captures a lesson learned through collaborative projects. They then recommend best practices for successful collaborations.

Knight, Jeanine. "Investing in Human Resources in Development: Strategic Planning for Success in Academic Libraries." In *Advances in Library Administration and Organization*, edited by Delmus E. Williams, Janine Golden, and Jennifer K. Sweeney, 1–42. Vol. 33. Bingley, UK: Emerald Publishing, 2015. Knight examines strategic planning in libraries, arguing for inclusion of human resource departments.

Kotter, John P. "What Leaders Really Do." In *On Leadership*, 37–56. Boston: Harvard Business Review Press, 2011. Kotter, a professor emeritus of leadership at Harvard Business School, emphasizes the differences between management and leadership and the key role of leadership, visioning.

Kurtz, Tony. "Leadership, Accountability, and Technological Change." In "Perspective: Leadership Skills for Archivists." *American Archivist* 74, no. 1 (2011): 110–15. Based on his experience as the head of a university archives and records management program, Kurtz identifies opportunities to exercise leadership in an environment where digital recordkeeping technology was bringing new concerns about compliant procedures, accountability, and staff training to the fore. The article describes opportunities within this context that Kurtz was taking to strengthen and expand the archives.

Kwan, Denise, and Libi Shen. "Senior Librarians' Perceptions of Successful Leadership Skills." In *Advances in Library Administration and Organization*, edited by Delmus E. Williams, Janine Golden, and Jennifer K. Sweeney, 89–134. Vol. 33. Bingley, UK: Emerald Publishing, 2015. Kwan and Shen interviewed ten senior librarians to collect demographic information and responses to open-ended questions on leadership skills for the twenty-first century. The interviews revealed that these librarians saw persuasion and collaborative skills as most important for libraries' leadership succession planning.

McCrea, Donna E. "Learning to Lead: Cultivating Leadership Skills." In "Perspective: Leadership Skills for Archivists." *American Archivist* 74, no. 1 (2011): 104–7. McCrea distills what she learned from the literature on leadership and from her own experiences and leadership training. This article cites books and articles she found most helpful and summarizes leadership responsibilities and attributes.

Seaman, John T., Jr., and George David Smith. "Your Company's History as a Leadership Tool." *Harvard Business Review* 90, no. 12 (December 2010): 44–52. Instead of treating a company's history as a marginal concern most useful for anniversaries, executives should use it to create a stronger identity and source of values for all employees. Citing many examples from their work with numerous corporations, the authors advocate the mental discipline of historical thinking that separates long-term trends from less important developments and that leads to discoveries of the roots of current problems.

Books

Ackerson, Anne W., and Joan H. Baldwin. *Leadership Matters.* Lanham, MD: AltaMira Press, 2014. The authors are both former museum directors. In this book, they draw on interviews with museum leaders to highlight characteristics of effective leadership in the museum field. They address leadership both for museum boards and museum directors.

Bastian, Jeannette A., Megan Sniffin-Marinoff, and Donna Webber. *Archives in Libraries: What Librarians and Archivists Need to Know to Work Together.* Chicago: Society of American Archivists, 2015. The book "provides an overview of basic archival concepts, policies and best practices for librarians and library directors, while also suggesting ways in which archivists working in libraries can describe their work and effectively advocate for archival needs." (5). Based on in-person and remote interviews with fifteen archivists and eight library directors, as well as on secondary literature. The authors use the interviews to present short illustrative vignettes and to highlight issues and viewpoints.

Bolman, Lee G., and Terence E. Deal. *How Great Leaders Think: The Art of Reframing.* San Francisco: Jossey-Bass, 2014. The authors focus on the thinking element in leadership and claim that good leaders have the ability to see problems from different perspectives. They apply this precept to four "frames" in which leadership must work: structural, human, political, and symbolic.

Caldera, Mary A., and Kathryn M. Neal, eds. *Through the Archival Looking Glass: A Reader on Diversity and Inclusion.* Chicago: Society of American Archivists, 2014. This book has ten chapters by archivists about diversity, identity, inclusion, community archives, and representation of different groups in the archives profession and archival institutions. Authors discuss these topics in terms of collection development, management of collections that document Native Americans, recruiting and hiring archivists from minority groups, use of archives, and archival education.

Childers, Thomas A. and Nancy A. Van House, *What's Good: Describing Your Public Library's Effectiveness.* Chicago and London: American Library Association, 1993. Childers and Van House argue that the library manager's primary tasks are to assess the library's effectiveness and to communicate that effectiveness to stakeholders. "The resources needed to keep the library going . . . depend not only on the library being good, but on others knowing that it is good" (71). Chapters of their book analyze topics such as evaluation, management tools for effectiveness, the nature of public libraries as institutions, and models for measuring effectiveness.

Curzon, Susan C. *Managing Change. A How-to-do-it Manual for Librarians.* New York: Neal-Schuman, revised edition 2005. In this revised edition of her 1989 book of the same title, Curzon presents change management through a cycle of phases of work starting with conceptualization and ending with evaluation. She breaks down each phase into discrete steps. This edition also includes an additional new section in which Curzon presents fifteen scenarios of change. A series of questions follow each scenario, intended to help users of the book develop a plan for managing the change described in the scenario.

Dadson, Emma. *Emergency Planning and Response for Libraries, Archives and Museums.* Lanham, MD: Scarecrow Press, 2012. Dadson uses the development on an emergency response plan as the framework for this book. She includes several case studies of emergencies at institutions in the United Kingdom, United States and Japan. She also devotes chapters to the response phases of incident control, recovery and collections salvage. In the final chapter about ensuring the usefulness of the emergency plan, Dadson discusses formatting, distribution, testing, training, and working with other organizations.

Dearstyne, Bruce. *Leadership and Administration of Successful Archival Programs.* Westport, CT: Greenwood Press, 2001. A collection of essays by seven archival leaders from different types of institutions, addressing a central theme of how effective leadership must operate within specific organizational settings. Dearstyne contributes two of his own essays, on leadership traits and on building archival programs.

Dearstyne, Bruce. *Leading the Historical Enterprise: Strategic Creativity, Planning and Advocacy for the Digital Age.* Lanham, MD: Rowman and Littlefield, 2015. Dearstyne addresses archives within the broader field of organizations devoted to historical stewardship: historical societies, museums, state historical agencies, and the like. The chapters address leadership itself as well as closely connected activities like innovation, advocacy, strategic planning, and digital engagement. A final chapter discusses what Dearstyne considers exemplary historical programs.

Dearstyne, Bruce. *Leading and Managing Archives and Records Programs: Strategies for Success.* London: Facet, 2008. In this book of essays by Dearstyne and thirteen contributing authors, leaders from a range of records and information programs analyze issues, challenges, and opportunities confronting leaders and managers. Dearstyne also provides an annotated list of sources on leadership and management from a number of different professions.

Dearstyne, Bruce. *Managing Historical Records Programs: A Guide for Historical Agencies.* Walnut Creek, CA: AltaMira Press, 2000. This book was written for those who want to start a historical records program within a historical agency or to strengthen an existing program. It is essentially a management primer but does include some material on leadership in a chapter about leadership and management.

Düren, Petra. *Leadership in Academic and Public Libraries: A Time of Change*. Oxford: Chandos Publishing, 2003. Düren analyzes case studies of organizational change to assess leaders as change managers.

Edwards, Richard L., John A. Yankey, and Mary A. Altpeter, eds. *Skills for Effective Management of Nonprofit Organizations*. Washington, DC: National Association of Social Workers, 1998. The editors use the competing values framework to organize the overall content as well as the contributions of many expert authors. In this framework, managers must continually choose between alternative desirable goals or values, using the general skills involved with boundary spanning, human relations, coordinating, and directing. As explained in an opening chapter written by the book's editors, each of these general skills entails two specific roles. The chapters by contributing authors explore the eight roles in detail.

Evans, Edward G., and Patricia L. Ward. *Leadership Basics for Librarians and Information Professionals*. Lanham, MD: Scarecrow Press, 2007. Addressing the future of information professions, the authors discuss teamwork, political skills, strategy, and "e-leadership." The book also includes survey responses from professionals in the field.

Hackman, Larry J., ed. *Many Happy Returns: Advocacy and the Development of Archives*. Chicago: Society of American Archivists, 2011. Hackman provides an essay summarizing his experience in advocating for archival programs at the New York State Archives and also a conclusion recommending changes in the way archivists, their professional organizations, and archival education programs practice advocacy. In between his contributions are thirteen case studies of archival advocacy and a summary of them.

Harvard Business Review Manager's Handbook: The 17 Skills Leaders Need to Stand Out. Boston: Harvard Business Review Press, 2017. *Harvard Business Review* authors compiled this survey of leadership and management skills for those who have recently become heads of teams or units within organizations. Although addressing work in for-profit companies, much of the book discusses skills and aptitudes broadly enough to apply to government and nonprofit environments as well. Particularly useful are chapters on emotional intelligence and communicating effectively.

Harvard Business Review on Leading Through Change. Boston: Harvard Business School Press, 2006. Eight essays about organizational change and what leadership approaches and styles help or hinder it. The majority of cases discussed in the essays come from the private sector. The authors are academics and business consultants.

Hernon, Peter, Joan Giesecke, and Camila A. Alire, eds. *Academic Librarians as Emotionally Intelligent Leaders*. Westport, CT: Libraries Unlimited, 2008. This book includes chapters by the editors and one additional author, mainly on the literature, research, and theoretical aspects of emotionally intelligent and resonant leadership in academic libraries.

Hernon, Peter, and Nancy Rossiter, eds. *Making a Difference: Leadership and Academic Libraries*. Westport, CT: Libraries Unlimited, 2007. Chapters by the editors and seven other authors about aspects of leadership cover topics of diversity, research on leadership, and assessment.

Hill, Linda A., and Kent Lineback. *Being the Boss: The Three Imperatives for Becoming a Great Leader*. Boston: Harvard Business Review Press, 2011. The authors (one an academic specializing in leadership studies and the other an executive in the private sector) divide this book into three parts that focus on managing yourself, your network, and your team. They include self-evaluation questions and pointers on how to improve as a leader.

Institute of Museum and Library Services, Office of Strategic Partnerships. *Making the Learning Connection: Museums, Libraries and 21st Century Skills*. Washington, DC: IMLS, 2009. This IMLS project applied basic leadership competencies to museum, library, and (by extension) archival leadership specifically. Through case studies and self-assessment tools, the project encourages leaders to develop essential skills, such as critical thinking, cross-disciplinary thinking, global awareness, and the like.

Kotter, John P. *Leading Change*. Boston: Harvard Business Review Press, 2012. In this book, Kotter builds on proposals he initially published in the late 1990s about leadership, change, and transformation. He lays out an eight-stage process of change and argues that this process can overcome obstacles and shortcomings that plague organizational efforts to change.

Kotter, John P., with Dan Cohen. *The Heart of Change: Real-Life Stories of How People Change Their Organizations*. Boston: Harvard Business Review Press, 2002. Kotter and Cohen focus on achieving major change quickly and assert that success depends on changing people's behavior by dealing with their emotions. They posit an eight-step process that transforming organizations go through to overcome inertia and embrace change. The book's thesis and findings are based on interviews with more than two hundred people, representing organizations around the world.

Kouzes, James M., and Barry Z. Posner. *The Leadership Challenge: How to Make Extraordinary Things Happen in Organizations*. 6th ed. Hoboken, NJ: John Wiley and Sons, 2017. In this latest edition of a popular book first published in 1995, Kouzes and Posner present leadership in terms of ten "commitments" and five practices. While the authors use examples from for-profit enterprises to illustrate the framework, the principles they discuss apply broadly to most organizations.

Kurtz, Michael J. *Managing Archival and Manuscript Repositories*. Chicago: Society of American Archivists, 2004. Kurtz's book was published as part of SAA's Archival Fundamentals Series II and remains an authoritative treatment of the management of archival programs. Kurtz discusses leadership as a component of management but includes useful overviews of several broad areas of responsibility: communications, internal and external relationships, strategic planning, and human resources.

Montiel-Overall, Patricia, Annabelle Villaescusa Nuñez, and Veronica Reyes-Escudero. *Latinos in Libraries, Museums and Archives*. Lanham, MD: Rowman and Littlefield, 2016. The authors emphasize the need for information agencies to better serve Latino clients and to better document the experiences of the Latino population in their holdings. According to them, the keys to accomplishing these ends are increasing the cultural competence of agencies' staff (primarily through better Spanish language skills) and understanding the Latino community's norms. In the chapter devoted to special collections and archives, the authors emphasize these aspects in terms of appraisal and acquisitions and in terms of collections digitization.

Phills, James. *Integrating Mission and Strategy for Non-Profit Organizations*. New York: Oxford University Press, 2005. Phills argues that the challenges facing nonprofits and private businesses are fundamentally similar. He uses the basic leadership functions of direction, motivation, and design to discuss how leaders carry out their responsibilities for mission, strategy, and execution.

Purcell, Aaron D. *Academic Archives: Managing the Next Generation of College and University Archives, Records, and Special Collections*. Chicago: Neal-Schuman, 2012. This book covers many aspects of running an academic archives and includes a chapter on creating a mission and vision; this chapter discusses the roles of manager and leader of an academic archives. Purcell also identifies trends in academic libraries that provide opportunities for leaders of their archival programs: merging of various units to form special collections departments, and the growth of digital libraries programs (in which archivists often take an active role), in particular.

Rubin, Rhea Joyce. *Demonstrating Results: Using Outcome Measurement in Your Library*. Chicago: American Library Association, 2006. Rubin's book is designed for use within the Public Library Association's framework, New Planning for Results. Based on user-focused outcomes, it explains a process for obtaining outcome measurements in library programs. Rubin includes sample forms, questionnaires, methodologies, and a glossary.

Sheldon, Brooke E. *Interpersonal Skills, Theory and Practice: The Librarian's Guide to Becoming a Leader*. Santa Barbara, CA: ABC-CLIO, 2010. Sheldon emphasizes such skills as listening, motivating, and resolving conflict among the things that aspiring leaders need to master. Within a framework that stresses the conceptual difference between a manager and a leader, Sheldon offers specific ways to develop the people skills that someone moving from a managerial to a chief executive level needs to succeed. He describes tools by showing how they might be used by hypothetical leaders.

Thomas, Lynne M., and Beth M. Whittaker, eds. *New Directions for Special Collections: An Anthology of Practice*. Santa Barbara, CA: Libraries Unlimited, 2017. This anthology consists of twenty-one chapters each written by separate authors, concerning various aspects of special collections librarianship: reference services, users, instruction programs, collection development, donor relations, volunteers, preservation/conservation, digital information, organizational change (reorganization of special collections on a functional basis into a larger library), copyright, privacy, succession planning, and leadership. Particularly relevant is the chapter by Athena Jackson, "Succession Planning for 21st-Century Special Collections Leadership: Initial Steps," 215–24.

Williams, Caroline. *Managing Archives: Foundations, Principles and Practice*. Oxford: Chandos, 2006. Addressing archives and records management in a British context, Williams covers the basic program functions of an archives but includes management (operations) functions (though not leadership) as well.

Wittenborg, Karin, Chris Ferguson, and Michael A. Keller. *Reflecting on Leadership*. Washington, DC: Council on Library and Information Resources, 2003. Three leaders of academic libraries write about their views of leadership and how they developed as the heads of their organizations.

Zamon, Christina. *The Lone Arranger: Succeeding in a Small Repository*. Chicago: Society of American Archivists, 2012. The opening chapter of this book discusses some management issues for small archives.

Leadership Development Programs and Resources

American Alliance of Museums offers online courses and conference sessions on topics concerning leadership. https://www.aam-us.org/, captured at https://perma.cc/7VL5-PCQ2.

American Association for State and Local History, History Leadership Institute. https://aaslh.org/programs/history-leadership-institute/, captured at https://perma.cc/U56A-Q72V.

American Library Association Leadership Institute. http://www.ala.org/educationcareers/leadership, captured at https://perma.cc/59D2-3WJ9.

Association of Research Libraries Leadership Fellows Program. http://www.arl.org/focus-areas/arl-academy/leadership-development-programs/arl-leadership-fellows-program#.W2YlKVOUv_R, captured at https://perma.cc/38AC-9LQY.

Center for Curatorial Leadership. This program is devoted to developing art museum curators into visionary leaders. https://www.curatorialleadership.org/, captured at https://perma.cc/GB9V-EB9C.

Getty Leadership Institute. Annually selects two groups of applicants for leadership development: experienced museum executives and midlevel managers aiming to become the next generation of executives. The institute is provided through the Claremont Graduate University. https://gli.cgu.edu/, captured at https://perma.cc/J4SU-V2UX.

Harvard University. John F. Kennedy School of Government. Executive Education. https://www.hks.harvard.edu/executive-education, captured at https://perma.cc/U5N5-FEAE.

Harvard University Leadership Institute for Academic Librarians. https://www.gse.harvard.edu/ppe/program/leadership-institute-academic-librarians, captured at https://perma.cc/9K2X-ZBSB.

Library Leadership and Management Association. "Leadership and Management Competencies." http://www.ala.org/llama/leadership-and-management-competencies#LLAMA%E2%80%99s%2014%20Foundational%20Competencies, captured at https://perma.cc/57MG-G8AM.

The Nonprofit Leadership Alliance offers its Certified Nonprofit Professional credential to prepare individuals for leadership positions. https://www.nonprofitleadershipalliance.org/about/, captured at https://perma.cc/NX6W-VJBK.

University of Virginia, Rare Book School. Course on Special Collections Library Leadership. https://rarebookschool.org/courses/library/l50/, captured at https://perma.cc /A8D5-WBBL.

University or college continuing education programs sometimes include professional certification programs in leadership. These can include specialized certificates for public managers, human resource management, and project management, for example, and any of these could be relevant for developing skills as an archival leader. See, for example, the University of Wisconsin's leadership certificate programs from its continuing education program: https://cfli.wisc.edu/, captured at https://perma.cc/B7AW-VZSS.

Websites, Blogs, and Podcasts

Better Library Leaders. www.betterlibraryleaders.com, captured at https://perma.cc/HN22-9DVD. Sarah Clark created this website in 2017. It includes podcasts and a blog. There is also a Facebook community. The site has information about various aspects of library leadership: leadership theory, symbolic leadership, leadership resources, and the like.

Lead Change. Weaving Influence, Inc. According to its own description: "[m]ore than a blog, Lead Change is a global, virtual platform showcasing great ideas and encouraging leaders in their professional growth . . . " https://leadchangegroup.com/about/, captured at https:// perma.cc/A82L-VUKN.

Leadership Freak. Dan Rockwell, a leadership consultant, coach, and author, started this blog in 2010; he discusses leadership attributes and behavior. https://leadershipfreak.blog/about/, captured at https://perma.cc/6VAH-LX7C.

Leadership Matters. Anne Ackerson and Joan Baldwin address leadership issues in US museums. https://leadershipmatters1213.wordpress.com/, captured at https://perma.cc/Y89D-AEE4.

Leading by Design: A Resource for Nonprofits. Anne Ackerson. Posts discuss aspects of nonprofit organization governance and leadership. http://leadingbydesign.blogspot.com/, captured at https://perma.cc/4SBN-TS9X.

About the Authors

DAVID W. CARMICHEAL is state archivist of Pennsylvania. He served previously as state archivist of Georgia and director of Records and Archives for Westchester County, New York. He is a past president of the Council of State Archivists and a Distinguished Fellow of the Society of American Archivists. He has overseen design and construction of two state archives buildings, led the national Intergovernmental Preparedness for Essential Records (IPER) project to protect government records, and served on NARA's Advisory Committee for the Electronic Records Archives.

PETER GOTTLIEB was state archivist of Wisconsin and director of the Library and Archives at the Wisconsin Historical Society prior to retiring in November 2010. Before starting these positions in 1991, he had worked as an archivist at West Virginia University (1977–1983) and at the Pennsylvania State University (1983–1990). He earned his BA (Honors) from the University of Wisconsin–Madison in 1971 and his MA (1974) and PhD (1977) in US history from the University of Pittsburgh.

JENNIFER I. JOHNSON is the senior archivist at Cargill, Incorporated. A University of Maryland graduate, she previously worked at the US Department of Energy and the Minnesota State Archives. Johnson has held leadership positions with the Society of American Archivists, Midwest Archives Conference, and Twin Cities Archives Round Table, and is a member of the Archives Leadership Institute 2011 cohort.

SARAH KOONTS has served as state archives and records administrator for North Carolina since 2012. Prior to that, she worked in a variety of units of the State Archives, including reference, imaging, local records management, and preservation programming. She has a BA from Simpson College in Indianola, Iowa, and an MA in public history from North Carolina State University. She and her husband, Russell, also an archivist, live in Apex, North Carolina, and have two grown children.

SAMANTHA NORLING is the digital collections manager at the Indianapolis Museum of Art at Newfields. In this role, she manages digital assets and data related to the museum's art, archival, and horticultural collections. Prior to moving into this role, Norling spent more than three years working as the institution's archivist, and she continues to collaborate closely with the Library and Archives department on born-digital records management and related projects. As a current member and former Chair of the SAA Committee on Public Awareness, she is particularly interested in raising the profile of the archival profession through advocacy and outreach.

MEGAN SNIFFIN-MARINOFF is the university archivist at Harvard University. Previously, she was deputy director at the Schlesinger Library at the Radcliffe Institute and institute archivist/head of Special Collections at MIT. From 1980 to 1999, she was college archivist and assistant professor at Simmons College GSLIS, where she founded and co-led the dual degree history/library and information science archives. She was president of the New England Archivists, member of the SAA Council, and board member of the University and Research Institution Archives Section of the International Council on Archives, and was named SAA Fellow. With Jeannette A. Bastian and Donna Webber, she coauthored *Archives in Libraries: What Librarians and Archivists Need to Know to Work Together* (Chicago: Society of American Archivists, 2015).

LYNETTE STOUDT served as the director of the Georgia Historical Society (GHS) Research Center during 2012–2018 and was responsible for leading library and archives staff, managing collections and preservation, administering reference and information services, overseeing donor relations and acquisitions, and managing facilities. Stoudt has been active in several professional organizations including Savannah Heritage Emergency Response, Regional Archival Associations Consortium, the Society of Georgia Archivists, and the Society of American Archivists. Prior to GHS, Stoudt held positions at the University of California San Diego, Irvine, and Berkeley, and with History Associates Incorporated. She holds an MLIS with an emphasis in archival studies from San Jose State University.

RACHEL VAGTS is the manager of Special Collections and Digital Archives at the Denver Public Library. She holds a master's degree in library and information studies with a concentration in archival administration from the University of Wisconsin–Madison. She held positions at the Wisconsin Historical Society and the University of Maryland before serving as college archivist at Luther College and head of Special Collections and Archives at Berea College. Vagts has served as the director of the Archives Leadership Institute from 2013 to 2018.

Index

CPSIA information can be obtained
at www.ICGtesting.com
Printed in the USA
FSHW020140160220
67168FS